Teach®
Yourself

# Esse
# Spa
# Vocabulary

Mike Zollo

EDHCC

D1464583

13

# Essential
# Spanish
# Vocabulary

For UK order enquiries: please contact Bookpoint Ltd, 130 Milton Park, Abingdon, Oxon OX14 4SB. *Telephone:* +44 (0) 1235 827720. *Fax:* +44 (0) 1235 400454. Lines are open 09.00–17.00, Monday to Saturday, with a 24-hour message answering service. Details about our titles and how to order are available at www.teachyourself.com

For USA order enquiries: please contact McGraw-Hill Customer Services, PO Box 545, Blacklick, OH 43004-0545, USA. *Telephone:* 1-800-722-4726. *Fax:* 1-614-755-5645.

For Canada order enquiries: please contact McGraw-Hill Ryerson Ltd, 300 Water St, Whitby, Ontario L1N 9B6, Canada. *Telephone:* 905 430 5000. *Fax:* 905 430 5020.

Long renowned as the authoritative source for self-guided learning – with more than 50 million copies sold worldwide – the *Teach Yourself* series includes over 500 titles in the fields of languages, crafts, hobbies, business, computing and education.

British Library Cataloguing in Publication Data: a catalogue record for this title is available from the British Library.

Library of Congress Catalog Card Number: on file.

Previously published in 2003 as Teach Yourself Spanish Vocabulary by Hodder Education, part of Hachette UK, 338 Euston Road, London NW1 3BH.

This edition published 2010.

The *Teach Yourself* name is a registered trade mark of Hodder Headline.

Typeset by Transet Ltd, Coventry, England.

Printed in Great Britain for Hodder Education, an Hachette UK Company, 338 Euston Road, London NW1 3BH.

The publisher has used its best endeavours to ensure that the URLs for external websites referred to in this book are correct and active at the time of going to press. However, the publisher and the author have no responsibility for the websites and can make no guarantee that a site will remain live or that the content will remain relevant, decent or appropriate.

Hachette UK's policy is to use papers that are natural, renewable and recyclable products and made from wood grown in sustainable forests. The logging and manufacturing processes are expected to conform to the environmental regulations of the country of origin.

Impression number 10 9 8 7 6 5 4 3 2 1

Year 2014 2013 2012 2011 2010

# Contents

..........................................................................................

# Credits

**Front cover:** © Oxford Illustrators

**Back cover and pack:** © Jakub Semeniuk/iStockphoto.com, © Royalty-Free/Corbis, © agencyby/iStockphoto.com, © Andy Cook/iStockphoto.com, © Christopher Ewing/iStockphoto.com, © zebicho – Fotolia.com, © Geoffrey Holman/iStockphoto.com, © Photodisk/Getty Images, © James C. Pruitt/iStockphoto,com. © Mohamed Saber – Fotolia.com

**Pack:** © Stockbyte/Getty Images

# Meet the author

Like so many people, you probably think you are no good at learning languages… yet you get by pretty well in English! You need to be patient with yourself: when you were acquiring language as a toddler, people were patient and supportive, and you were even allowed to make mistakes! Spanish native speakers are very appreciative and supportive of anyone who makes the effort to speak their language, and it is OK to make mistakes if you can at least make yourself understood. A minimum of language is what is needed, plus a healthy dose of **coraje**!

Vocabulary is, of course, the major building block of language, but you will need to think about how to go about learning it. Think back to how you learned a particular word as a youngster, along with its nuances and associations. Take the word 'orange'… You will certainly have heard the sound first, when first you were given orange as a drink. Then you came to associate the taste and the sensation of drinking orange juice with the word. Later, when you were given a segment of orange to chew, the sensation of texture was added, and at some stage you attempted to say the word for the first time, probably struggling with the pronunciation. Then later you will have experienced the sight and feel of a whole orange, the sensation of peeling it, and will have acquired the idea of orange as a colour, and other connotations and associations after that. In other words, you gained layer upon layer of associations related to 'orange'. Ask the average person nowadays what the word conjures up for them and they will probably reply 'a mobile phone service'!

So, words are multi-faceted and, like the child, you need to build up whatever associations and contexts are relevant and meaningful to you. That is why we have given you so many suggestions on how to learn vocabulary, and have placed so much emphasis on learning each new word with an attached 'memory-hook'. You need to learn thoughtfully and intelligently, feeding each dimension of your learning skills whenever possible: learning by seeing, hearing, doing and thinking. **¡Suerte!**

**Mike Zollo**

# Only got a minute?

Although many British people visit Spain, relatively few make the effort to speak the language, so Spaniards are delighted when you can communicate in their language. Indeed, the ability to speak Spanish will open doors and will be rewarding in many unexpected ways. Besides, Spanish is one of the best languages for an English speaker to learn, providing the beginner with a great rate of progress in the early stages.

Spanish is rewarding for many reasons, not least that its systems of spelling and pronunciation are so logical and regular that, once learned, they are extremely reliable. Besides, Spanish has very few sounds which are different from English, so even a beginner can achieve authentic pronunciation. Once you have learned a few basic rules, you will be able to pronounce new words accurately, and there are no awkward exceptions to the rules of spelling and stress!

For the beginner, all this is reason enough to choose to learn Spanish, but there are many other attractions! The Spanish-speaking world has a huge variety of landscapes, a rich culture in all its aspects, a long and varied history, a fantastic climate for whatever activity appeals to you, an amazing range of architecture and, of course, wonderful people in whichever Spanish-speaking country you visit. Indeed, because Spain had a huge empire in bygone centuries, its language and cultural heritage was spread around the world... and enhanced by all the cultures with which it merged. Then of course there is the fantastic variety of culinary experience, the beautiful beaches, the sports facilities, and the terrific range of music and dance.

Plus which, whatever Hispanic country you visit, the wonderfully welcoming and hospitable people will very much appreciate the chance to meet and communicate with you, whether you are a beginner or an experienced speaker of Spanish. ¡**Que te diviertas!**

# 5 Only got five minutes?

Many English speakers nowadays think that everyone in the world speaks English, but of course this is not so. Whilst many Spaniards in tourist areas can indeed communicate adequately and are often keen to try out their English, elsewhere you may not find anyone with even a basic grasp of English.

Many Spanish-speaking people do not speak a foreign language, especially in rural areas and in the more remote communities of Latin America. Also, you may hear a local dialect or even a non-Spanish language being spoken, although Castilian Spanish is readily spoken and understood throughout the Hispanic world. Firstly, many Spanish native speakers have little or no need to speak other languages, still less English. Secondly, Castilian Spanish (standard Spanish) is in most regions the language of the people who once dominated and / or colonized, so although it is the 'official language' throughout Hispanic countries, local languages still flourish for everyday communication among the local people. However, don't be put off by this, as Spanish is at the very least a 'lingua franca', and will usually be the accepted mode of communication with strangers.

This means that speaking Spanish in Hispanic countries is a considerably more rewarding experience than speaking the language of many other European countries (where your efforts may be met with quite fluent English in response, which is rather demotivating!). Spanish-speaking people are more likely to be quite surprised and pleased – indeed appreciative – when a foreigner makes an effort to speak their language. If you make mistakes, most will display a supportive attitude, listening patiently and helping you along, filling in any gaps and correcting basic errors only if you ask them to.

All of this means that it is worth acquiring as much basic vocabulary as possible in the time you have available, as your efforts to use it will be met with appreciation and encouragement by sympathetic native listeners, which in turn will speed up your learning. Don't forget that we already use a number of Spanish words and phrases in English, which will help you to 'get into the mood' and provide practical experience of many elements of Spanish spelling and pronunciation, such as **fiesta, paella, vino, hasta luego, gracias** and **adiós**. In the same way, Spanish has borrowed lots of words from English, usually with similar if not identical pronunciation and spelling. You will soon get used to the characteristic Spanish spellings, particularly the endings of words; notice that most of those above end in a vowel, as the majority of Spanish words do.

Most of the words you learn first are likely to be those of immediate use to you, phrases and nouns such as **por favor** (*please*) and **un billete** (*a ticket*); 'discourse markers' such as **¿Algo más?** (*Anything else?*) or set phrases such as **Ya está todo, gracias** (*That's all, thanks*). The obvious reason is that much of the language you will need to learn early on is what is known as 'transactional' language (i.e. the language used to get what you need, find something out, buy something or get something done).

We should mention that in Spanish there are polite forms of the word for *you*. **Usted** (*you*, singular) and **ustedes** (*you*, plural), are often used in formal situations, for example in shops, hotels and banks, and with strangers. They can be confusing at first, especially because you have to remember to use the third person (*he / she / they*) form of the verb with them. However, you will quickly get used to them and to deciding which form of 'you' to use.

Here is a brief 'toolkit' of some basic phrases that you are likely to need. (Notice how Spanish uses inverted question marks and exclamation marks at the beginning of the phrase or sentence as well as right-way-up ones at the end.)

| | |
|---|---|
| **¡Hola!** | *Hello / Hi* |
| **¡Buenos días!** | *Good day* |
| **¡Buenas tardes!** | *Good afternoon / evening* |
| **¡Adiós!** | *Goodbye* |
| **Díga(me)** | *Hello (on the phone)* |
| **¿Algo más?** | *Anything else?* |
| **Basta así, gracias** | *That's all, thanks* |
| **¿En qué puedo ayudarle?** | *How can I help you?* |
| **Esta tarde** | *This evening* |
| **¿A quién le toca?** | *Who's next?* |
| **¡A mí!** | *Me!* |
| **Cien gramos de...** | *100 grams of...* |
| **Una botella de...** | *A bottle of...* |
| **Un vaso de...** | *A glass of...* |
| **Pequeño/a** | *Small* |
| **Mediano/a** | *Medium* |
| **Grande** | *Large* |
| **¿Qué hora es?** | *What time is it?* |
| **Es la... Son las...** | *It's...* |

**Uno, dos, tres, cuatro, cinco, seis, siete, ocho, nueve, diez, once, doce**
*One, two, three, four, five, six, seven, eight, nine, ten, eleven, twelve*

Although the above words are mostly the kind you will use in shops and public situations, you will progress quickly to 'interactional' (usually social) language, because you will usually find that once people realize that you can speak Spanish or want to have a go, they will want to find out about you and your family, to tell you about themselves – and even, if you are on a train or bus, to share their lunch with you! If they do, you can refuse by replying **'No gracias, ¡que aproveche!'** (*No thanks, may it do you good!*)

Fewer people in Spanish-speaking societies leave their home town or region, which may be part of the reason why regional dialects and even languages still flourish, rather than being 'watered down' by population movement. However, as already explained, almost all Spanish-speakers understand and speak standard Spanish (**castellano**) as well, and when they realize you are a foreigner and are learning, they will switch into standard Spanish to help you!

To sum up, the best way to learn Spanish is to get out there and use it – you will be amazed at how quickly you learn once you are 'in at the deep end'!

**Buena suerte...**

# 10 Only got ten minutes?

## History

Spain is a country with a strong identity resulting from centuries of glorious and sometimes not so glorious history. Its language has spread around the world as a result of Spain's huge former empire, and it is still expanding rapidly in the many 'young' Spanish-speaking communities, including the huge Hispanic population of the USA, the fourth largest Spanish-speaking community in the world. There are currently around 400 million Spanish speakers in the world in 25+ countries. Spanish is therefore very much a world language, and one whose use is expanding rapidly thanks to its widespread use on the Internet and in other modern modes of communication.

Spain has many speakers of dialects of 'standard Spanish', which is actually Castilian, the language of the region which eventually dominated the rest of Spain. The main languages spoken in the Iberian peninsula are, of course, Spanish and Portuguese, but within the Spanish territory, a handful of other Hispanic languages are well-established. Catalan, Galician and Basque have their own distinctive cultures and many centuries of history.

Catalan is a sort of half-way-house between Castilian Spanish and French, with recognizable features of each. Similarly, Galician sits between Castilian and Portuguese, and like Catalan is fairly easy for a competent Spanish speaker to read. By contrast, Basque – Euskera – bears little or no relationship to these other Romance languages (derived from Latin) apart from modern 'borrowings'. Indeed, it is believed to be one of the oldest languages in Europe, spoken by a people whose special physiological characteristics point to origins way before the influx of other races into Western Europe. The Basques were largely unaffected by other races, because they remained in the high valleys of the western Pyrenees as other people's battles raged backwards and forwards past them. In more recent times they have spread out into northern Spain and south-western France, yet preserving their unique identity. These regional languages faded to an extent during much of the 20th century, but liberal reforms in education and broadcasting have led to revival and expansion; curiously, young Basques and Catalans are more likely to speak and write their language than many of their elders!

There is not space here to describe dialects of Castilian Spanish, but it is necessary to point out one major variation: 'c' before 'e' and 'i' is pronounced 'th' in most of Spain, but in southern and south-west Spain, this is pronounced as 's'; these features are known as **ceceo** and **seseo** respectively, and the latter is the pronunciation used in the Canary Islands and in all of Hispano-America – i.e. by the overwhelming majority of Spanish speakers.

Although Spanish is a well-established language in its own right, with a huge literary heritage, it has deep roots and many 'inputs'. These include many Arabic words resulting from the many centuries when Moors lived in Spain, and 'imports' from Latin-American native languages. The most important source of Spanish is, of course, Latin. Indeed, of the modern European Romance languages descended from Latin, Spanish is one of the closest in terms of its linguistic and grammatical links to its 'parent language'.

---

## Links with Latin

Many feminine words are identical in the singular to their Latin equivalent:

| | |
|---|---|
| **casa** (f) house | **la casa** |
| **villa** (f) large house | **la villa** |
| **piscina** (f) swimming pool, fish pool | **la piscina** |

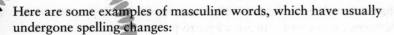

Here are some examples of masculine words, which have usually undergone spelling changes:

**panis** (m) bread        **el pan**
**liber** (m) book        **el libro**
**carbo** (m) carbon, coal        **el carbón**

Some words are slightly different, usually because of sound changes that have happened over the centuries in the transition from classical Latin to modern Spanish, but are nevertheless immediately recognizable. English spellings often tend to be closer to the Latin original than those of Spanish. This is because of one or other of the peculiar quirks of Spanish such as the following (can you recognize them?):

- words beginning in Latin / English with **sc-**, **sp-**, **st-** have **sc-**, **sp-**, **st-** in Spanish: **escuela, español, estudiante**;

- words in Latin / English having **-e-** or **-o-** change to **-ie-** and **-ue-** respectively in Spanish: **bene** →**bien** (*well*); **ovum** → **huevo** (*egg*);

- words with **ph** and **th** in Latin / English simplify their spelling to **f** and **t** in Spanish: **teatro**; **farmacia**.

---

## Stress

Two factors make Spanish a 'comfortable' and relatively easy language to learn. Firstly, Spanish spelling and pronunciation are completely regular and reliable once a few basics have been learned: it is a phonetic language – what you see is what you say, and what you say or hear is what you write. Secondly, the majority of its words conform to similar sound patterns, which, once mastered, are a 'confidence-booster' to good pronunciation and intonation. All words of more than one syllable have one which is stressed, pronounced louder than the others – just as in English.

What makes this even easier is that there are three simple rules which ensure that you can see where to put the stress in a new word. Here they are:

**1** Words ending with a vowel, **n** or **s** have the stress on the last but one syllable.

**niño, hacen, consejo, diccionario, posesiones**

**2** Words ending with a consonant except **n** or **s** have the stress on the last syllable.

**Madrid, mujer, papel, reloj, conocer, desayunar**

**3** Words which break rules 1 and 2 have a written accent to show where the stress falls.

**miró, champán, pájaro, condición, champú, hacéis**

This gives Spanish an attractive, slightly musical quality which somewhat resembles English in its cadences.

---

## Pronunciation of individual letters and phonemes

As mentioned previously, there are a few easy rules on the pronunciation of Spanish letters and phonemes, and these can be mastered quite quickly, with the result that you can acquire fluency and accurate pronunciation in the very early stages of language learning – a relatively unusual advantage for a beginner! Almost uniquely among languages, almost every letter is pronounced and has its own 'value'. The exceptions are **h** – never pronounced – and **u** when following **q**. The majority of the consonants are pronounced either exactly as in English or very similarly, with a couple of exceptions:

## Consonants

**c** is pronounced like the English 'k' except before 'i' or 'e', when it is pronounced 'th' (**ceceo** as described above) or 's' (**seseo**, in southern Spain and Hispano-America); **z** is always pronounced the same as **ceceo** or **seseo**, whichever is the local preference

**ch** is pronounced exactly as in English

**d** is pronounced like a hard 'th' as in 'this' when between two vowels or at the end of a word.

**g** is pronounced like the English 'g' except **before** 'e' or 'i', when it becomes a quite harsh sound a bit like the end of Scottish 'lo**ch**'; **j** is always pronounced like this

**h** is always silent

**k** is only encountered in a few words but is pronounced like the English 'k'

**r** is pronounced in a similar way to the Scottish 'r' except that it is usually trilled or rolled once when a single 'r', and several times when doubled or at the start of a word

**ll** is pronounced as a sort of 'lya' sound wherever it occurs in a word

**v** is often pronounced like a 'b' in northern and central Spain, especially at the beginning of a word; this is softer in much of Spain, and is often pronounced as a 'v' in the south and in much of Hispano-America

## Vowels

The vowels in Spanish are **a, e, i, o** and **u**, as in English, but they all have only one pure sound as follows:

**a** is pronounced similarly to the English word 'ah', but shorter.

**e** is pronounced either like the short 'e' in 'bed' or slightly longer, like the sound in the English word 'eh'

**i** is pronounced like the 'i' in 'machine' or the 'ea' in 'cream'

**o** is sometimes pronounced like the 'o' in English 'oh', but is sometimes more like a slightly shortened version of the English word 'or'

**u** is pronounced like the 'oo' in the English word 'cool'

Note that when two vowels occur together, each retains its normal pronunciation, but they simply merge from one into the other. Try **Buenos días.** So, none of the variation and inconsistency of English here!

You may be aware that we use intonation – the way the voice rises and falls – to add to or modify the meaning of a sentence. Spanish does the same: the voice rises at the end of a question, and before a comma in a long sentence, and falls at the end of a statement. A brief note about punctuation here: Spanish places an inverted question mark at the start of a question and an inverted exclamation mark at the start of an exclamation to let you know that a question or exclamation is coming, so that you can adjust your intonation accordingly: very useful if you are reading a long sentence or question. How considerate is that?!

## Pronunciation practice

You are almost certainly familiar with the general 'tone' of Spanish pronunciation for a couple of good reasons. Even if you have never been to Spain or a Spanish-speaking country, you will have heard lots of Spanish on TV, in films and in songs; Spanish is often used in songs for its 'romantic' quality, and has featured in songs by stars from the Beatles to Madonna. You may also know snippets of Spanish songs or even opera. Then you will have seen odd Spanish words and phrases used on menus (**paella, sangría**), on labels of Spanish products (**turrón, vino tinto**), or being used as names of cars or other products (**fiesta, sierra**). But also, of course, we have 'borrowed' lots of Spanish words into English, and have usually preserved at least the impression of Spanish pronunciation, such as in **España, Hasta la vista, Adiós**, and **tapas**. You might be surprised to know that even 'cowboy' English as heard in Westerns is full of words of Spanish origin: **corral, lassoo (lazo), hombre** and so on.

So plenty of good reasons to be confident of acquiring a good accent. Here for good measure are some words for you to practise saying, using the rules you have just read. You should be able to say all of these words correctly now, using the guidelines in this section. Don't forget to keep an eye out for the Spanish peculiarities such as *c* and *g* before *e* and *i*, and remember the stress rules so that you don't get stressed!

**arriba, Alicante, eso, chica, ¡Hola!, cura, ¡Buenos días!, cinco, muchacho, Madrid, Málaga, hija, jardín zoológico, calle, llave, ¿Qué tal?, raro, burro, corer, Valladolid, Valencia, Cádiz**

## Confidence

One of the biggest barriers to linguistic progress is lack of confidence. Most early learners of a new language are held back by three factors:

a) lack of vocabulary

b) uncertainty as to how to pronounce words, leading to hesitancy and lack of fluency

c) lack of understanding on the part of interlocutors, who either correct them or answer back in English

None of these factors should be a barrier to learning Spanish, because the vocabulary is easy to acquire, the spelling is regular, and the pronunciation follows a distinct set of easily-learned rules and features almost no sounds which are 'foreign' to the English native speaker. More good news: if and when you start to get involved in learning Spanish grammar, you will also find that, at least in the early stages, Spanish grammar is both logical and straightforward to understand and learn.

Another big factor which will help you to gain confidence and fluency (possibly the biggest factor) is that the listeners are overwhelmingly sympathetic and (very importantly!) unlikely to respond in English, for the simple reason that not many of them can speak it. So as a mother-tongue English speaker learning Spanish, you should find that you gain confidence and fluency more quickly in Spanish than you would (or have!) in any other language.

**¡Mucha suerte!**

# Introduction

There have been many studies carried out into the way we learn vocabulary. The Swiss, who are generally acknowledged as experts in multi-language learning are also leaders in the understanding of the processes of language acquisition and some of their findings may be of interest to people wanting to broaden their vocabulary.

**Studies have shown that the most successful way [of learning vocabulary] is when the student is able to relate the new word to a concept and to integrate it into a conceptual system.**

(Wokusch, 1997)

Put simply this means that the most successful way of learning vocabulary is to put the new language into a context.

When a child first learns a language they are learning the concepts as well as the language at the same time. If you give a child an ice cream and say 'ice cream' they are learning the word and the concept at the same time, associating the word and the object. An adult has the advantage of already having the concept. An ice cream already conjures up other words: cold, vanilla, strawberry, like, don't like, size, price, etc.

Similarly if you decide to learn about a computer or a car you probably already know the parts or expressions you want to learn and can visualize them before you meet the word. In fact you already have the 'concept' and you can 'place' the new words within that concept.

It is for this reason that the vocabulary in this book has been given in context rather than, as in a dictionary, in alphabetical order. The words have been chosen as the words most likely to be useful or of interest to the learner.

One of the most useful tips in learning a new language is to look for ways of remembering a word: find a 'hook' to hang your new word or phrase on.

_____

## How this book works

This book is more than just a list of words – it is a key to open the door to better communication. It is designed to give you the confidence you need to communicate better in Spanish by increasing your knowledge of up-to-date vocabulary and at the same time showing you how to use the new words you are learning.

The first part of the book includes some useful learning tips, rules on pronunciation and shortcuts to look out for when learning new words. The toolbox provides you with the tools you need to speak a language. It includes basic information about the structure of the language and useful tips, including how to address people, how to ask questions, how to talk about what you have done and what you are going to do, useful expressions, and shortcuts to language learning. This part of the book is designed to be used for general reference.

The main part of the book is divided into topic areas: personal matters, family, work, education, etc. The selected words are the ones which our research has shown are the ones which are likely to be the most useful or most relevant to the learner of today. The words have been carefully arranged, grouped with other related words, nouns, verbs, adjectives etc. and useful expressions with up-to-date notes about language fashions where relevant, so that the new language can be used immediately.

## Make learning a list of words more interesting

- First decide which list you are going to look at today.
- See how many words you know already and tick them off.
- Choose which new words you want to learn – don't try to do too many at once!
- Count them so you know how many you are going to try to learn.
- Say them aloud; you could even record yourself saying them.

## Remembering new words

- Try to associate new words with words that sound similar in English: **plato** (*plateau*).
- Try to associate the words with pictures or situations, e.g. try to imagine a picture of a rose when you say the word: *rosa*
- See if you can split the word into bits, some of which you know already: **super-mercado**.
- Look for words related to ones you know already: **día** (*day*), **diario** (*daily newspaper*); **zapato** (*shoe*), **zapatería** (*shoe shop*).
- Look for words related to the English ones: **mano** (*manual*); **bicicleta** (*bicycle*).
- Learn the value of typical beginnings and endings used to alter the meaning of words: <u>**des**</u>**honesto** (<u>*dis*</u>*honest*), <u>**im**</u>**posible** (<u>*im*</u>*possible*), **independ**<u>**encia**</u> (*independ*<u>*ence*</u>), **capac**<u>**idad**</u> (*capac*<u>*ity*</u>).
- Copy a list of the most important words onto A4 paper with a broad felt tip; stick it on the wall so that you can study it when doing some routine activity such as washing up, ironing, shaving or putting on make-up.
- For names of objects around the house, you could write the word on a sticky label or post-it note and attach it to the actual object.
- Copy lists of words in Spanish and English in two columns. First, say each word aloud, then cover up one column, and try to remember each word in the other column.
- Do something else for half an hour and then come back and see how many you can still remember.

- Write down the first letter of each new word and put a dot for each missing letter, cover the word up and see if you can complete the word.
- Pick a few words you find difficult to remember: write each one down with the letters jumbled up; leave them for a while, then later try to unscramble each one.
- In your list, mark the difficult words: ask someone else to test you on the ones you have marked.

---

## Spelling tips

These don't always work but they may help!

- Words which begin with **esc, esp** or **est** – take off the e: **escalar** (*to scale, climb*); **España** (*Spain*); **estudiante** (*student*).
- Words beginning with **ll** – try *cl, fl* or *pl*: **llama** (*flame*); **llano** (*plain*).
- If a word begins with **f** + a vowel, try *ph*: **farmacia** (*pharmacy*)
- If a word begins with **t**, try *th*: **teatro** – *theatre*.
- Where you see a word with the letters **ie** in the middle, try replacing them with just **e**: **prefiero** (*I prefer*); **diez** (*ten*, related to decimal).
- Where you see a word with the letters **ue** in the middle, try replacing them with **o**: **puerto** (*port*).
- Words which begin with **con-, dis-, im-, in-, re-, sub-** in Spanish usually begin with *con-, dis-, im-, in-, re-, sub-* in English; words beginning with **des-** in Spanish begin with *dis-* in English.
- Many words which end in **-able** and **-ible** in Spanish usually have the same ending in English; other similar English-Spanish endings are:

| Spanish | -ero/-era, -or/-ora | -miento | -aje | -oso/a | -ista | -ción | -al |
|---------|---------------------|---------|------|--------|-------|-------|-----|
| English | -er | -ment | -age | -ous | -ist | -tion | -al |

# Write words down

## Short cuts: looking for patterns

Certain letter patterns reveal important facts about the type of word you are trying to learn.

- Most words in Spanish ending in -o (except verbs) are masculine, belonging to the same group of words as real masculine words such as **chico** (*boy*) and **toro** (*bull*)
- Most words in Spanish ending in -a (except verbs) are feminine, belonging to the same group of words as real feminine words such as **chica** (*girl*) and **vaca** (*cow*)
- Most masculine words end in -o.
- Most feminine words end in -a.
- Words ending in -aje, -or, and -án are masculine.
- Words ending in -ión, -dad are feminine.
- Almost all verb forms end in a vowel, s or n, r or d: -a, -e, -i, -o; -as, -es, -áis, -éis, ís, -mos; -an, -en, -ron, -rán; -ar, -er, -ir; -ad, -ed, -id.

Other patterns can be seen in Spanish which are similar to those in English:

- Words ending in -**mente** (adverbs) are similar to English words ending in -**ly**, such as **rápidamente** (*rapidly*); **normalmente** (*normally*); as you can see, in Spanish and English they are based on adjectives, in this case **rápido** (*rapid*) and **normal** (*normal*), simply with the endings -**mente** and -**ly**.
- Sometimes if you know a basic Spanish word, it is easy to work out an adapted version. Here are some examples showing how this works:

| | | | |
|---|---|---|---|
| -ero | = -er | **granja** (*farm*), | **granjero** (*farmer*) |
| -or | = -er | **conducir** (*to drive*), | **conductor** (*driver*) |
| -oso/a | = -ous | **fábula** (*fable*), | **fabuloso** (*fabulous*) |
| -ista | = -ist | **guitarra** (*guitar*), | **guitarrista** (*guitarist*) |

- Similarly, some Spanish words can be converted by adding a syllable at the beginning, and most work the same as in English, as follows:

| | | |
|---|---|---|
| **con-** | = *con-* | **tener** (to *have, hold*), **contener** (to *contain implies within*) |
| **re-** | = *re-* | **inventar** (to *invent*), **reinventar** (to *reinvent*) |

- the following syllables added to the beginning of a word cause it to have the opposite or negative meaning:

| | | |
|---|---|---|
| **dis-/des-** = *dis-* | | **aparecer** (to *appear*), **desaparecer** (to *disappear*) |
| **im-** | = *im-* | **posible** (*possible*), **imposible** (*impossible*) |
| **in-** | = *in-* | **tolerante** (*tolerant*), **intolerante** (*intolerant*) |

---

## The alphabet

This is the English alphabet with Spanish pronunciation, which is useful if you need to spell out your name, surname, address and so on. The letters peculiar to the Spanish alphabet are listed separately at the end.

a  **a** as in c**a**t
b  **be** as in **b**erry
c  **the** as in **the**spian (soft)
d  **de** as in **d**en, or **the** as in **the**n
e  **e** as in **e**gg
f  **efe** as in e**f**fective
g  **je** – rough **h** sound as in clearing your throat
h  **atche**
i  **ee** as in p**ee**p
j  **hota** starting with rough **h** sound

k  **ca** as in **c**at
l  **ele** as in **el**ephant
m  **eme** as in **em**ery board
n  **ene** as in **en**emy
o  **o** as in c**o**t
p  **pe** as in **pe**ar
q  **cu** as in **cu**ckoo
r  **erre** as in he**r**etic, with rolled **r**
s  **ese** as in **es**sence
t  **te** as in **te**rrible
u  **oo** as in cuck**oo**
v  **oove: oo** as in cuck**oo** and **e** as in **e** above
w  **oovedoble: oove** as in the above, plus **dobblei**
x  **eckeess**
y  **ee griyega** (Greek **i**)
z  **theta** as in **the**spian

The following are letters peculiar to the Spanish alphabet, though only ñ appears separately in the dictionary.

ch  **che** as in **ch**erry
ll  **ellye**
ñ  **enye**

In addition, you may need to say some of the following if you have to spell out something more complicated:

| | |
|---|---|
| *punctuation* | la puntuación |
| *full stop* | el punto final |
| *comma* | la coma |
| *colon* | dos puntos |
| *semi colon* | punto y coma |
| *question mark* | el signo de interrogación |
| *exclamation mark* | el signo de admiración |
| *inverted commas* | comillas |
| *capital letter* | la mayúscula |
| *small letter, lower case* | la minúscula |
| *hyphen* | el guión |

| | |
|---|---|
| *paragraph* | el párrafo |
| *sentence* | la frase |
| *line* | la línea |
| *dash* | la raya |
| *dot-dot-dot* | los puntos suspensivos |
| *full stop, new sentence* | punto y seguido |
| *full stop, new paragraph/line* | punto y aparte |
| *next word* | a continuación |
| *space* | el espacio |
| *blank* | el espacio |
| *forward slash* | la barra oblicua |
| *backward slash* | la barra inversa |
| *@/at* | la arroba |
| *computer keyboard* | el teclado |
| *control* | la tecla Control |
| *alt* | la tecla Alt |
| *delete* | la tecla de borrado, de supresión |
| *enter* | la tecla Entrar-Retorno |
| *return* | la tecla de retorno |

## Pronunciation

If you wish to speak Spanish with a good accent, the following tips will be useful.

**1** Vowels: all are pure and always sound the same (see **the alphabet** above). Where two or more vowels occur together, each is pronounced with its normal value and in the correct order.

..........................................................

buenos días = booenos deeas
adiós, hasta luego = adeeos, hasta looego

..........................................................

**2** Consonants are **always** pronounced, with one notable exception: **h**, which is never pronounced. Most of the consonants are pronounced as indicated in **the alphabet** above, but note that some have sounds which are different from English.

**3** Note and learn the pronunciation of the following consonants:

................................................................

**c**: hard **c** before **a**, **o** and **u**: **c**asa, **c**omo, **c**ulebra
**BUT:** soft **th** (**ceceo**) before **e** and **i**: **c**ero, do**c**e, **c**ine, vi**c**io
(pronounced the same as **z**, **but** replaced by **seseo**
(**s** sound) in Southern Spain and all of Latin America)
**g**: hard **g** before **a**, **o** and **u**: **g**ato, **g**orra, **g**uerra
**BUT:** rough **h** sound before **e** and **i**: **g**eneral, **G**inebra
(this is pronounced the same as **j**)

................................................................

- In verb forms, to preserve hard **c** sound, the **c** is changed to **qu** before **e**: e.g. sacar → sa**qué**;
- Similarly, to preserve hard **g** before **e** and **i**, Spanish inserts a **u** to protect the **g**: cargar → car**gué**
- Also, note that **z** is often used for the soft **th** sound where verb forms would otherwise affect the **c**, and **j** replaces **g** where necessary:

hacer → hizo
coger → cojo

**4** Note the following consonants and combinations of consonants and their pronunciation.

................................................................

**cc** – as in a**cc**ión: pronounced as a**cth**ión
**ll** – as in **ll**ave and ca**ll**e, pronounced as **-ly-**
**nn** – each **n** is pronounced with normal value
**rr** – pronounced as a double trill of the tongue
(compare pe**r**o and pe**rr**o)
**ch** – pronounced as in English: **ch**ico, azaba**che**
................................................................

**5** Finally, an extra hint:

> **q** is always followed by **u**, which are pronounced as **k**
> que = **k**e; NEVER as in English **qu**ick

**6** Spanish intonation: the voice rises towards a comma, and towards the end of a question, but falls towards the end of a statement.

**7** Stress: all words of more than one syllable have one syllable stressed more than the rest. There are three hard and fast rules, but it is worth learning each new word with its stress pattern:

**1** Words ending with a **vowel**, **n** or **s** have the stress on the **last but one** syllable.
   **ni**ño, **ha**cen, con**se**jo, diccio**na**rio, pose**sio**nes

**2** Words ending with a **consonant except n** or **s** have the stress on the **last** syllable.
   Ma**drid**, mu**jer**, pa**pel**, re**loj**, cono**cer**, desayu**nar**

**3** Words which break rules 1 and 2 have a **written accent** to show where the stress falls.
   mi**ró**, cham**pán**, **pá**jaro, condi**ción**, cham**pú**, ha**cé**is

- When a word gains a syllable when made plural, an accent may either be lost or gained to keep the stress in the right place:

   condición → condiciones
   autobús → autobuses
   examen → exámenes

Needless to say, this happens a great deal with verb forms.

- Accents are also used to distinguish between pairs of otherwise identical words.

| | | | |
|---|---|---|---|
| *you* (object) | te | té | *tea* |
| *your* | tu | tú | *you* (subject) |
| *if* | si | sí | *yes* |

To sum up, once you are familiar with all of the above rules, Spanish spelling and pronunciation are very reliable. Of course you won't learn them overnight, and it may be best to concentrate on learning and practising one at a time. Another useful method is to record and listen to spoken Spanish as often as possible. Here are some ideas as to how you can make recordings of natural spoken Spanish:

- Take a portable cassette player and some blank cassettes every time you go to Spain. Try recording from the local radio, or even people speaking, though you ought to ask their permission first!
- Try playing around with your radio tuner to find a Spanish radio station, and if you do, try to record some Spanish.
- If you have Spanish friends, ask them to make recordings for you, perhaps sending you messages with their family news, or giving their views on topics of interest to you.
- If you have satellite TV, see if you can also receive Spanish radio, and if not, talk to your local TV shop to ask if it is worth re-tuning your satellite equipment.
- If you have access to the internet, try to find Spanish radio broadcasts, which are sometimes possible via radio station websites.
- Once you have some recordings, listen to them as often as possible, and try to repeat what you hear, imitating the sounds, and repeating short chunks of Spanish. You might try writing out small sections, saying them aloud and comparing your version with the original.
- If you have Spanish friends, try recording short messages on cassette, send them to your friends, and ask them to comment on, and correct your pronunciation.
- When speaking direct to Spanish people, ask them to correct your pronunciation when possible.

# Toolbox

## Nouns – gender and plurals

All Spanish nouns – names of things or people – are either masculine or feminine, as explained above. Most end in -o (masculine) or -a (feminine), though there are exceptions to this rule and there are also other common masculine and feminine endings. However, all nouns form their plural by adding -s or, if the noun ends in a consonant, adding -es. Adjectives behave in exactly the same way – see Section C.

| | |
|---|---|
| libro / libros | book / books |
| rosa / rosas | rose / roses |
| coche (m) / coches | car / cars |
| llave (f) / llaves | key / keys |
| reloj / relojes | watch / watches |

Many nouns, notably those referring to people, have specific masculine and feminine forms. Some of these have been used in the following table to show typical masculine, feminine, singular and plural forms:

| masculine singular | feminine singular | masculine plural | feminine plural |
|---|---|---|---|
| **chico** boy | **chica** girl | **chicos** boys | **chicas** girls |
| **hijo** son | **hija** daughter | **hijos** sons | **hijas** daughters |
| **hermano** brother | **hermana** sister | **hermanos** brothers | **hermanas** sisters |
| **tío** uncle | **tía** aunt | **tíos** uncles | **tías** aunts |
| **secretario** secretary | **secretaria** secretary | **secretarios** secretaries | **secretarias** secretaries |

| estudiante | estudiante | estudiantes | estudiantes |
|---|---|---|---|
| *student* | *student* | *students* | *students* |
| **profesor** | **profesora** | **profesores** | **profesoras** |
| *teacher* | *teacher* | *teachers* | *teachers* |

## Articles and other determiners

Nouns are often preceded by an article, in English either *the* (definite article) or *a / an* (indefinite article). There are more articles in Spanish, because there are masculine, feminine, singular and plural forms as set out below. It is very useful to learn nouns with their definite or indefinite article, so that you know its gender:

| **un libro** | *a book* | **el libro / los libros** | *the book / books* |
|---|---|---|---|
| **una rosa** | *a rose* | **la rosa / las rosas** | *the rose / roses* |
| **un coche** | *a car* | **el coche / los coches** | *the car / cars* |
| **un reloj** | *a watch* | **el reloj / los relojes** | *the watch / watches* |

Of course, nouns can have other so-called 'determiners' (modifying words) in front of them, expressing possession or specifying which of two or more is referred to. Notice how, in the following table, nouns, articles and determiners are set out in columns: whichever column the noun is in, you can only use it with articles and determiners from that same column, so that they match the noun in gender and number (for example, **nuestra madre**). The table also includes a couple of adjectives (*old*, *young*) to show how they fit into this pattern.

| meaning | masculine singular | feminine singular | masculine plural | feminine plural |
| --- | --- | --- | --- | --- |
| child / children | niño | niña | niños | niñas |
| father(s) + mother(s) | padre | madre | padres | madres |
| old | viejo | vieja | viejos | viejas |
| young | joven | joven | jóvenes | jóvenes |
| the | el | la | los | las |
| a/an; some (in plural) | un | una | unos | unas |
| my | mi | mi | mis | mis |
| your (familiar) | tu | tu | tus | tus |
| his / her / its / your (formal) | su | su | sus | sus |
| our | nuestro | nuestra | nuestros | nuestras |
| your | vuestro | vuestra | vuestros | vuestras |
| their | su | su | sus | sus |
| this / these | este | esta | estos | estas |
| that those | ese | esa | esos | esas |
| that / those | aquel | aquella | aquellos | aquellas |

Here are some more examples:

**No es mi amigo – es tu amigo.** *He's not my friend, he's yours.*

**Nuestros hijos jóvenes van a esta escuela.** *Our young children go to this school.*

**No me gusta este vestido; prefiero aquella falda.** *I don't like this dress; I prefer that skirt.*

14

## Adjectives

Adjectives are describing words which add information about nouns. They have to match the noun in gender and number, so they also follow the pattern set out in the previous table. Thus, in masculine form most adjectives end in -o, and in feminine form most end in -a. Adjectives that end in -e can be used either with a masculine or a feminine noun without change; there are several other possible adjective endings. All adjectives form their plural by adding -s or -es, just as for nouns.

Unlike English, Spanish usually places adjectives just after the noun they describe, but a few can go in front. They can also be used in other situations, such as after the verb *to be*.

| | |
|---|---|
| **el jardín grande** | *the large garden* |
| **la casa pequeña** | *the small house* |
| **los melones baratos** | *the cheap melons* |
| **las bicicletas caras** | *the expensive bikes* |
| **el chico es gordo** | *the boy is fat* |
| **las manzanas son deliciosas** | *the apples are delicious* |

The table opposite shows how a couple of adjectives fit into the pattern of possible forms for nouns, adjectives, articles and determiners.

It is worth learning a few set phrases to help you remember the need for agreement and some typical endings:

**masc. singular:** un toro negro; el río grande; este libro interesante; tu viejo amigo

**fem. singular:** una paloma blanca; la isla bonita; esa chica guapa; nuestra tía tonta

**masc. plural:** unos vinos tintos; los ángeles buenos; aquellos chicos malos; mis hijos feos

**fem. plural:** unas mujeres elegantes; las vegas fértiles; estas peras maduras; sus casas modernas

Here is a list of useful adjectives for describing people; remember, those ending in -o change to -a for the feminine form, and all add -s for the plural; one or two are invariable (inv.), i.e. the same form is used for masculine and feminine forms:

| | | | |
|---|---|---|---|
| *tall / big* | **alto** | *short* | **bajo** |
| *thin* | **delgado** | *fat* | **gordo** |
| *old* | **viejo / anciano** | *young* | **joven** |
| *happy (contented)* | **contento** | *sad* | **triste** |
| *happy (nature)* | **feliz** | *unhappy* | **infeliz** |
| *quiet / shy* | **tímido** | *loud* | **extrovertido** |
| *relaxed / laid back* | **relajado** | *stressed* | **estresado** |
| *nice, pleasant* | **simpático** | *nasty* | **antipático** |
| *kind* | **amable** | *unhelpful* | **poco amable** |
| *self-centred / egoistic* | **egoísta** (inv.) | *considerate / helpful* | **atento** |
| *sporty / active* | **deportista** (inv.) | *lazy* | **perezoso** |
| *good looking* | **guapo / hermoso** | *ugly* | **feo** |
| *outstanding / exceptional* | **extraordinario** | *ordinary / un-remarkable* | **ordinario** |
| *smart* | **elegante** | *scruffy* | **descuidado** |
| *well-behaved* | **que se porta bien** | *naughty* | **travieso** |
| *polite* | **cortés, educado** | *rude* | **grosero** |

The following adjectives can be used to describe things:

| | | | |
|---|---|---|---|
| *old* | **viejo** | *new* | **nuevo** |
| *good* | **bueno** | *bad* | **malo** |
| *cheap* | **barato** | *expensive* | **caro** |
| *fast* | **rápido** | *slow* | **lento** |
| *in good condition* | **en buen estado** | *damaged* | **en mal estado** |
| *flimsy* | **poco sólido** | *solid* | **sólido** |
| *rough* | **áspero** | *smooth* | **liso** |
| *shiny* | **brillante** | *matt* | **mate** |

| nice | **agradable** | *horrible* | **horrible** |
| *soft* | **blando** | *hard* | **duro** |
| *interesting* | **interesante** | *boring* | **aburrido, pesado** |

Often, we use adjectives to compare one thing or person with another, or with all others. To say something is ...-*er* than another, we use the comparative form of the adjective, and to say it is the ...-*est*, we use the superlative form. The comparative of most Spanish adjectives is formed by simply putting **más** in front of the adjective, and the superlative uses **el / la / los / las más** in front of the adjective. Some examples can be seen in the following table. Four Spanish adjectives – for *big*, *small*, *good* and *bad* – have different forms in the comparative and superlative, and these are shown at the end of the table. However, please note that in practice **más grande** or **más pequeño** etc. are often used instead of **mayor** or **menor** etc.

| adjective | | comparative | | superlative | |
|---|---|---|---|---|---|
| *big* | **grande, grandes** | *bigger* | **mayor mayores** | *biggest* | **el / la mayor los/las mayores** |
| *small* | **pequeño/a pequeños/as** | *smaller* | **menor menores** | *smallest* | **el / la menor los/las menores** |
| *good* | **bueno/a buenos/as** | *better* | **mejor mejores** | *best* | **el/la mejor los/las mejores** |
| *bad* | **malo/a malos/malas** | *worse* | **peor peores** | *worse* | **el/la peor los/las peores** |
| *ugly* | **feo** | *uglier* | **más feo** | *ugliest* | **el más feo** etc |
| *intelligent* | **inteligente** | *more intelligent* | **más inteligente** | *most intelligent* | **el más inteligente** etc. |
| *useful* | **útil** | *more useful* | **más útil** | *most useful* | **el más útil** etc. |

## Verbs

### Infinitives and present tense

Verbs are words which describe actions, including abstract states or changes. Most verb forms tell you who is doing the action and when it is done, as well as what is being done (the **www** address of the verb!). Whilst in English the who idea is expressed mostly by a person word (I, you, he, she, it, we, they) in front of the verb, in Spanish the verb ending is enough to show this, and person words (subject pronouns) are only used **when** clarification or emphasis is needed. The subject pronouns are included in the tables below just for clarity. The verb endings also show when the action is done – past, present or future. Here are examples, of the three main types of Spanish verb in the **present** tense. The headings of the tables show the **infinitive** of the verb, the part of the verb without the person ending, and the form found in dictionaries and wordlists meaning 'to ...'.

| pronoun | hablar (infinitive) | *to speak* |
|---|---|---|
| yo | hablo | *I speak* |
| tú* | hablas | *you speak (familiar)* |
| él / ella / usted* | habla | *he / she speaks, you speak (formal)* |
| nosotros/as | hablamos | *we speak* |
| vosotros/as* | habláis | *you speak (familiar plural)* |
| ellos / ellas / ustedes* | hablan | *they speak you speak (formal plural)* |

| pronoun | comer (infinitive) | *to eat* |
| --- | --- | --- |
| yo | como | *I eat* |
| tú* | comes | *you eat (familiar)* |
| él / ella / | come | *he / she eats,* |
| usted* | | *you eat (formal)* |
| nosotros/as | comemos | *we eat* |
| vosotros/as* | coméis | *you eat (familiar plural)* |
| ellos / ellas / | comen | *they eat* |
| ustedes* | | *you eat (formal plural)* |

| pronoun | vivir (infinitive) | *to live* |
| --- | --- | --- |
| yo | vivo | *I live* |
| tú* | vives | *you live (familiar)* |
| él / ella / | vive | *he / she lives,* |
| usted* | | *you live (formal)* |
| nosotros/as | vivimos | *we live* |
| vosotros/as* | vivís | *you live (familiar plural)* |
| ellos / ellas / | viven | *they live* |
| ustedes* | | *you live (formal plural)* |

* **usted** and **ustedes** are the 'formal' or 'polite' ways of saying *you*, singular and plural. For historical reasons, they are used with the he/she/it form of the verb. The 'informal' or 'familiar' words for *you* are **tú** and **vosotros/as** (the latter has masculine and feminine forms). In most cases, strangers will address you as **usted**, though when speaking to friends and younger people, **tú** is used. If in doubt, use **usted** until and unless invited to use **tú**. A Spanish person may invite you to use **tú** by saying **Podemos tutearnos, ¿no?**

Throughout this book when verb forms are translated, *you* is translated as either **tú** or **usted**, depending on which is most likely for the expression translated; sometimes both are given, but if you see *, it is to remind you that you need to decide on which to use. The object pronoun for **tú** is **te**, and for **usted** is **le**. Both are usually given, for you to choose.

The *I* form is known as the first person singular, *you* as the second person singular, *he / she / it* as the third person singular, *we* as the first person plural, *you* (plural) as the second person plural, and *they* as the third person plural.

It is useful to learn these verb patterns by heart, so that using them, and choosing the correct one becomes automatic.

Here are the patterns for some other useful verbs in the present tense:

| | | |
|---|---|---|
| ser* | *to be* | soy, eres, es, somos, sois, son |
| estar* | *to be* | estoy, estás, está, estamos, estáis, están |
| tener | *to have* | tengo, tienes, tiene, tenemos, tenéis, tienen |
| ir | *to go* | voy, vas, va, vamos, vais, van |
| hacer | *to do* | hago, haces, hace, hacemos, hacéis, hacen |

*There are two verbs for *to be* in Spanish: *ser* is used for *permanent* notions, often describing the *essence* of something or somebody; *estar* is used to describe *where* somebody or something is, or what *state* they are in.

Here are the infinitives and first person (*I* form) of 26 of the most useful verbs. In the majority of cases you can probably work out the other forms for yourself, but because some are less predictable (irregular) it is worth checking them in a good dictionary, grammar book or verb book:

| | |
|---|---|
| *to answer* | **contestar; contesto** |
| *to arrive* | **llegar; llego** |
| *to ask* | **preguntar; pregunto** |
| *to be able to* | **poder; puedo** |
| *to bring / fetch* | **traer; traigo** |
| *to call (phone)* | **llamar; llamo** |
| *to cancel* | **anular; anulo** |
| *to find* | **encontrar; encuentro** |

| | |
|---|---|
| *to forget* | **olvidar; olvido** |
| *to give* | **dar; doy** |
| *to go in* | **entrar; entro** |
| *to go out* | **salir; salgo** |
| *to have to* | **tener que...; tengo que...** |
| *to know (a person, place)* | **conocer; conozco** |
| *to know (a fact, how to...)* | **saber; sé** |
| *to leave* | **irse; me voy** |
| *to look for* | **buscar; busco** |
| *to need* | **necesitar; necesito** |
| *to put* | **poner; pongo** |
| *to regret* | **lamentar; lamento** |
| *to remember* | **recordar; recuerdo** |
| *to reserve / book* | **reservar; reservo** |
| *to see* | **ver; veo** |
| *to take* | **tomar; tomo / coger; cojo** |
| *to want* | **querer; quiero** |
| *to write* | **escribir; escribo** |

Note how the *I* form always ends in -o, except **soy, estoy, voy** and **doy**. As you come to learn more verbs forms, you will find more patterns like this.

### Reflexive verbs

Some verbs have a special 'person word' in front of them where the action described in some way 'bounces back', affecting the person doing the action. In English, these are called reflexive verbs and have a 'self' word attached, i.e. *I wash myself*.

Here is a typical reflexive verb set out in full; remember that the subject pronoun in the first column is not usually needed but the reflexive pronoun (in the second column) is always used:

| subject pronoun | reflexive pronoun | lavarse (infinitive) | to wash oneself |
|---|---|---|---|
| yo | me | lavo | *I wash myself* |
| tú | te | lavas | *you wash yourself* (familiar) |
| él/ella/ usted | se | lava | *he / she washes himself / herself, you wash yourself* (formal) |
| nosotros/as | nos | lavamos | *we wash ourselves* |
| vosotros/as | vos | laváis | *you wash yourselves* (familiar plural) |
| ellos/ellas/ ustedes | se | lavan | *they wash themselves you wash yourselves* (formal plural) |

Here are some more useful reflexive verbs. Notice the **se** attached to the end of the infinitive – this reminds you that the verb is reflexive. You will also recognize that many reflexive verbs describe everyday routine actions we do to ourselves. The first person form of each verb is also given to you.

| | | | |
|---|---|---|---|
| *to wake up* | **despertarse** | **me despierto** | *I wake up* |
| *to get up* | **levantarse** | **me levanto** | *I get up* |
| *to wash oneself* | **lavarse** | **me lavo** | *I wash myself* |
| *to have a shower* | **ducharse** | **me ducho** | *I have a shower* |
| *to dress oneself* | **vestirse** | **me visto** | *I get dressed* |
| *to have a shave* | **afeitarse** | **me afeito** | *I have a shave* |
| *to comb one's hair* | **peinarse** | **me peino** | *I comb my hair* |
| *to put on make-up* | **maquillarse** | **me maquillo** | *I put on make-up* |
| *to have a bath* | **bañarse** | **me baño** | *I have a bath* |
| *to go to bed* | **acostarse** | **me acuesto** | *I go to bed* |
| *to go to sleep* | **dormirse** | **me duermo** | *I go to sleep* |
| *to go for a walk* | **pasearse** | **me paseo** | *I go for a walk* |
| *to be called* | **llamarse** | **me llamo** | *I am called* |

| to leave / go away | **irse** | **me voy** | I'm going / leaving |
| to fall (down) | **caerse** | **me caigo** | I fall down |

NB The reflexive form of some other verbs is used to express the idea of, for example, two people seeing each other: nos vemos todos los días – we see each other every day.

---

## Talking about the past

Verbs have past tense forms to indicate actions which have already been done. With the exception of the perfect tense, the past tenses are formed by adding an ending to the stem of infinitive. Here are some examples with **hablar** – *to speak*:

| tense | use | example | endings |
| --- | --- | --- | --- |
| preterite | single completed actions | I spoke | hablé, hablaste, habló, hablamos, hablasteis, hablaron |
| imperfect | ongoing, repeated action | I was speaking | hablaba, hablabas, hablaba, hablábamos, hablabais, hablaban |
| perfect | single, completed recent actions | I have spoken | he hablado, has hablado, ha hablado, hemos hablado, habéis hablado, han hablado |

Note that each tense has some very definite distinguishing features, the sign of that tense, either in its shape (perfect: two words), in its spelling (imperfect: -ab- or -í-) or its stress pattern (the preterite mostly has stress on the first syllable of its endings). The perfect tense is very straightforward in Spanish: the present tense of the verb **haber** is used for the first part of it, together with the past participle of the main verb.

As you can see, for single, completed actions at a specific time in the past, you can use the perfect tense if the action was recent, or the preterite if not recent. You use the imperfect tense when you are talking about something that was happening, or used to happen, or for descriptions in the past.

Here are ten useful verbs in the preterite:

| infinitive | meaning | forms | meaning |
|---|---|---|---|
| ir / ser | to go / to be | fui, fuiste, fue, fuimos, fuisteis, fueron | I went etc. |
| venir | to come | vine, viniste, vino, vinimos, vinisteis, vinieron | I came etc. |
| entrar | to go in, to enter | entré, entraste, entró, entramos, entrasteis, entraron | I entered etc. |
| salir | to go out | salí, saliste, salió, salimos, salisteis, salieron | I went out etc. |
| despertarse | to wake up | me desperté, te despertaste, se despertó, nos despertamos, os despertasteis, se despertaron | I woke up etc. |
| tomar | to take (also to eat/drink) | tomé, tomaste, tomó, tomamos, tomasteis, tomaron | I took etc. |

| levantarse | to get up | me levanté, | I got up etc. |
| | | te levantaste, | |
| | | se levantó, | |
| | | nos levantamos, | |
| | | os levantasteis, | |
| | | se levantaron | |
| comer | to eat | comí, comiste, | I ate etc. |
| | | comió, comimos, | |
| | | comisteis, comieron | |
| beber | to drink | bebí, bebiste, | I drank etc. |
| | | bebió, bebimos, | |
| | | bebisteis, bebieron | |
| divertirse | to enjoy yourself | me divertí, te divertiste, | I enjoyed myself etc. |
| | | se divirtió, | |
| | | nos divertimos, | |
| | | os divertisites, | |
| | | se divirtieron | |

Here are 15 useful verbs in the imperfect tense. Only the first three are given in full, since, once you have the first person (I) form, the remaining forms of the rest follow predictably, with the exception of ser and ir.

| | |
|---|---|
| I was | **era, eras, era, éramos, éramos, erais, eran** |
| I was going | **iba, ibas, iba, íbamos, ibais, iban** |
| I had | **tenía, tenías, tenía, teníamos, teníais, tenían** |
| I could | **podía** |
| I was drinking | **bebía** |
| I was working | **trabajaba** |
| I was studying | **estudiaba** |
| I was eating | **comía** |
| I was talking | **hablaba** |
| I was travelling | **viajaba** |
| I used to live | **vivía** |
| I used to visit | **visitaba** |
| I used to see | **veía** |

| | |
|---|---|
| *I used to want* | **quería** |
| *I used to know* | **sabía** |

---

## Talking about the future

The future tense is always formed by adding the appropriate endings to the infinitive or an adopted form of it. Therefore, its distinguishing feature is always an -r- before the appropriate ending. The endings are the same for all verbs, without exception.

hablaré, hablarás, hablará, hablaremos, hablaréis, hablarán

There is another way of talking about future events if they are on the point of happening. As in English, you can use the present tense of **ir** (*to go*) with **a** and the infinitive of the main verb:

| | |
|---|---|
| *I am going to sing* | **voy a cantar** |
| *you are going to listen* | **vas a escuchar** |
| *he is going to play* | **va a jugar** |
| *we are going to watch* | **vamos a mirar** |
| *you (pl.) are going to go out* | **vais a salir** |
| *they are going to finish* | **van a terminar** |

Here are some of the most commonly used verbs in the future tense; note that some have slight spelling changes to the infinitive, though the endings are all the same as those shown previously. Only the first person form is given – you can work out the others.

| | | | |
|---|---|---|---|
| *to go* | **ir** | *I will go* | **iré** |
| *to arrive* | **llegar** | *I will arrive* | **llegaré** |
| *to know* | **saber** | *I will know* | **sabré** |
| *to want* | **querer** | *I will want* | **querré** |
| *to go out* | **salir** | *I will go out* | **saldré** |
| *to put* | **poner** | *I will put* | **pondré** |

| | | | |
|---|---|---|---|
| to have | **tener** | I will have | **tendré** |
| to come | **venir** | I will come | **vendré** |
| to say | **decir** | I will say | **diré** |
| to do | **hacer** | I will do | **haré** |

Here are some useful phrases in the future tense:

| | |
|---|---|
| I will go – will you be going to the meeting? | **Iré yo; ¿vas a ir a la reunión?** |
| I will be OK. Will you be all right? | **Estaré bien. Y tú, ¿vas a estar bien?** |
| I will do it. Will you do it? | **Voy a hacerlo. ¿Lo harás tú?** |
| Will you take the bus? | **¿Vas a coger el autobús?** |
| How will you go? | **¿Cómo vas a ir?** |
| When will you arrive? | **¿A qué hora llegarás?** |
| When will you leave? | **¿Cuándo te irás?** |
| What will the weather be like? | **¿Qué tiempo hará?** |
| How much will it cost? | **¿Cuánto costará?** |
| Will it be suitable for children? | **¿Será adecuado para los niños?** |
| What will he do? | **¿Qué hará él?** |
| What will he have to drink? | **Él, ¿qué va a tomar?** |
| What will you take? | **¿Qué vas a llevar?** |
| When will it be? | **¿Cuándo será?** |
| Is it going to rain? Or will it snow? | **¿Lloverá, o va a nevar?** |
| Will it be fine? | **¿Hará buen tiempo?** |
| Will there be much traffic? | **¿Habrá mucho tráfico?** |
| There will be a lot of work. | **Habrá mucho trabajo.** |

## Conditional and subjunctives

Special verb forms are used for expressing conditions, wishes and so on. Here are examples of these:

me **gustaría**  I would like
no quiero que **vayas**  I don't wish you to go

The first of these is a good example of the conditional. You may have spotted that, as with the future, the ending is put after the whole of the infinitive. Therefore all forms have an -r- in them. You may also recognize the ending – the same as the imperfect endings for –er and –ir verbs. Here are some useful expressions, using all forms of the conditional:

| | | |
|---|---|---|
| *to prefer* | **preferir** | **Preferiría ir al bar.** |
| | | *I would prefer to go to the bar.* |
| *to feel like* | **apetecer** | **¿Te apetecería un café?** |
| | | *Do you feel like a coffee?* |
| *to like* | **gustar** | **¿Le gustaría un aperitivo?** |
| | | *Would you like an aperitif?* |
| *to appreciate* | **apreciar** | **El apreciaría tu ayuda.** |
| | | *He would appreciate your help.* |
| *to be able to* | **poder** | **Ella podría ir mañana.** |
| | | *She could go tomorrow.* |
| *to go* | **ir** | **Iríamos si pudiéramos.** |
| | | *We would go if we could.* |
| *to have* | **tener** | **¿Tendríais tiempo?** |
| | | *Would you have time?* |
| *to be* | **ser** | **Ustedes serían bienvenidos.** |
| | | *You would be welcome.* |
| *to do* | **hacer** | **Ellos lo harían mañana.** |
| | | *They would do it tomorrow.* |
| *to take* | **coger** | **Ellas cogerían el primer tren.** |
| | | *They would catch the first train.* |

The subjunctive is a special verb form used where there is doubt or uncertainty, and in some command forms, and it has its own forms and endings. Here are some useful expressions using the subjunctive:

| | |
|---|---|
| **¡No hagas eso!** | *Don't do that!* |
| **¡No me mires así!** | *Don't look at me like that!* |
| **¡Hable despacio, por favor!** | *Speak slowly, please!* |

| | |
|---|---|
| **Deme un kilo de azúcar, por favor.** | *Give me a kilo of sugar, please.* |
| **Dígame, ¿dónde está Correos?** | *Tell me, where is the post office?* |
| **Te digo que no salgas.** | *I'm telling you not to go out.* |
| **Quiero que cierres la puerta.** | *I want you to close the door.* |
| **Nos dicen que no vayamos.** | *They are telling us not to go.* |
| **Le dijeron que no entrara.** | *They told him not to go in.* |
| **No queríais que él fuera a España.** | *You didn't want him to go to Spain.* |

---

## Negative expressions – saying you don't!

The Spanish word **no** means both *no* and *not*, and it is often used by itself. Other negative expressions are given below, and **no** is used in front of the verb to introduce a negative. Negative expressions can also be used by themselves in front of the verb. Here are some useful negative expressions:

| | |
|---|---|
| **No como carne, no me gusta.** | *I don't eat meat, I don't like it.* |
| **No, no quiero salir.** | *No, I don't want to go out.* |
| **No tiene nada.** | *He has nothing. / He hasn't got anything.* |
| **No vale nada.** | *Nothing is any good.* |
| **No vio a nadie.** | *She saw nobody.* |
| **Nadie va a aquella tienda.** | *No one goes to that shop.* |
| **No trabajamos nunca en casa.** | *We never work at home.* |
| **Jamás voy en autobús.** | *I never go by bus.* |
| **No rompí ninguna ventana.** | *I broke no windows.* |
| **No tiene ni familia ni amigos.** | *He has neither family nor friends.* |

Here are some further useful examples of negative expressions:

| | |
|---|---|
| *My friend doesn't have a car.* | **Mi amigo no tiene coche.** |
| *I don't have a bike.* | **No tengo bicicleta.** |
| *I don't watch TV.* | **No veo la tele.** |
| *I don't smoke.* | **No fumo.** |

| | |
|---|---|
| *I don't go there any more.* | **Ya no voy allí.** |
| *I won't see him / her any more.* | **Ya no lo / la veré más.** |
| *I don't play any more.* | **Ya no juego.** |
| *Didn't you book a table?* | **¿No reservaste una mesa?** |
| *No they didn't answer the phone.* | **No, no contestaron el teléfono.** |
| *Didn't you get to the bank?* | **¿No llegaste al banco?** |
| *No, it wasn't open.* | **No, no estaba abierto.** |
| *Didn't you speak to him?* | **¿No hablaste con él?** |
| *Didn't you get tickets for the match?* | **¿No conseguiste entradas para el partido?** |
| *No, there weren't any left.* | **No quedaban.** |
| *Didn't you see your friend?* | **¿No viste a tu amigo?** |
| *No, he wasn't in.* | **No estaba.** |
| *Don't walk on the grass.* | **No pisar la hierba.** |
| *No entry* | **Prohibido entrar** |
| *No exit* | **Prohibido salir por aquí** |
| *No admission* | **No hay acceso** |
| *No smoking* | **No fumar** |
| *No dogs* | **Prohibido el acceso a perros** |
| *Don't do it!* | **¡No lo haga(s)!** |
| *Don't eat it!* | **¡No lo coma(s)!** |
| *Don't open the window.* | **No abra(s) la ventana.** |
| *Don't cross the road.* | **Prohibido cruzar la carretera.** |
| *... is not allowed / permitted* | **no se permite ...** |

---

## Interrogative – asking questions

In English we sometimes ask questions by reversing the subject (person) and verb, so that, for example, the statement 'He is in a meeting' becomes 'Is he in a meeting?' as a question. In Spanish this is not practical, because the subject pronoun is not usually used. In spoken Spanish, the rise and fall of the voice (intonation) shows whether a question or a statement is intended – the voice rises at the end of a question, falls at the end of a statement. As a result, an ordinary sentence and a question can have the same words in the same order. In written Spanish an upside-down question mark shows a question is on the way. Thus:

| | |
|---|---|
| **¿Hablas inglés?** | *Do you speak English?* |
| **Hablas inglés.** | *You speak English.* |
| **Te gustan las manzanas.** | *You like apples.* |
| **¿Te gustan las manzanas?** | *Do you like apples?* |

Here are some more examples of questions; the normal answer expected would begin with **sí** or **no**:

| | |
|---|---|
| *Did you go to town?* | **¿Fuiste a la ciudad?** |
| *Have you seen him?* | **¿Le viste?** |
| *Did you try the steak?* | **¿Probaste el bistec?** |
| *Have you seen the film?* | **¿Has visto la película?** |
| *Do you drive a car?* | **¿Conduces un coche?** |
| *Do you smoke?* | **¿Usted fuma?** |
| *Do you prefer red or white wine?* | **¿Prefiere usted vino tinto o blanco?** |
| *Do you eat fish?* | **¿Comes pescado?** |
| *Are you taking medication?* | **¿Está tomando medicina / medicamento?** |

There are several words which can introduce a question, as you can see in the following examples:

| | |
|---|---|
| **¿Quién** abrió la puerta? | *Who opened the door?* |
| **¿Qué** tienes en la mano? | *What have you got in your hand?* |
| **¿Por qué** haces eso? | *Why are you doing that?* |
| **¿Para qué** lo quieres? | *What do you want it for?* |
| **¿Dónde** está tu amiga? | *Where is your girlfriend?* |
| **¿Cuál** quieres? | *Which one do you want?* |
| **¿Cuáles** quieres? | *Which ones do you want?* |
| **¿Cuándo** va a llegar el tren? | *When will the train arrive?* |
| **¿Cuánto** dinero necesitas? | *How much money do you need?* |
| **¿Cuántas** manzanas quieres? | *How many apples do you want?* |

¿Durante **cuánto** tiempo estás allí? *How long are you there for?*

Remember that you need to consider whether you are addressing the other person formally (**usted**) or informally (**tú**), as this will affect the form of the verb.

## Adverbs

You will remember that adjectives add information about nouns. In the same way, the main use of adverbs is to add information about actions. Many useful adverbs are based on adjectives: just as in English we add *–ly* to the adjective, Spanish adds **-mente** to the feminine form (if there is one – otherwise use the masculine). There are a few adverbs which don't follow this pattern – you will just have to learn these separately. The following table shows some useful adverbs (both regular and irregular in the way they are formed).

| *adjective* | *adjective* | *adverb* | *adverb* |
| --- | --- | --- | --- |
| | | muy | *very* |
| | | bastante | *quite* |
| mucho | *much* | más | *more, most* |
| poco | *little* | menos | *less, fewer* |
| bueno | *good* | bien | *well* |
| bueno | *good* | mejor | *better, best* |
| malo | *bad* | peor | *worse, worst* |
| malo | *bad* | mal | *badly* |
| rápido | *quick, fast, rapid* | rápidamente | *quickly, fast, rapidly* |
| lento | *slow* | lentamente | *slowly* |
| inmediato | *immediate* | inmediatamente | *immediately* |
| completo | *complete* | completamente | *completely* |

| | | | |
|---|---|---|---|
| repentino | *sudden* | de repente, repentino | *suddenly* |
| silencioso | *noiseless* | silenciosamente | *noiselessly* |
| doloroso | *painful* | dolorosamente | *painfully* |
| feliz | *happy* | felizmente | *happily* |
| condescend-iente | *condescending* | con condescen-cia | *condescend-ingly* |
| apropiado | *appropriate* | apropiadamente | *appropriately* |
| económico | *economic* | económicamente | *economically* |
| técnico | *technical* | técnicamente | *technically* |
| triste | *sad* | tristemente | *sadly* |
| frecuente | *frequent* | frecuentemente | *frequently* |
| previo | *previous* | previamente | *previously* |
| temprano | *early* | más temprano | *earlier* |
| próximo | *next* | próximamente | *next* |

Here are some additional adverbs and adverbial phrases, which do not fit into any pattern:

| | |
|---|---|
| **pocas veces** | *rarely* |
| **de vez en cuando** | *occasionally* |
| **a veces** | *sometimes* |
| **a menudo** | *often* |
| **muy a menudo** | *very often* |
| **ahora** | *now* |
| **ya** | *already* |
| **pronto** | *soon* |
| **antes** | *before* |
| **después** | *afterwards* |
| **entonces, luego** | *then* |
| **temprano** | *early* |
| **tarde** | *late* |
| **más tarde** | *later* |
| **un poco** | *a little* |

Just like adjectives, adverbs can also have comparative and superlative forms. They are formed in the same way, as shown in the first two examples in the following table; note also the special forms based on **bien** and **mal**:

| adverb | comparative | superlative | adverb | comparative | superlative |
|--------|-------------|-------------|--------|-------------|-------------|
| rápida-mente | más rápida-mente | lo más rápidamente | *fast* | *faster* | *fastest* |
| lenta-mente | más lenta-mente | lo más lenta-mente | *slow* | *slower* | *slowest* |
| bien | mejor | lo mejor | *well* | *better* | *best* |
| mal | peor | lo peor | *badly* | *worse* | *worst* |

## Colours and sizes

### *Colours* **los colores**

Here is a list of common colours. Remember, these are all adjectives, so they go after the noun and follow the usual rules of agreement with nouns. To remind you, those ending in –o can also have the endings –a (fem), -os (masc. plural) and –as (fem. plural); those ending in any other vowel or a consonant just have a plural ending in –es. There are also three which are invariable, marked (inv.), which don't change at all.

| | |
|--|--|
| *black* | **negro** |
| *blue* | **azul** |
| *brown* | **marrón** |
| *green* | **verde** |
| *grey* | **gris** |
| *mauve* | **malva (inv.)** |
| *orange* | **naranja (inv.)** |

| pink | rosa (inv.) |
| purple | purpúreo |
| red | rojo |
| white | blanco |
| yellow | amarillo |

Here are examples of colours in use:

| a red car | un coche rojo |
| a black suit | un traje negro |
| a pink jumper | un jersey rosa |
| a pink blouse | una blusa rosa |
| a blue shirt | una camisa azul |
| blue trainers | zapatillas azules |
| grey shoes | zapatos grises |
| brown gloves | guantes marrones |

Finally, here is a list of most of the other colours you are likely to need.

| cream / ivory | color crema | emerald | verde esmeralda |
| scarlet | (color) escarlata | olive green | verde oliva |
| | | dark green | verde oscuro |
| lilac | (color) lila | ruby | (color) rubí |
| light/pale blue | azul claro | salmon pink | color salmón |
| navy blue | azul marino | fuchsia | fucsia |
| royal blue | azul real | burgundy | granate |
| dark blue | azul oscuro | bright red | rojo fuerte / vivo |
| turquoise | azul turquesa | blue-grey | gris azulado |
| sapphire | azul zafiro | bottle green | verde botella |
| khaki | caqui | pale green | verde claro |
| | | beige | (color) beige |

## Sizes

Sizes too are adjectives, and follow the normal rules on position and agreement.

| | |
|---|---|
| *very small* | **muy pequeño, pequeñito, chico** |
| *small* | **pequeño** |
| *medium, average* | **mediano** |
| *large* | **grande** |
| *very large* | **muy grande** |
| *wide* | **ancho** |
| *narrow* | **estrecho** |
| *long* | **largo** |
| *short (people / stature)* | **bajo** |
| *short (objects)* | **corto** |

---

# Numbers, times, days and dates

### *Cardinal numbers* **los números cardinales**

| | | |
|---|---|---|
| 1 uno / una | 11 once | 21 veintiuno/a |
| 2 dos | 12 doce | 22 veintidós |
| 3 tres | 13 trece | 23 veintitrés |
| 4 cuatro | 14 catorce | 24 veinticuatro |
| 5 cinco | 15 quince | 25 veinticinco |
| 6 seis | 16 dieciséis | 26 veintiséis |
| 7 siete | 17 diecisiete | 27 vientisiete |
| 8 ocho | 18 dieciocho | 28 veintiocho |
| 9 nueve | 19 diecinueve | 29 veintinueve |
| 10 diez | 20 veinte | 30 treinta |

31 treinta y uno / una etc
40 cuarenta etc
50 cincuenta
60 sesenta
70 setenta
80 ochenta
90 noventa
100 cien (*on its own and before nouns*); ciento (*before numbers*)

| | |
|---|---|
| 101 ciento uno | 400 cuatrocientos |
| 102 ciento dos | 500 quinientos |
| 110 ciento diez | 1,000 mil |
| 150 ciento cincuenta | 2,000 dos mil |
| 200 doscientos/as | 2,100 dos mil diez |
| 300 trescientos | 5,000 cinco mil |
| | 10,000 diez mil |

million un millón
billion un billón (*also* mil millones)

- Numbers written as figures just as in English, except that 7 is always crossed 7.

- When saying a long number aloud, such as a telephone number, Spanish people either say each number individually or they split the numbers into pairs (note that if there is an odd number, the first three may be expressed as hundreds):

   9865423 = nueve-ocho-seis-cinco-cuatro-dos-tres
   or   novecientos ochenta y seis, cincuenta y cuatro, veintitrés

- In Spanish, as in most other European countries, a full stop is used to indicate thousands instead of a comma, and a comma is used where we use a decimal point.

   tres mil doscientos quince = 3.215
   dieciséis coma cuatro = 16,4

*Ordinal numbers* **los números ordinales**

These are adjectives … so remember the rules!

| | | | |
|---|---|---|---|
| *first* | **primero** | *fifth* | **quinto** |
| *second* | **segundo** | *tenth* | **décimo** |
| *third* | **tercero** | *21st* | **veintiún** (e.g. |
| *fourth* | **cuarto** | | *21st* |
| | | | *birthday* **el** |
| | | | **veintiún** |
| | | | **cumpleaños**) |

Here are some fractions:

| | | | |
|---|---|---|---|
| *half* | **la mitad** | *quarter* | **el cuarto** |
| *third* | **el tercio** | *fifth* | **el quinto** |

### Dates **fechas**

| | |
|---|---|
| *the century* | **el siglo** |
| *the nineteen hundreds* | **el siglo diecinueve** |
| *the 20th century* | **el siglo veinte** |
| *the 21st century* | **el siglo veintiuno** |
| *the 22nd century* | **el siglo veintidós** |
| *the millennium* | **el milenio** |
| *the 1990s* | **los años noventa** |
| *the year 2000* | **el año dos mil** |
| *the year 2010* | **el año dos mil diez** |
| *next year* | **el año próximo, el año que viene** |
| | *(counted from now)* |
| *last year* | **el año pasado** |
| *the year before last* | **el año antepasado** |
| *the year after next* | **el año que viene no, el siguiente** |

*Days and months* **días y meses**

In Spanish days of the week and months of the year are written with a small letter, (except for when they start a sentence). They are all masculine.

| | | | |
|---|---|---|---|
| *Monday* | **lunes** | *Saturday* | **sábado** |
| *Tuesday* | **martes** | *Sunday* | **domingo** |
| *Wednesday* | **miércoles** | *on Thursday* | **el jueves** |
| *Thursday* | **jueves** | *on Saturdays* | **los sábados** |
| *Friday* | **viernes** | | |

| | | | |
|---|---|---|---|
| *January* | **enero** | *July* | **julio** |
| *February* | **febrero** | *August* | **agosto** |
| *March* | **marzo** | *September* | **septiembre** |
| *April* | **abril** | *October* | **octubre** |
| *May* | **mayo** | *November* | **noviembre** |
| *June* | **junio** | *December* | **diciembre** |

## Expressions of time

| | |
|---|---|
| *day* | **el día** |
| *week* | **la semana** |
| *month* | **el mes** |
| *year* | **el año** |
| *last year / month* | **el año / mes pasado** |
| *last week* | **la semana pasada** |
| *next week* | **la semana que viene** |
| *next month / year* | **el mes / el año que viene** |
| *yesterday* | **ayer** |
| *the day before yesterday* | **anteayer** |
| *today* | **hoy** |
| *tomorrow* | **mañana** |
| *the day after tomorrow* | **pasado mañana** |
| *early morning* | **la madrugada** |
| *morning* | **la mañana** |
| *afternoon* | **la tarde** |

| | |
|---|---|
| *evening* | **la tarde** |
| *night* | **la noche** |
| *tomorrow morning* | **mañana por la mañana** |
| *yesterday afternoon* | **ayer (por la) tarde** |
| *this afternoon* | **esta tarde** |
| *tonight* | **esta noche** |

### The seasons **las estaciones**

| | | | |
|---|---|---|---|
| *spring* | **la primavera** | *autumn* | **el otoño** |
| *summer* | **el verano** | *winter* | **el invierno** |

### The clock  **el reloj**

| | |
|---|---|
| *What time is it?* | *¿Qué hora es?* |
| *midday / midnight* | *es mediodía / medianoche* |
| *1 o'clock* | *es la una* |
| *2 o'clock* | *son las dos* |
| *3.05* | *son las tres y cinco* |
| *4.10* | *son las cuatro y diez* |
| *5.15* | *son las cinco y cuarto* |
| *6.20* | *son las seis y veinte* |
| *7.25* | *son las siete y veinticinco* |
| *8.30* | *son las ocho y media* |
| *9.35* | *son las diez menos veinticinco* |
| *10.40* | *son las once menos veinte* |
| *11.45* | *son las doce menos cuarto* |
| *12.50* | *es la una menos diez* |
| *13.55* | *son las dos menos cinco* |

You can see that Spanish uses **es …** before 1 o'clock, midday and midnight, which is quite logical since all are singular, then **son las…** for the rest, which are plural. You will also by now have worked out that from the hour to half past, you simply add **y** and the number, **cuarto** or **media,** and then use **menos** from half past up to the hour, calculating backwards from the next hour as in English. You can also add **de la madrugada, de la mañana, de la tarde** and **de la noche** to be precise, such as in the example:

*It is four o'clock in the afternoon.* Son las cuatro de la tarde.

The 24-hour clock is also used very widely in Spain, especially on the radio and for transport. In these instances the times are expressed pretty much as in English:

| | |
|---|---|
| *It is 0900 hours.* | **Son las cero nueve horas.** |
| *It is 1315.* | **Son las trece quince (horas).** |
| *It is 2245.* | **Son las veintidós cuarenta y cinco.** |

Finally, some extra vocabulary and expressions to do with time:

| | | | |
|---|---|---|---|
| *second* | **el segundo** | *hour* | **la hora** |
| *minute* | **el minuto** | *half hour* | **la media hora** |
| *clock, watch* | **el reloj** | *alarm clock* | **el despertador** |

| | |
|---|---|
| *What time is it?* | **¿Qué hora es?** |
| *Have you got the time?* | **¿Tiene hora?** |
| *early* | **temprano** |
| *late* | **tarde** |
| *sooner or later* | **tarde o temprano** |
| *Better late than never!* | **¡Más vale tarde que nunca!** |
| *sunset* | **la puesta del sol** |
| *sunrise* | **la salida del sol** |
| *dawn / daybreak* | **el alba (f)/ el amanecer** |
| *dusk / nightfall* | **el anochecer** |
| *telling the time* | **decir la hora** |
| *My watch has stopped.* | **No anda mi reloj. / Mi reloj no funciona.** |
| *... is (... minutes) fast / slow* | **va (... minutos) adelantado / atrasado** |

## Quantity

| | | | |
|---|---|---|---|
| weight | **el peso** | length | **la longitud** |
| height | **la altura / la estatura** | size | **la talla** (clothes), **el número** (shoes) |

*Weights and measures* **los pesos y las medidas**

| | |
|---|---|
| kilo | **el kilo** |
| half a kilo | **el medio kilo** |
| 500 grams | **quinientos gramos / medio kilo** |
| a pound | **una libra** |

| | | | |
|---|---|---|---|
| a litre | **un litro** | a kilometre | **un kilómetro** |
| a metre | **un metro** | a pair | **un par** |
| a centimetre | **un centímetro** | a dozen | **una docena** |
| bottle | **una botella** | box | **una caja** |
| jar | **un bote** | pot | **un pote / tarro** |
| tin | **una lata** | package | **un paquete** |

| | |
|---|---|
| lots of (e.g. sugar) | **mucho (azúcar)** |
| lots of (e.g. meat) | **mucha (carne)** |
| lots of (e.g. lemons) | **muchos (limones)** |
| lots of (e.g. apples) | **muchas (manzanas)** |
| a little ... | **un poco de ...** |
| a few ... | **unos cuantos/as ...** |
| more of ... | **más ...** |

| | | | |
|---|---|---|---|
| a portion of | **una ración de** | about 20 | **una veintena** |
| about 10 | **una decena** | about 100 | **un centenar** |
| about 15 | **una quincena** | about 1,000 | **un millar** |

# Exclamations, giving orders and being polite

## How to say please and thank you!

| | |
|---|---|
| *Thank you* | **¡Gracias!** |
| *Please* | **Por favor** |

Bear in mind that Spanish people don't use please or thank you quite as often with close family and friends, where relationships tend to be 'warmer', and they are deemed not to be as essential. Therefore, if a Spaniard says to you in English *Give me the salt!*, he is not being impolite or unfriendly – he is simply expressing himself the way he would in Spanish. You could even assume it is showing that he considers you close enough not to need a formula of politeness, the 'lubricating oil' of relationships!

However, you will find that Spanish people say far more often than we do: ¡de nada!, or ¡no hay de que! when you say thank you – two ways of saying *don't mention it*.

## Giving orders / commands

You will remember that Spanish has four ways of saying you: familiar singular (**tú**), polite singular (**usted**), familiar plural (**vosotros/as**) and polite plural (**ustedes**). Look back at the Verbs section above to remind yourself when to use each form. In general, when giving orders to strangers you need to use the formal or polite forms.

| | |
|---|---|
| *Help!* | **¡Socorro!** |
| *Fire!* | **¡Fuego!** |
| *Cheers! (with drink)* | **¡Salud!** |
| *Cheers! (thanks)* | **¡Gracias!** |
| *Cheers (goodbye)* | **¡Chao!** |
| *Cheerio* | **¡Chao!** |
| *Please* | **Por favor** |

| | |
|---|---|
| *Wait!* | **¡Espere!** |
| *Stop!* | **¡Pare!** |
| *Listen!* | **¡Escuche!** |
| *Look!* | **¡Mire!** |
| *Pass me a knife.* | **Deme un cuchillo.** |
| *Fetch a glass.* | **Traiga / tráigame un vaso.** |
| *Take the chocolates.* | **Tome los chocolates.** |
| *Bring me my bag.* | **Tráigame mi bolso.** |
| *Excuse me (listen to me).* | **Oiga. / Oígame. / Por favor.** |
| *Excuse me (sorry).* | **Perdone / Perdón.** |
| *Excuse me (I want to pass).* | **Con permiso.** |
| *I'm sorry.* | **Lo siento.** |
| *I didn't mean it.* | **Fue sin querer.** |
| *I didn't know.* | **No lo sabía.** |
| *I didn't understand.* | **No (le) comprendí(a) / entendí(a).** |
| *Sorry I'm late.* | **Siento llegar tarde / con retraso.** |

### Being polite

| | |
|---|---|
| *yes, please* | **sí, por favor** |
| *no, thank you* | **no, gracias** |
| *don't mention it* | **de nada** |
| *not at all* | **no hay de qué** |
| *Pardon? (please repeat)* | **¿cómo?** |
| *I didn't catch what you said.* | **No le oí bien.** |
| *I don't understand.* | **No entiendo / comprendo.** |
| *Can I help you?* | **¿En qué puedo ayudarle?** |
| *Can you help me?* | **¿Me puede ayudar?** |
| *Can you say it again?* | **Repita, por favor.** |
| *Can you speak more slowly please?* | **Hable más despacio, por favor.** |
| *Please will you write it down?* | **Por favor, escríbalo.** |

# Spanish spelling quirks

This section offers tips to help you cope with the 'spelling quirks' of Spanish, and the peculiarities of Spanish punctuation. First a few odd points:

- Many English words containing a double consonant (such as *accent*) have a single consonant in Spanish (**acento**).
- Spanish accents do not alter the sound of the letter that carries one, but the syllable in which it occurs is pronounced more loudly than the rest of the word (see the Pronunciation section above). This can be crucial in verb forms, such as: **hablo** *I speak*; **habló** *he / she / you spoke*.
- As you have seen in the section on Days and months above, Spanish uses capital letters less than English, notably not on names of days and months, nationalities and names of languages.
- Punctuation is mostly the same as in English, except for the use of upside-down question marks and exclamation marks at the beginning of a question or exclamation. This serves to show that a question or exclamation follows, so that if you are reading aloud you can adjust your intonation accordingly. In a question the voice rises towards the end, whilst in a normal statement, it rises before a comma, but falls at a colon, semi-colon or full stop. In an exclamation, the most important words are spoken with more emphasis.

If you are aware of the following 'spelling quirks' you will be able to work out the meaning of many more Spanish words. The meaning of some of the Spanish words are given, but where the meaning is not given it is because it should be obvious!

### 'Vowel stretching' of e and o

When these two letters are stressed, they often change and 'stretch' in the Spanish version of a similar word in English:

........................................................................

*e* → **ie,** and *o* → **ue**; and sometimes *e* → **i**, *o* → **u** and *u* → **ue**

*e* → **ie**: b**ie**n = *well*; compare with Latin / Italian b**e**ne, English b**e**neficial

*o* → **ue**: b**ue**no = *good*; compare with French b**o**n, English b**o**nus

*e* → **i**: p**i**do = *I ask for*, from p**e**dir; compare with p**e**tition

*o* → **u**: d**u**rmió = *he slept*, from d**o**rmir; compare with d**o**rmitory

*u* → **ue**: ag**üe**ro = *aug**u**r*

Some of these can also work the other way round:

pr**e**cio = *price*; d**e**scuento = *discount*

........................................................................

### esc-, esp-, est-

Many words in English and French which begin with *sc-*, *sp-* and *st-* begin in Spanish with **esc-, esp-, est-**. So, to guess at new words with these beginnings, simply take off the **e-**. You'll be surprised at how many new words you will now be able to work out.

........................................................................

**e** + **sc**: **esc**uela = *school*

**e** + **sp**: **esp**añol = *Spanish*

**e** + **st**: **est**udiante = *student*

........................................................................

Spanish replaces **y** in English with an **i**, and **-ía** or **-ia** at the end of a word.

........................................................................

s**i**stema = *s**y**stem*; r**i**tmo = *rh**y**thm*; s**í**ntoma = *s**y**mptom*

biolog**ía** = *biolog**y***; farmac**ia** = *pharmac**y***; Ital**ia** = *Ital**y***

........................................................................

## Double consonants

Spanish has fewer double consonants than in English. However, **cc**, **ll** and **rr** are all very common in Spanish; **nn** occurs in a few words, usually those beginning with the prefix **in-**.

............................................................................

abadía (*abbey*), aceptar, efecto, balón, mamut, opresor, profesor, psicología, melancólico, caótico, ciencia, conciencia
N.B. **inn**ecesario – *unnecessary* (**in-** negating / opposite);
**inn**ovar = *to innovate* (**in-** meaning *into*)
**cc** = **ct**: acción, diccionario, elección

............................................................................

### f/ph

Spanish does not have **ph** spellings, and uses **f** instead.

............................................................................

atmósfera; farmacia; filosofía; geografía; profeta; semáforo

............................................................................

### g/w

Spanish has problems with **w** sounds, especially at the beginning of words; it tends to use **g** (**g** or **gu**) instead.

............................................................................

**w → g**: (el País de) **G**ales = *Wales*; c.f. Galicia
**gu**erra = *war*; c.f. **gu**errilla / guerrillero
*whisky* is often pronounced or written **güi**sky

............................................................................

## j/x

Spanish usually uses **j** where English uses **x**.

**x → j**: Mé**j**ico = *Mexico*; fi**j**o = *fixed*

## ll

Spanish often uses **ll** instead of **cl**, **fl**, and **pl** at the beginning of words.

*cl* → **ll**: **ll**amar = *to call*; c.f. *exclaim* (*call out*)
*fl* → **ll**: **ll**ama = *flame*
*pl* → **ll**: **ll**ano = *plain*

## t/th

Spanish does not have **th** spellings and uses **t** instead.

**t**eología, **t**erapia, **t**eatro, a**t**eo (*atheist*), simpa**t**ía

---

## Tips on Spanish

In the Introduction you were given some handy hints to help you learn – and more to the point – remember words. The 'spelling quirks' of Spanish were covered in the previous section to help you to see connections which might otherwise be hidden. This section will give you some further hints to help you understand how words work in Spanish.

As we've already discussed there is a large overlap between Spanish and English vocabulary. This exists because about 60 per cent of English words come from Latin, and at least 90 per cent of Spanish words come from Latin: there is bound to be an overlap of words which both languages have taken from Latin – the so-called cognates! Apart from words which came into English from Norman French – words like *veal*, *beef*, *hostel* and *tailor*, – many Latin words were imported into English at a later stage to create terminology for newly defined aspects of art, literature and philosophy, such as *sculpture*, *epigram*, *ideology* and later science, such as *species*, *genus*, *geology*, and technology such as *astronaut*, *chronometer*, *spectroscope*.

In addition, English can be described as a 'layered' language: we often have two words for the same thing. There is often an everyday word of Anglo-Saxon origin, and a completely different 'Latinate' equivalent with a similar meaning, but used in more 'learned' or specialized language. 'Step up' in level of language from speed and you find a word meaning the same – velocity – which you probably would not use in everyday language. Since Spanish mostly comes directly from Latin, but with adapted spellings, the 'higher level' English words are often close to the everyday Spanish words, because Spanish does not have as many 'language layers'. For example:

| | |
|---|---|
| **a gran velocidad** | *at great speed* |
| **a toda velocidad** | *at top speed* |
| **velocidad económica** | *cruising speed* |
| **exceder la velocidad permitida** | *to exceed the speed limit* |
| **tercera velocidad** | *third gear* |

In a nutshell, the longer the English word is (i.e. the more specialized and 'learned') the more likely it is to be similar to the Spanish word! So, working from English to Spanish, think of a more 'upmarket' word with the same meaning, and the Spanish word you need will often be similar in spelling. Working from Spanish to English, try saying the word with an English accent, and you will sometimes find that you can understand it with no problem, but that the word you want in English will be the more downmarket synonym, the one with the same meaning used in everyday English.

Besides this there are, of course, lots of Spanish words we have 'borrowed', and lots of English words 'imported' into Spanish. The following list starts with these, which you will understand instantly, and moves on to types of word with less obvious connections, that need a bit more effort. The meanings of the Spanish words are only given if they are not obvious.

- English words imported into Spanish, with the same meaning
  e.g. álbum, récord, líder, fútbol, mánager.

- Words which English has borrowed from Spanish:
  e.g. paella, matador, fiesta, aficionado

- Words used in Spanish and English with the same spelling:
  e.g. hotel, panorama, taxi, normal

- Words similar in form to their English equivalent but with Spanish 'spelling quirks' as described above:
  e.g. documento, militar, sistema, clima, movimiento, millón

- Verbs whose basic part ('stem') is identical to or similar to English,
  e.g. admirar, contener, consistir, aplaudir, desarrollar
  (*to develop, unroll*)

- Words with common prefixes at the beginning and suffixes on the end; note the similarity between the English and Spanish in this list of the most common prefixes and suffixes:

| | |
|---|---|
| **a-** = *a-/ab-* | e.g. **amoral** (*amoral*); **anormal** (*abnormal*) |
| **con-** = *con-* | e.g. **considerar** (*to consider*); **concierto** (*concert*) |
| **des-/dis-** = *dis-* | e.g. **desventaja** (*disadvantage*); **distinguir** (*to distinguish*) |
| **il-** = *il-* | e.g. **ilegal** (*illegal*); **ilógico** (*illogical*) |

| | |
|---|---|
| in- = im- | e.g. **inmediato** (*immediate*); **inmoderado** (*immoderate*) |
| in- = in- | e.g. **insuficiente** (*insufficient*); **inseparable** (*inseparable*) |
| in- = un- | e.g. **innecesario** (*unnecessary*); **ininteligible** (*uninteligible*) |
| ir- = un- | e.g. **irreal** (*unreal*); **irrepetible** (*unrepeatable*) |
| ir- = ir- | e.g. **irregular** (*irregular*); **irreducible** (*irreducible*) |
| re- = re- | e.g. **reinventar** (*reinvent*); **recuperar** (*to recuperate*) |
| sub- = sub- | e.g. **subsistir** (*subsist*); **subdividir** (*subdivide*) |
| -able = -able | e.g. **probable** (*probable*); **culpable** (*culpable*) |
| -ción = -tion | e.g. **acción** (*action*); **elección** (*election*) |
| -dad = -ty | e.g. **ciudad** (*city*); **capacidad** (*capacity*) |
| -ble = -ible | e.g. **imposible** (*impossible*); **susceptible** (*susceptible*) |
| -ía, -ia = -y | e.g. **energía** (*energy*); **farmacia** (*pharmacy*) |
| -ismo = -ism | e.g. **turismo** (*tourism*); **fascismo** (*fascism*) |
| -m(i)ento = -ment | e.g. **apartamento** (*apartment*); **desplazamiento** (*displacement*) |

Once you have learnt a few Spanish words well, you will begin to realize that many words are built on other base words: if you know the base word, you can work out the meaning of the 'derived' form for yourself by 'undressing' the word to get back to the basics! You might have noticed this in the list above.

- Here are some clear examples of base words with their 'derivatives', whose meaning is adapted by common prefixes or suffixes added to the base word you already know:

**des-: hacer** (*to do*) → **deshacer** (*to undo*)
**dis-: continuo** (*continuous*) → **discontinuo** (*discontinuous*)
**in-/im-: correcto** (*correct*) → **incorrecto** (*incorrect*)
 **posible** (*possible*) → **imposible** (*impossible*)

re-: **volver** (*to [re]turn*) → **revolver** (*to revolve, turn round*)
sub-: **marino** (*marine*) → **submarino** (*submarine*)
-able-: **salud** (*health*) → **saludable** (*healthy*)
miento-: **pensar** (*to think*) → **pensamiento** (*thought*)
-oso: **arena** (*sand*) → **arenoso** (*sandy*)

- There are many nouns describing people, places of work and occupations based on, for example, the product involved or the verb describing what the person does. Here are some useful examples:
  **zapato** (*shoe*) → **zapatero, zapatería** (*shoemaker, shoe-shop*)
  **pescado** (*fish*) → **pescadero, pescadería** (*fishmonger, fish-shop*)
  **pescar** (*to fish*) → **pescador** (*fisherman*)
  **jugar** (*to play*) → **jugador** (*player*)
  **pintar** (*to paint*) → **pintor** (*painter*)
  **piano** (*piano*) → **pianista** (*pianist*)

- As explained earlier (see the Adverbs section above) most adverbs in Spanish are formed by adding the ending **-mente** to an adjective:
  e.g. **total** → **totalmente** (*total, totally*); **activo** → **activamente** (*active, actively*)

- A number of adjectives are formed with the ending **-able** or **-ible** added to the stem of a verb; many of them are almost the same as their English counterparts:
  e.g. **imaginar** → **imaginable**; **admirar** → **admirable**

- Other adjectives have the ending **-oso/-osa** added to a base noun; again, they are easily identifiable:
  e.g. **religión** → **religioso**; **furia** → **furioso**; **vicio** → **vicioso**

- Many adjectives of nationality or origin have the ending **-és/esa**, **-(i)ense**, **-eno/a**, **-eño/a** on the end of the basis of the name of the country or region:
  e.g. **Japón** → **japonés**; **Canadá** → **canadiense**; **Chile** → **chileno**, **Brasil** → **brasileño**

- You will easily recognize the diminutive forms ending in -ito, -illo, -ico derived from known words:
  e.g. **señorito, panecillo, casita, perrito**

- Similarly, there are augmentative (= bigger) and pejorative (= nasty) suffixes such as **-ón/ona, -azo, -ucho**:
  e.g. **hombrón** (*a big man*) **mujerona** (*big woman*); **manotazo** (*slap, smack – with the hand*); **casucha** (*hovel – horrible house!*)

- Spanish has many compound nouns, often consisting of combinations of verbs and nouns, in the order verb-noun, unlike English noun-verb!
  e.g. **abrelatas** (*bottle-opener*); **sacacorchos** (*cork-scre*w); **cortacésped** (*lawn-mower*)

- There are many words derived from adjectives:
  e.g. **tranquilo** → **tranquilizar** (*to tranquilize*); **blanco** → **blanquear** (*to whiten*); **sucio** → **ensuciar** (*to dirty*); **limpio** → **limpieza** (*cleaning*)

- Equally, look out for words derived from verbs, with endings -ante or -ente:
  e.g. **cantar** → **cantante** (*singer*); **oír** → **oyente** (*listener*)

- Many place names are spelt in a similar way to the English equivalent:
  e.g. **Italia, América, Brasil, Argentina, Grecia, Londres, Cornualles, Edimburgo**

- Note that common acronyms and initials in Spanish may be in reverse order compared to English, following the different order of noun and adjective:
  e.g. UNO = ONU – **Organización de las Naciones Unidas**
  NATO = OTAN – **Organización del Tratado del Atlántico del Norte**
  Note also the abbreviation for the USA is **EEUU – los Estados Unidos**. Plural abbreviations double the initials used.

To persuade you how useful all this knowledge is, and just for fun, here is an alphabetical list of words with the commonest derivative ending, **-ción** or **-ión**, added to a base word. Most can also be considered cognates, since English has a version of most of them. The idea of this list is to prove a point and to give you confidence in your understanding of how Spanish words work ... but there are *hundreds* more, so see how many you can add to the lists!

..................................................................................................

**A** adición, adicción, admiración, anticipación
**B** bendición
**C** condición, comprensión, continuación, creación
**D** dedicación, dominación, definición
**E** elevación, evaluación, estimación
**F** fabricación, formación
**G** generación, graduación
**H** habitación
**I** iniciación, introducción, invitación
**J** jubilación, jerarquización
**L** limitación, levitación
**M** motivación
**N** nominación
**O** oposición, opinión
**P** producción, participación
**R** renovación, reunión, reservación, restauración
**S** sensación, simplificación, situación
**T** tentación, testificación
**U** ubicación, utilización, usurpación
**V** verificación, vacación
**Y** yuxtaposición
**Z** zonación

..................................................................................................

# 1

## Personal matters

### 1.1 Titles, greetings and making arrangements

**Core vocabulary**

| Titles | *Fórmulas de tratamiento* |
|---|---|
| *Mr* | **señor (Sr)** |
| *Mrs* | **señora (Sra)** |
| *Miss* | **señorita (Srta)** |
| *Sir / Mr* | **Don (D)** |
| *Madam / Mrs* | **Doña (Dª)** |

### Insight

• **Señor** is used for both *Mr* and *Sir*; the latter is used to a stranger by e.g. a shop assistant, and by a serviceman to a senior officer; **señora** is used for both *Mrs* and *Madam* in the same way, and **señorita** is always used for *Miss*. All of these are used with the person's surname, whether or not their first name is also being used, and are preceded with **el** or **la** except when you are speaking directly to him / her:

> **el señor Juan Ribera; la señora Jiménez;**
> **'¡Hola, señorita López!'**

- Spanish also has two other courtesy titles – **don / doña**: these are reserved for someone of some status or age, and must be used with the person's first name. You can also use them with **señor(a)** and the surname, provided the first name is also used.

> **el señor don Paco Peña; Señora doña Blanca López Román** (*on a letter*); '**¡Buenos días, don José!**'

- Spanish people usually use doctor(a) when referring to or addressing a doctor, even though the normal word for the profession is **médico/a**. A lawyer is referred to as **abogado/a**, and teachers can be addressed as **profesor(a)**. The normal word for boss is **jefe / jefa**.

| **Greetings** | *Los saludos* |
| --- | --- |
| *Hello, hi* | **¡Hola!** |
| *Good morning* | **¡Buenos días!** |
| *Good afternoon, Good evening* | **¡Buenas tardes!** |
| *Good night* | **¡Buenas noches!** |
| *Goodbye* | **¡Adiós!, ¡chao! (informal)** |

## Insight

Note that **tarde** is used both for *afternoon* and *evening*, and lasts from lunchtime until dinner time, which is usually around 9 or 10 p.m. **Buenas noches** can be used when you meet up with someone late in the evening, as well as when you are leaving them to go home or to bed.

## Insight
### How to say *you*
### Tutear / hablar de usted / tratar de usted

In Spanish, you need to decide how to address the person you
are speaking to. The informal **tú** is used for family, close friends
and acquaintances, and in most cases anyone of an age and status
similar to yours, even if you don't yet know them. The formal
**usted** is used for strangers and those older than you or senior in
status. In Spain this is more relaxed than it used to be, but if in
doubt when meeting someone for the first time, use **usted** until
invited to use **tú**. Your new acquaintance will probably use an
expression such as **podemos tutearnos** or **me puedes hablar de tú**
to invite you to be informal.

| Introducing someone | Presentar a alguien |
|---|---|
| *This is ...* | **Éste / ésta es ...,** |
| *May I introduce ... ?* | **Te / le presento a ...** |
| *Are you (Mr ... )?* | **¿Es usted (el señor ...)?** |
| *Do you know (Mr ...)?* | **¿Conoce(s) a ...? / ¿Conoce(s) al señor / a la señora ...?** |
| *Mr What's-his-name* | **el señor fulano** |
| *Mrs What's-her-name* | **la señora fulana** |
| *Pleased to meet you.* | **¡Encantado/a! / ¡Mucho gusto!** |
| **I am ...** | *Soy ...* |
| single | **soltero/a** |
| married | **casado/a** |
| divorced | **divorciado/a** |
| separated | **separado/a** |
| widowed | **viudo/a** |

| Making plans | Hacer planes |
|---|---|
| *What shall we do this evening?* | **¿Qué vamos a hacer esta tarde?** |
| *May I invite you to a ...?* | **¿Puedo invitarte/le a ...?** |
| *Why don't we go to ...?* | **¿Por qué no vamos a ...?** |
| bar | **un bar** |
| nightclub | **un club nocturno** |

| | |
|---|---|
| restaurant | un restaurante |
| theatre | (al) teatro |
| cinema | (al) cine |
| dance | un baile |
| discothèque | una discoteca |
| drink | tomar algo |
| meal / lunch / dinner | comer / cenar |
| dance | bailar |
| show | un espectáculo |
| play | una obra de teatro |
| musical | un musical |
| comedy | una comedia |
| concert | un concierto |
| What would you like to do? | ¿Qué te / le gustaría hacer? |
| Where would you like to go? | ¿Adónde te / le gustaría ir? |
| When / where shall we meet? | ¿Cuándo / dónde nos vemos / quedamos? |
| | |
| I will pick you up. | Iré a buscarte/le. |
| to arrange a meeting | citarse |
| to book a table | reservar una mesa |
| to go to the cinema | ir al cine |
| to go to the theatre | ir al teatro |
| to go out | salir |
| to go to a night club | ir a un club nocturno |
| to watch a video | ver un vídeo |

## Useful phrases

| | |
|---|---|
| How are you? | ¿Cómo estás / está usted? |
| How's it going? | ¿Qué tal? (Informal) |
| Very well thank you. | Muy bien, gracias. |
| Have a nice day / weekend etc. | ¡Que tengas un buen día / fin de semana! |
| | |
| May I sit here? | ¿Puedo sentarme aquí? |
| Are you alone? | ¿Está(s) solo/a? |
| See you soon. | Hasta pronto. |
| See you later. | Hasta luego. |

58

| | |
|---|---|
| *See you next time.* | **Hasta la vista.** |
| *See you tomorrow.* | **Hasta mañana.** |
| *See you Saturday.* | **Hasta el sábado.** |
| *Excuse me* | **Discúlpame / discúlpeme** |
| *Pardon?* | **¿Cómo?** |
| *I don't understand* | **No entiendo / comprendo** |
| *(Speak) more slowly please* | **(Habla / hable) más despacio por favor** |
| *I apologize* | **Lo siento** |
| *I'm sorry* | **Lo siento** |
| *I beg your pardon* | **Perdóname / perdóneme** |
| *I didn't mean it* | **Lo hice sin querer** |
| *Forgive me* | **Perdóname / perdóneme** |
| *Sorry, it was my fault* | **Lo siento, fue culpa mía** |
| *It was your fault* | **Fue culpa tuya / suya** |
| *Thank you very much* | **Muchas gracias** |
| *Don't mention it / You're welcome / That's OK* | **De nada / No hay de qué** |
| *I enjoyed it very much* | **Me gustó mucho** |
| *I had a lovely time* | **Lo pasé muy bien** |
| *We must do it again sometime* | **Deberíamos hacerlo otra vez** |
| *I will see you tomorrow / later* | **Te / le veré mañana / más tarde** |
| *I would like to see you again* | **Me gustaría verte/le/la otra vez** |
| *It's a pleasure* | **Es un placer** |
| *Have a good time!* | **¡Que te diviertas / se divierta!** |
| *Have a safe journey* | **Buen viaje** |
| *Good luck* | **¡Mucha suerte!** |
| *All the best* | **¡Que tenga suerte!** |

**Useful verbs**

| | |
|---|---|
| *to introduce* | **presentar, introducir** |

## 1.2  Where are you from?

### Core vocabulary

| **Where do you come from?** | **¿De dónde eres? /** |
| | **¿De dónde es usted?** |
| *I come from ...* | **Soy de ...** |
| *I am ...* | **Soy ...** |
| *I speak ...* | **hablo ...** |

| | | | |
|---|---|---|---|
| *Austria* | **Austria** | *Austrian* | **austriaco/a** |
| *Belgium* | **Bélgica** | *Belgian* | **belga** |
| *Eire* | **Irlanda** | *Irish* | **irlandés, irlandesa** |
| *England* | **Inglaterra** | *English* | **inglés, inglesa** |
| *France* | **Francia** | *French* | **francés, francesa** |
| *Germany* | **Alemania** | *German* | **alemán, alemana** |
| *Greece* | **Grecia** | *Greek* | **griego/a** |
| *Holland* | **Holanda** | *Dutch* | **holandés, holandesa** |
| *Italy* | **Italia** | *Italian* | **italiano/a** |
| *Portugal* | **Portugal** | *Portuguese* | **portugués, portuguesa** |
| *Scotland* | **Escocia** | *Scottish* | **escocés, escocesa** |
| *Spain* | **España** | *Spanish* | **español(a)** |
| *Switzerland* | **Suiza** | *Swiss* | **suizo/a** |
| *Wales* | **El País de Gales** | *Welsh* | **galés, galesa** |

### Insight

In each case the masculine form of the nationality is the name of the language, except in the case of countries which do not have their own language.

| | | | |
|---|---|---|---|
| Africa | **África** | African | **africano/a** |
| America | **América** | American | **americano/a** |
| Australia | **Australia** | Australian | **australiano/a** |
| Croatia | **Croacia** | Croatian | **croata** |
| Denmark | **Dinamarca** | Danish | **danés, danesa** |
| Finland | **Finlandia** | Finnish | **finlandés, finlandesa** |
| Hungary | **Hungría** | Hungarian | **húngaro/a** |
| India | **India** | Indian | **indio/a** |
| New Zealand | **Nueva Zelanda/ Zelandia** | New Zealander | **neocelandés neocelandesa** |
| Norway | **Noruega** | Norwegian | **noruego/a** |
| Poland | **Polonia** | Polish | **polaco/a** |
| Russia | **Rusia** | Russian | **ruso/a** |
| Sweden | **Suecia** | Swedish | **sueco/a** |

### Extras

There are a number of British geographical names for which there is a Spanish version:

| | |
|---|---|
| the United Kingdom | **el Reino Unido** |
| Great Britain | **Gran Bretaña** |
| England | **Inglaterra** |
| Wales | **el País de Gales** |
| Scotland | **Escocia** |
| Northern Ireland | **Irlanda del Norte** |
| London | **Londres** |
| Edinburgh | **Edimburgo** |
| Thames | **el Támesis** |
| Cornwall | **Cornualles** |

There are also a number of foreign cities which have a Spanish version:

| | |
|---|---|
| Rome | **Roma** |
| Genoa | **Génova** |
| New York | **Nueva York** |

| | |
|---|---|
| *Moscow* | **Moscú** |
| *Paris* | **París** |
| *Berlin* | **Berlín** |
| *Brussels* | **Bruselas** |
| *Geneva* | **Ginebra** |
| *Stockholm* | **Estocolmo** |
| *Hamburg* | **Hamburgo** |
| *the Hague* | **La Haya** |

## Useful phrases

| | |
|---|---|
| *Do you speak English?* | **¿Hablas inglés? / ¿Habla usted inglés?** |
| *What languages do you speak?* | **¿Qué idiomas / lenguas habla(s)?** |
| *What nationality are you?* | **¿De qué nacionalidad eres / es usted?** |
| *Where are you from?* | **¿De dónde eres / es usted?** |
| *I'm from...* | **Soy de ...** |
| *Where were you born?* | **¿Dónde naciste / nació usted?** |
| *I was born in ...* | **Nací en ...** |
| *I live ...* | **Vivo ...** |
| *in the north / south /east / west* | **en el norte / sur / este / oeste** |
| *in the middle* | **en el centro** |
| *near the sea / the city* | **cerca del mar / de la ciudad** |
| *on the coast* | **en la costa** |
| *in the mountains* | **en las montañas** |
| *in the city* | **en la ciudad** |
| *in a village* | **en un pueblo / una aldea** |
| *in the suburbs* | **en los barrios** |
| *in the country* | **en el campo** |

## Useful verbs

| | | | |
|---|---|---|---|
| *to be (from)* | **ser** | *I am from...* | **soy de ...** |
| *to live* | **vivir** | *I live ...* | **vivo ...** |
| *to speak* | **hablar** | *I speak ...* | **hablo ...** |
| *to be born* | **nacer** | *I was born in ...* | **nací en ...** |

## 1.3 Personal appearance

### Core vocabulary

| | |
|---|---|
| *What are you like?* | **¿Cómo eres? / ¿Cómo es usted?** |
| *I am a ...* | **Soy un(a) ...** |
| *What is he / she like?* | **¿Cómo es?** |
| *He /she is a ...* | **Es ...** |
| man | **un hombre** |
| woman | **una mujer** |
| girl | **una chica** |
| boy | **un chico** |
| teenager | **un / una adolescente** |
| young person | **un / una joven** |
| child | **un niño / una niña** |
| baby | **un bebé** |

## Insight

Use the following grids to help you to build up what you need to be able to say to describe yourself and someone you know well:

| *I am* **Soy** | (*quite* **bastante**) | *tall* **alto/a** |
|---|---|---|
| *Are you?* **¿Eres? /** | | |
| **¿Es usted?** | (*very* **muy**) | *small* **pequeño/a** |
| | | *short* **bajo/a** |
| | | *average* **mediano/a** |
| *He / She is* | | |
| **Él / ella es ...** | | |

| *I have* **tengo** | *short / long hair* | **(el) pelo corto / largo** |
|---|---|---|
| *He has* **(Él)** | *medium-length* | **(el) pelo mediano** |
| **tiene ...** | *hair* | |
| *She has* **(Ella)** | *blonde hair* | **(el) pelo rubio** |
| **tiene ...** | *brown hair* | **(el) pelo castaño** |
| | *dark hair* | **(el) pelo oscuro** |
| | *blue / brown eyes* | **(los) ojos azules / marrones** |

| | | | |
|---|---|---|---|
| *attractive* | **atractivo/a** | *unattractive* | **no atractivo/a** |
| *fashionable* | **de moda** | *unfashionable* | **pasado de moda** |
| *fit* | **en buena forma** | *unfit* | **en mala forma** |
| *good looking* | **hermoso/a** | *ugly* | **feo/a** |
| *neat* | **aseado/a** | *untidy* | **descuidado** |
| *smart* | **elegante** | *scruffy* | **dejado** |
| *ordinary* | **ordinario** | *different* | **diferente** |
| *tall* | **alto/a** | *short* | **bajo/a** |
| *underweight* | **de peso insuficiente** | *overweight* | **gordo** |
| *well built* | **fornido/a** | *weak / skinny* | **flaco/a** |
| *anorexic* | **anoréxico/a** | *obese* | **obeso** |
| *right-handed* | **diestro** | *left-handed* | **zurdo** |
| *short-sighted* | **miope / corto de vista** | *long-sighted* | **présbita** (inv) |
| *agoraphobic* | **agorafóbico** | *claustrophobic* | **claustrofóbico** |

Here are some of the more colloquial words used in Spain to describe people:

| | |
|---|---|
| *butch (man)* | **macho** |
| *butch (woman)* | **marimacha** |
| *getting on a bit* | **de cierta edad** |
| *teenager* | **el / la adolescente** |
| *brat, kid, youngster* | **el mocoso / crío / la mocosa / cría** |
| *bird (girl)* | **la pollita** |

### Useful phrases

| | |
|---|---|
| *How much do you weigh?* | **¿Cuánto pesas / pesa usted?** |
| *I weigh 75 kg* | **Peso 75 kg (kilos)** |
| *How tall are you?* | **¿Cuánto mides / mide usted?** |
| *I am 1.59 m* | **Mido 1.59 m (un metro y cincuenta y nueve centímetros)** |

## Useful verbs

| | |
|---|---|
| *to look like someone* | **parecerse a alguien** |
| *to put on weight* | **engordar** |
| *to lose weight* | **adelgazar** |
| *to get fit* | **ponerse en forma** |

## 1.4 What sort of person are you?

### Core vocabulary

**Insight**

*Character and feelings* **Carácter y sentimientos**

If you are describing somebody, you need to decide whether you are talking about their character, in which case you need an expression with the verb **ser**, or you are talking about how they are or how they feel, in which case you need an expression with the verb **estar** (see Toolbox, patterns for verbs **ser** and **estar**). Remember also that the adjectives have to agree with the noun (male or female, singular or plural).

| | | | |
|---|---|---|---|
| *I am* | **soy** | *shy / talkative* | **tímido / hablador** |
| *are you...?* | **¿eres / es usted...?** | *happy / unhappy* | **feliz / infeliz** |
| *he is* | **(él) es** | *friendly / unfriendly* | **amistoso / poco amistoso** |
| *she is* | **(ella) es** (+ fem adj) | *nice / nasty* | **simpático / antipático** |
| *I am* | **estoy** | *happy / sad* | **contento / triste** |
| *are you* | **¿estás / está usted?** | *awake / tired* | **despierto / cansado** |
| *he is* | **(él) está** | *smart / scruffy* | **guapo / mal vestido** |
| *she is* | **(ella) está** (+ fem adj) | *in a good / bad mood* | **de buen / mal humor** |

Here are some extra adjectives you could use to describe people.
Can you decide whether they go with the verb **ser** or **estar**?

| | | | |
|---|---|---|---|
| *good* | **bueno** | *bad* | **malo** |
| *hard-working* | **trabajador** | *lazy* | **vago / perezoso** |
| *interesting* | **interesante** | *boring* | **aburrido / pesado** |
| *quiet* | **tranquilo** | *loud* | **ruidoso** |
| *strong* | **fuerte** | *weak* | **débil** |
| *capable* | **competente** | *useless* | **inútil** |
| *confident* | **seguro de sí mismo** | *nervous* | **nervioso** |
| *generous* | **generoso** | *mean* | **tacaño** |
| *helpful* | **atento** | *unhelpful* | **poco servicial** |
| *odd* | **raro** | *normal* | **normal / corriente** |
| *polite* | **cortés** | *rude* | **descortés / grosero** |
| *practical* | **práctico** | *unpractical* | **poco práctico** |
| *reliable* | **fiable** | *unreliable* | **poco fiable** |
| *relaxed* | **relajado** | *up-tight* | **tenso** |
| *sensible* | **sensato** | *stupid* | **estúpido** |
| *sensitive* | **sensible** | *unfeeling* | **insensible** |
| *serious* | **serio** | *frivolous* | **frívolo** |
| *sincere* | **sincero** | *insincere* | **insincero / poco sincero** |
| *strong-willed* | **decidido** | *weak* | **débil** |
| *well-behaved* | **que se porta bien** | *badly-behaved* | **que se porta mal** |
| *up-to-date* | **de moda** | *out-of-date* | **fuera de moda** |

**The five senses** *Los cinco sentidos*

| | | | | | |
|---|---|---|---|---|---|
| *sight* | **la vista** | *to see* | **ver** | *I see* | **veo** |
| *hearing* | **el oído** | *to hear* | **oír** | *I hear* | **oigo** |
| *taste* | **el gusto** | *to taste* | **probar** | *I taste* | **pruebo** |
| *smell* | **el olfato** | *to smell* | **oler** | *I smell* | **huelo** |
| *touch* | **el tacto** | *to touch* | **tocar** | *I touch* | **toco** |

## Useful phrases

| He / She has ... | (Él / Ella) tiene ... |
|---|---|
| a sense of humour | un buen (sentido del) humor |
| plenty of will power | mucha fuerza de voluntad |
| a kind-heart | buen corazón |
| a weakness for ... | debilidad por ... |
| a good imagination | una buena imaginación |

## Useful verbs

| to get bored | aburrirse | I am getting bored | me aburro |
|---|---|---|---|
| to be interested in something | interesarse por algo | I am interested in ... | me intereso por ... |
| to be worried about something | estar preocupado por algo | I am worried about ... | me preocupo por ... |

## Insight

Note how, whilst English uses *to be* + an adjective (such as *to be angry*), Spanish often has a special verb for these, usually in reflexive form, e.g. **enfadarse, enojarse**

## Extras

| angry | enfadado |
|---|---|
| annoyed | enojado |
| kind | amable |
| unkind | poco amable |
| laid-back | despreocupado |
| dynamic | dinámico |

### False friends

You may have noticed a couple of **falsos amigos** *false friends* in this area. This table should help you:

| **English** | **Spanish** |
| *sensitive* | sensible |
| *sensible* | sensato |
| *nice, kind* | simpático |
| *sympathetic* | comprensivo |

## 1.5 My things

### Core vocabulary

| things | **las cosas** |
| bag | **el bolso / la bolsa** |
| briefcase | **la cartera** |
| cheque book | **el talonario de cheques** |

| | |
|---|---|
| credit cards | **las tarjetas de crédito** |
| diary | **la agenda** |
| driving licence | **el permiso de conducir** |
| glasses / sunglasses | **las gafas (de sol)** |
| keys | **las llaves** |
| notebook | **la libreta / el bloc** |
| passport | **el pasaporte** |
| pen | **la pluma** |
| purse | **el monedero** |
| wallet | **la cartera** |
| watch | **el reloj** |

## Insight

The words for *your* (fam. sing.) / *his* / *her*, *their* / *your* (formal plural) follows the same pattern as the word for *my*, but the pattern for *our* and *your* (fam. plural) is a bit more complex; this is because the former do not have separate feminine forms, whilst the latter do:

| | |
|---|---|
| *my* | mi, mis |
| *your* (familiar) | tu, tus |
| *his, her, your* (formal) | su, sus |
| *our* | nuestro, nuestra, nuestros, nuestras |
| *your* | vuestro, vuestra, vuestros, vuestras |
| *their, your* (formal) | su, sus |

## My friends — *Mis amigos / amigas*

| | |
|---|---|
| (girl) friend | **mi amiga** |
| girl friends (f) | **mis amigas** |
| (boy) friend | **mi amigo** |
| boy friends (m) | **mis amigos** |
| friends (m&f) | **mis amigos** |
| girlfriend | **mi novia** |
| boyfriend | **mi novio** |
| colleagues | **mis colegas** |

| **On my desk** | **En mi escritorio** |
|---|---|
| computer | **el ordenador, la computadora** |
| hard drive | **el disco duro** |
| mobile | **el (teléfono) móvil, celular** |
| mouse | **el ratón** |
| laptop | **el (ordenador) portátil, laptop** |
| palm-top | **el ordenador de bolsillo** |
| PC | **el PC** |
| phone | **el teléfono** |
| printer | **la impresora** |
| scanner | **el escáner** |

| **At home** | **En casa** |
|---|---|
| dvd | **el disco de vídeo polivalente, el DVD** |
| CD | **el disco compacto, el CD** |
| CD / DVD player | **el lector de CD / DVD** |
| discs | **discos** |
| camera | **la cámara, la máquina fotográfica** |
| video camera | **la cámara de vídeo** |
| digital camera | **la cámara digital** |
| film | **la película** |
| roll of film | **el carrete / rollo** |
| photos | **las fotos** |

## Insight

Here are a few expressions used in colloquial Spanish:

| | |
|---|---|
| *bike* | la bici |
| *TV* | la tele |
| *motorbike* | la moto |
| *photo* | la foto |
| *other half* | la media naranja |
| *kids* | los críos |

Note how the first four of these have an apparently odd gender; this is because all of them are abbreviated forms; the gender is as for the full forms: **la bicicleta, la televisión, la motocicleta, la fotografía.**

### Useful phrases

| | |
|---|---|
| *Have you got a ... ?* | **¿Tienes / tiene usted un(a) ... ?** |
| *I have lost my ...* | **He perdido mi ...** |
| *I can't find my ...* | **No encuentro mi ...** |
| *Have you seen my ...?* | **¿Has visto mi ...?** |

### Useful verbs

| | |
|---|---|
| *to lose / mislay* | **perder** |
| *to find* | **encontrar** |
| *to forget* | **olvidar** |

## 1.6 I think, I feel

### Core vocabulary

| | | | | | |
|---|---|---|---|---|---|
| to like | (gustar*) | liking | (el gusto) | I like | (me gusta) |
| to like a lot | (encantar*) | | | I like a lot | (me encanta) |
| to love | amar | love | el amor | I love | amo |
| to prefer | preferir | preference | la preferencia | I prefer | prefiero |
| to dislike | (no gustar) | dislike | la antipatía | I dislike | (no me gusta) |
| to hate | odiar | hate | el odio | I hate | odio |

## Insight

*The verb **gustar** is used to express the idea of liking, but it has to be used back-to-front, because it really means *to please*! So what you really say is *this car pleases me* **me gusta este coche**. Study the table and learn the examples to help you remember how to use this expression. Note how the person word changes, and that only two verb endings are used, to match the thing or things liked, not the person liking. It really is back to front!

| | singular things | plural things |
|---|---|---|
| *I like* | me gusta | me gustan |
| *you like* (familiar sing.) | te gusta | te gustan |
| *he / she likes / you like* (formal sing.) | le gusta | le gustan |
| *we like* | nos gusta | nos gustan |
| *you like* (familiar pl.) | os gusta | os gustan |
| *they / you like* (formal pl.) | les gusta | les gustan |

Among other expressions like this are:

encantar → me encanta – *I really like*
chiflar → me chifla – *I really like* (colloquial)
interesar → me interesa – *I'm interested in*

In each case, note that what you are really saying is that
something pleases / delights / interests you!

........................................................................

| | |
|---|---|
| *I like wine* | **me gusta el vino** |
| *you like beer* | **te gusta la cerveza** |
| *he likes football* | **le gusta el fútbol** |
| *we like Spain* | **nos gusta España** |
| *you like working* | **os gusta trabajar** |
| *they like travelling* | **les gusta viajar** |
| *I like tomatoes* | **me gustan los tomates** |
| *you like oranges* | **te gustan las naranjas** |
| *she likes sweets* | **le gustan los caramelos** |
| *we like Spanish people* | **nos gustan los españoles** |
| *you like public holidays* | **os gustan las fiestas** |
| *they like holidays* | **les gustan las vacaciones** |

........................................................................

| | | | | | |
|---|---|---|---|---|---|
| *to believe* | creer | *belief* | la creencia | *I believe* | creo |
| *to think* | pensar | *thought* | el pensamiento | *I think* | pienso |
| *to feel* | sentirse | *feeling* | el sentimiento | *I feel* | me siento |
| *to worry* | preocuparse | *worry* | la preocupación | *I worry* | me preocupo |
| *to advise* | aconsejar | *advice* | el consejo | *I advise* | aconsejo |
| *to encourage* | animar | *encouragement* | el ánimo | *I encourage* | animo |
| *to exaggerate* | exagerar | *exaggeration* | la exageración | *I am exaggerating* | exagero |
| *to joke* | bromear | *joke* | la broma | *I am joking* | hablo en broma |
| *to lie* | mentir | *lie* | la mentira | *I am lying* | miento |
| *to promise* | prometer | *promise* | la promesa | *I promise* | prometo |

........................................................................

## Insight

Note that **aconsejar** and **animar** need a subjunctive verb after them if there is a subordinate clause (see Toolbox, Conditional and subjunctives in the Verbs section). The same is true of **creer** and **pensar** when used in the negative:

| | |
|---|---|
| **te aconsejo que no vayas** | *I advise you not to go* |
| **le voy a animar a que trabaje** | *I am going to encourage him to work* |
| **no creo que esté allí** | *I don't believe he is there* |
| **no pienso que tengan miedo** | *I don't think they are afraid* |

### Useful verbs

### Negative and positive experiences

| | | | |
|---|---|---|---|
| *to be disappointed* | estar desilusionado | *to be relieved* | estar aliviado |
| *to be lucky* | tener suerte | | |
| *to be depressed* | estar deprimido | *to be elated* | estar eufórico |
| *to be stressed* | estar estresado | *to be relaxed* | estar relajado |
| *to be discouraged* | estar desanimado | *to be encouraged* | estar animado |
| *to be embarrassed* | estar avergonzado | *to be at ease* | estar a gusto |
| *to be nervous* | estar nervioso | *to be confident* | estar seguro |
| *to be worried* | estar preocupado | *to be reassured* | estar tranquilo |
| *to be sad* | estar triste | *to be happy* | estar contento |
| *to be ashamed* | estar avergonzado | *to be proud* | estar orgulloso |
| *to be unfortunate* | tener mala suerte | *to be fortunate* | ser afortunado |

## Verbs which are used with another verb

| | | | |
|---|---|---|---|
| to want to | querer | *I want to go* | quiero ir |
| to be able to | poder | *I can go in* | puedo entrar |
| to have to | tener que | *I must leave* | tengo que irme |
| to need to | necesitar | *I need to go out* | necesito salir |
| to 'ought' to | deber | I should stay | debería quedarme |
| | | at home | en casa |

## Insight

Unlike the case of **aconsejar** and **animar** (see above), if there is no change of subject the verb does NOT need to be in subjunctive form; instead the infinitive is used.

e.g. *I want to go to the beach* **Quiero ir a la playa** (no change of subject, so infinitive is used after **quiero**)
*I want you to go to the cinema* **Quiero que vayas al cine** (change of subject, so subjunctive after **quiero**)

### What is it like?

| | | | |
|---|---|---|---|
| *acceptable* | **aceptable** | *comfortable* | **cómodo** |
| *considerable* | **considerable** | *probable* | **probable** |
| *possible* | **posible** | *preferable* | **preferible** |
| *remarkable* | **extraordinario** | *responsible* | **responsable** |
| *tolerable* | **tolerable** | | |

Most words which end in **-able** or **-ible** are the same in English and in Spanish, but in Spanish remember to pronounce the vowels clearly and to stress the **a** of **-able** or the **i** of **-ible**.

## Insight

Note that the prefix in Spanish is not necessarily the same as in English, e.g. **inaceptable**, *unacceptable*.

## 1.7 Expressing an opinion

### Core vocabulary

| | |
|---|---|
| to believe | **creer** |
| to consider | **considerar** |
| to think | **pensar** |
| to agree/ disagree | **estar de acuerdo / no estar de acuerdo** |
| to argue | **discutir / pelearse** |
| to ask | **preguntar** |
| to dispute | **disputar** |
| to question | **cuestionar** |
| to quote | **citar** |
| to request | **pedir** |
| to suggest | **sugerir** |

| | | | |
|---|---|---|---|
| to compare | **comparar** | I compare | **comparo** |
| to contrast | **contrastar** | I contrast | **contrasto** |
| to differ | **diferir** | I differ | **difiero** |
| to discuss | **discutir** | I discuss | **discuto** |
| to conclude | **concluir** | I conclude | **concluyo** |

| | |
|---|---|
| firstly | **primero / en primer lugar** |
| secondly | **segundo / en segundo lugar** |
| finally | **finalmente / por último** |
| actually | **efectivamente / en realidad** |
| basically | **básicamente / fundamentalmente** |
| clearly | **evidentemente** |
| consequently | **por consecuencia** |
| fortunately / unfortunately | **afortunadamente / desafortunadamente** |
| generally | **generalmente** |
| honestly | **francamente** |
| mainly | **principalmente** |

| | |
|---|---|
| normally | **normalmente** |
| obviously | **obviamente** |
| particularly | **especialmente** |
| principally | **principalmente** |
| really | **verdaderamente** |
| usually / unusually | **normalmente / excepcionalmente** |

## Useful phrases

| | |
|---|---|
| in my / his / her opinion | **en mi / su / opinión** |
| above all | **sobre todo** |
| although | **aunque** |
| as a result | **como resultado** |
| as well as | **además de** |
| however | **sin embargo** |
| in many respects | **en muchos aspectos / sentidos** |
| in spite of | **a pesar de** |
| instead of | **en lugar de** |
| nevertheless | **no obstante** |
| otherwise | **de lo contrario** |
| similarly | **igualmente** |
| the reason is | **es porque** |
| to tell the truth | **a decir verdad** |
| I wish I could agree | **ojalá pudiera estar de acuerdo** |
| I beg to differ | **siento tener que disentir** |
| I mean | **quiero decir** |
| I maintain | **mantengo / sostengo** |
| for example | **por ejemplo** |
| etc. | **etcétera** |
| in brief | **en breve** |
| the advantages | **las ventajas** |
| the disadvantages are | **las desventajas / los inconvenientes son** |
| the pros and cons | **los pros y los contras** |
| to conclude | **para concluir** |
| bad / good | **malo / bueno** |

| comfortable / uncomfortable | **cómodo / incómodo** |
| better / worse | **mejor / peor** |
| nice / not very nice | **agradable / desagradable** |
| too hard / easy | **demasiado difícil / fácil** |

## 1.8 I do (I + useful action verbs) **hago**

### Useful verbs

| to wake up | **despertarse** | I wake up | **me despierto** |
| to get up | **levantarse** | I get up | **me levanto** |
| to take a shower | **ducharse** | I take a shower | **me ducho** |
| to get dressed | **vestirse** | I get dressed | **me visto** |
| to eat | **comer** | I eat | **como** |
| to drink | **beber** | I drink | **bebo** |
| to work | **trabajar** | I work | **trabajo** |
| to go home | **regresar / volver** | I go home | **regreso / vuelvo** |
| | **(a casa)** | | **a casa** |
| to play | **jugar** | I play | **juego** |
| to watch | **ver la** | I watch | **veo la** |
| television | **tele(visión)** | television | **tele(visión)** |
| to read | **leer** | I read | **leo** |
| to get washed | **lavarse** | I get washed | **me lavo** |
| to go to bed | **acostarse** | I go to bed | **me acuesto** |
| to laugh | **reír** | I laugh | **río** |
| to smile | **sonreír** | I smile | **sonrío** |
| to giggle | **reírse** | I giggle | **me río** |
| | **tontamente** | | **tontamente** |
| to sleep | **dormir** | I sleep | **duermo** |
| to dream | **soñar** | I dream | **sueño** |

### Insight

How many of the verbs above are reflexive? Can you identify them? (See Toolbox, Reflexive verbs)

## Coming and going verbs — *Verbos de ir y venir*

| | | | |
|---|---|---|---|
| to walk | **andar** | I walk | **voy andando** |
| to run | **correr** | I run | **corro** |
| to ride | **montar /<br>ir en / a** | I ride | **monto /<br>voy en / a** |
| to drive | **conducir / llevar<br>el coche** | I drive | **conduzco / llevo<br>el coche** |
| to arrive | **llegar** | I arrive | **llego** |
| to depart | **irse** (person),<br>**salir** (e.g. train) | I depart | **me voy /<br>salgo** |
| to enter | **entrar** | I enter | **entro** |
| to leave | **salir** | I leave | **salgo** |
| to come | **venir** | I come | **vengo** |
| to go | **ir** | I go | **voy** |
| to go up | **subir** | I go up | **subo** |
| to go down | **bajar** | I go down | **bajo** |
| to stay | **quedar** | I stay | **quedo** |
| to return | **volver** | I return | **vuelvo** |

## Communicating — *Comunicar*

| | |
|---|---|
| to speak | **hablar** |
| to repeat something | **repetir algo** |
| to talk to someone | **hablar con alguien** |
| to whisper to someone | **susurrar a alguien** |
| to shout at someone | **gritar a alguien** |
| to ask a question | **hacer una pregunta / preguntar** |
| to ask for something | **pedir algo** |
| to respond to a question | **contestar / responder** |
| to tell a story | **contar un cuento** |
| to enjoy yourself | **divertirse** |
| to get angry | **enfadarse** |
| to have trouble / difficulty | **tener dificultad(es)** |
| to get depressed | **ponerse deprimido/a** |
| to know / meet someone | **conocer a alguien** |
| to know something | **saber algo** |
| to cheat | **estafar** |

| to trick | **engañar** |
| to challenge | **desafiar** |
| to compliment | **felicitar** |
| to neglect | **descuidar** |

### Useful phrases

Spanish also uses a number of impersonal expressions with similar sorts of meaning. There are a number of impersonal expressions in Spanish which consist of an adjective followed by an infinitive.

| it's necessary | es necesario llegar a las diez | it's necessary to arrive at ten |
| it's vital | es imprescindible hacerlo | it's vital to do it |
| it's obligatory | es obligatorio pagar la cuenta | it's obligatory to pay the bill |
| it's possible | es posible salir | it's possible to go out |
| it's impossible | es imposible saber | it's impossible to know |
| it's dangerous | es peligroso bañarse aquí | it's dangerous to swim here |
| it's horrible | es horrible verle así | it's horrible to see him like this |
| it's prohibited | está prohibido fijar carteles | it's prohibited to put up posters |

## 1.9 Don't panic!

### Core vocabulary

| Help! | **¡Socorro!** |
| Listen! | **¡Escucha / escuche!** |
| Danger | **Peligro** |
| Watch out! | **¡Cuidado!** |
| Warning | **Aviso / Advertencia** |
| No entry | **Prohibido entrar / la entrada** |

## Useful phrases

| | |
|---|---|
| *Do you understand me?* | **¿Me comprende(s) / entiende(s)?** |
| *Do you understand?* | **¿Comprende(s)?** |
| *Can you help me?* | **¿Puede(s) ayudarme?** |
| *Do you speak English?* | **¿Habla(s) inglés?** |
| *Can you say it more slowly?* | **Dilo / dígalo más despacio.** |
| *I didn't catch what you said.* | **No oí lo que dijiste / dijo.** |
| *Please can you find someone who speaks English?* | **¿Puede(s) buscar a alguien que hable inglés?** |
| *Can you write it down for me please?* | **¿Puede(s) escribirlo, por favor?** |
| *How do you spell it?* | **¿Cómo se escribe?** |
| *Have you got the phone number for the ...?* | **¿Tiene(s) el número de teléfono de ...?** |
| police | **la policía** |
| fire brigade | **los bomberos** |
| ambulance | **la ambulancia** |
| doctor | **el médico** |
| breakdown services | **los servicios de asistencia en carretera** |
| *What do I need to dial first?* | **¿Qué tengo que marcar primero?** |
| *What is the code for...?* | **¿Cuál es el prefijo de / para ...?** |
| *How do I get an outside line?* | **¿Cómo puedo obtener una línea exterior?** |

## Insight

A reminder: generally when speaking to strangers it is best to use the **usted** (formal) form. However, increasingly the **tú** (informal) form is becoming quite acceptable with strangers, especially if you are speaking to someone in the same age group as yourself or younger.

# Test yourself

Unjumble these sentences so that they make sense. Check your answers against the solutions (see the *Test yourself Answer key* at the end of the book). It is a good idea to translate each sentence to make sure you understand the meaning, and didn't just get lucky!

**a** mi mujer. presento Te a
**b** vamos tarde? a ¿Qué hacer esta
**c** te ir? gustaría ¿Adónde
**d** favor, despacio. más hable Por
**e** qué ¿De eres? nacionalidad
**f** encuentro No bolsa. mi
**g** gustan las mucho vacaciones. Nos
**h** miedo. No tengan pienso que
**i** acuerdo. estar pudiera Ojalá que de
**j** aquí. peligroso bañarse Es

# 2

Family

## 2.1 My family

### Core vocabulary

| My family and relatives | Mi familia y mis parientes / familiares |
|---|---|
| my mother | mi madre |
| my father | mi padre |
| my parents | mis padres |
| my son | mi hijo |
| my daughter | mi hija |
| my children | mis hijos |
| my sister | mi hermana |
| my brother | mi hermano |
| my younger brother/sister | mi hermano/a menor |
| my older brother/sister | mi hermano/a mayor |
| my half-brother/sister | mi hermanastro/a |
| my step-brother/sister | mi hermanastro/a |
| my twin brother/sister | mi hermano/a gemelo/a |
| my grandfather/mother | mi abuelo/a |
| my grandparents | mis abuelos |
| my great-grandparents | mis bisabuelos |
| my grandson/daughter | mi nieto/a |
| my grandchildren | mis nietos |
| my uncle/aunt | mi tío/a |

| | |
|---|---|
| *my cousin* | **mi primo/a** |
| *my nephew/niece* | **mi sobrino/a** |
| *my husband* | **mi marido** |
| *my wife* | **mi mujer / esposa** |
| *my ex-husband* | **mi ex-marido** |
| *my ex-wife* | **mi ex-mujer** |
| *my father/mother-in-law* | **mi suegro/a** |
| *my brother/sister-in-law* | **mi cuñado/a** |
| *my partner* | **mi pareja** |
| *my friend* | **mi amigo/a** |
| *my boy/girlfriend* | **mi novio/a** |
| *my godson/daughter* | **mi ahijado/a** |
| *a married couple* | **un matrimonio** |
| *widow/er* | **el/la viudo/a** |
| *divorcee* | **el/la divorciado/a** |

## Insight

As with **mis padres**, where relevant, the *masculine* plural
form of the above is used for both / all (**mi madre y mi padre**,
*my mother and my father*), e.g. **mis hijos** = *my children*, **mis
tíos** = *my uncle(s) and aunt(s)*. However, **mis hijos** could
also mean *my sons*, and **mis tíos** could mean *my uncles*. The
feminine forms can only refer to the females, e.g. **mis hijas** =
*my daughters*, and **mis tías** = *my aunts*.

### Useful phrases

| | |
|---|---|
| *May I introduce my ...* | **Te presento a mi ... / Éste/a es mi ...** |
| *Pleased to meet you.* | **¡Encantado! / ¡Mucho gusto!** |
| *I am sorry to hear about your* | **Lamento lo de tu / su** |
| *separation* | **separación** |
| *divorce* | **divorcio** |
| *bereavement* | **pérdida** |
| *Will you go out with me?* | **¿Quieres salir conmigo?** |
| *I am going out with ...* | **Salgo con ...** |
| *We are just good friends* | **Somos amigos nada más** |

## Useful verbs

| | |
|---|---|
| to like someone | **gustar*** |
| to flirt | **ligar / coquetear** |
| to kiss | **besar** |
| to go out with someone | **salir con alguien** |
| to get on with someone | **llevarse bien con alguien** |
| to have a good time | **divertirse** |
| to have intercourse / sex | **tener relaciones sexuales** |
| to get married | **casarse** |
| to get on each other's nerves | **ponerse los nervios de punta / sacar de quicio el uno al otro** |
| to look after someone | **cuidar de alguien** |
| to quarrel | **pelearse** |
| to separate | **separarse** |
| to divorce | **divorciarse** |

*see Unit 1, Section 1.6.

| **Pet names** | *Nombres de cariño* |
|---|---|
| *darling* | **querido/a** |
| *darling (for a woman only)* | **nena** |
| *sweetheart\** | **cariño, mi amor** |

........................................................................................

## Insight

Note that these translations of *sweetheart* are ALWAYS masculine, since they describe the quality embodied by the person addressed, whether male or female!

........................................................................................

| *honey* | **mi vida** |
|---|---|
| *daddy\** | **papaíto** |
| *mummy\** | **mamaíta, mami, mamita, mamacita** |
| *grandpa\** | **abuelito** |

| | |
|---|---|
| *grandma, nan\** | **abuelita** |
| *kiddy\** | **chiquillo/a** |

> ## Insight
>
> Note that the forms marked * are diminutives, which are often used to express affection. This is often done with names, some of which have popular diminutive forms, such as:
>
> Ana – Anita, Eva – Evita
> Juan – Juanito, Carlos – Carlitos
>
> You will see diminutive forms of all sorts of nouns, not just names of people.

> ## Insight
> Tips for remembering words
>
> • Remember that lots of words for family members can be grouped in similar pairs – **hermano/a, hijo/a** and so on.
> • Try to associate the words with members of your own family – you could draw your own family tree and label it.
> • Think of **padre** as being a word we use for a *priest* (Father ...) and as being related to our word *paternal* similarly with **madre** and *maternal*.
> * Think of **primo/a** as being *first* cousin.

## 2.2 Children

### Core vocabulary

| | |
|---|---|
| *baby* | **el bebé** |
| *infant* | **el niño / la niña** |
| *child* | **el niño / la niña** |
| *boy* | **el muchacho / el chico / el niño** |

86

| girl | la muchacha / la chica / la niña |
| twin | el gemelo / la gemela |
| teenager | el / la  adolescente / joven |
| adolescent | el / la adolescente |

## Insight

As you can imagine, the masculine plural forms of the above words are used to refer to a mix of males and females. Thus, just as **los tíos** means *uncle(s) and aunt(s)*, **los niños** refers to *children (boys and girls)*.

| pregnancy | el embarazo |
| birth | el nacimiento |
| newborn baby | el recién nacido |
| nanny | la niñera |
| childminder | la niñera |
| babysitter | el / la canguro |
| midwife | la comadrona |
| crèche | la guardería |
| playschool | el jardín de infancia |
| baby's bottle | el biberón |
| teat | la tetina |
| dummy | el chupete |
| bib | el babero |
| babymilk | la leche para niños |
| high chair | la silla alta |
| nappy | el pañal |
| carrycot | el moisés |
| cot | la cuna |
| pram | el cochecito (de niño) |
| pushchair | la sillita de paseo |
| toy | el juguete |
| wind | el flato |
| colic | el cólico |

| | |
|---|---|
| an only child | **un hijo único / la hija única** |
| an adopted child | **un niño adoptado / hijo adoptivo** |
| an orphan | **un huérfano** |
| children's playground | **el patio de recreo** |
| swing | **el columpio** |
| slide | **el tobogán** |
| roundabout | **el carrusel** |

## Useful verbs

| | |
|---|---|
| to be expecting a baby | **estar encinta** |
| to breastfeed | **amamantar, criar a los pechos** |
| to burp | **eructar** |
| to change a nappy | **cambiar un pañal** |
| to cry | **llorar** |
| to feed | **dar de comer** |
| to give a bottle | **dar el biberón** |
| to rock | **acunar, mecer** |
| to teethe | **echar los dientes** |
| to look after | **cuidar a** |
| to babysit | **hacer de canguro** |

## Useful phrases

| | |
|---|---|
| I am pregnant. | **Estoy embarazada.** |
| It's a boy / girl. | **Es un niño / una niña.** |
| sibling rivalry | **la rivalidad entre hermanos** |
| family planning | **la planificación familiar** |
| a spoilt child | **un niño mimado** |
| I need ... | **Necesito ...** |
| a cream for a sore bottom | **una crema para un culito dolorido** |
| sun cream for children | **un bronceador para niños** |
| shampoo for children | **un champú para niños** |
| something for wind | **algo para flato** |
| something for children teething | **algo para la dentición** |

## Insight

### Word-building

You may notice that often one word will have another word or words based on it; here are some examples:

| child | **el niño** | **la niñera** | *nanny* |
| to drink | **beber** | **el biberón** | *baby's bottle* |
| chair | **silla** | **sillita** | *little chair* |
| to watch over | **guardar** | **guardería** | *crèche* |

The point is that you will come to recognize the members of these 'word families' without needing a dictionary.

## 2.3 Anniversaries, marriage and death

### Core vocabulary

| | |
|---|---|
| *birthday* | **el cumpleaños** |
| *engagement* | **el noviazgo** |
| *marriage* | **el matrimonio** |
| *birth* | **el nacimiento** |
| *death* | **la muerte** |
| *the wedding* | **la boda** |
| *church* | **la iglesia** |
| *town hall* | **el ayuntamiento** |
| *engagement ring* | **el anillo de compromiso** |
| *wedding invitation* | **la invitación de boda** |
| *wedding day* | **el día de la boda** |
| *bride* | **la novia** |
| *bridegroom* | **el novio** |
| *bridesmaid* | **la dama de honor** |
| *wedding dress* | **el traje de novia** |
| *wedding ceremony* | **la ceremonia nupcial** |
| *wedding ring* | **el anillo de boda** |
| *wedding certificate* | **el certificado nupcial** |
| *wedding cake* | **el pastel de la boda** |

| | |
|---|---|
| honeymoon | **la luna de miel** |
| married life | **la vida matrimonial** |
| separation | **la separación** |
| divorce | **el divorcio** |
| heterosexual | **heterosexual** |
| homosexual | **homosexual** |
| lesbian | **lesbiana** |
| death | **la muerte** |
| funeral | **el funeral** |
| corpse | **el cadáver** |
| coffin | **el ataúd** |
| cemetery | **el cementerio** |
| burial | **el entierro** |
| cremation | **la cremación** |
| grave | **la sepultura** |
| death duties | **el impuesto de sucesiones** |
| death certificate | **la partida de defunción** |
| will | **el testamento** |

## Useful verbs

| | |
|---|---|
| to get engaged | **prometerse** |
| to get married | **casarse** |
| to die | **morir** |
| to be buried | **ser enterrado** |
| to be in mourning | **estar de luto** |
| to commit suicide | **suicidarse** |

## Useful phrases

| | |
|---|---|
| Congratulations! | **¡Felicitaciones!** |
| Happy birthday | **Feliz cumpleaños** |
| Merry Christmas | **Feliz Navidad** |
| Happy New Year | **Feliz Año Nuevo** |
| Congratulations on your engagement | **Felicitaciones por tu noviazgo** |

| | |
|---|---|
| *wedding* | **boda** |
| *anniversary* | **aniversario** |
| *We would like to wish you every future happiness.* | **Os / les deseamos la más completa felicidad para el futuro.** |
| *We would like to send you our best wishes.* | **Os / les mandamos la enhorabuena.** |
| *I would like to convey my condolences.* | **Te / le acompaño en el sentimiento.** |
| *I am very sorry to learn of your sad loss.* | **Quiero expresar mi tristeza por tu / su pérdida.** |

# Test yourself

Identify the odd word or phrase in each series. You may check your answers with the *Test yourself Answer key* at the end of the book.

1 a mi abuela b mi hermano c mi anillo d mi novia e mi marido
2 a mi cuñado b mi hijo c mi mujer d mi suegro e mi hermanastra
3 a mi mujer b mi esposo c mi pareja d mi marido e mi esposa
4 a el viudo b el matrimonio c la boda d la luna de miel e el divorcio
5 a pelearse b separarse c divorciarse d querido e besarse
6 a la sillita b la niñera c el canguro d eructar e el biberón
7 a divertirse b amamantar c mecer d llorar e cuidar
8 a el cólico b el flato c la dentición d el biberón e el embarazo
9 a abuelito b mamaíta c chiquilla d papaíto e Madrid
10 a el noviazgo b el ayuntamiento c el cumpleaños d la boda e el funeral

# 3

## Work

### 3.1 Job titles

#### Core vocabulary

| | |
|---|---|
| accountant | **el / la contable** (m+f) |
| actor / actress | **el actor / la actriz** |
| architect | **el arquitecto** |
| builder | **el / la albañil** (m+f) |
| businessman | **el hombre de negocios** |
| businesswoman | **la mujer de negocios** |
| civil servant | **el funcionario (del estado)** |
| computer operator | **el operador de ordenador** |
| computer programmer | **el programador de ordenadores** |
| dentist | **el / la dentista** (m+f) |
| doctor | **el médico** |
| driver | **el conductor** |
| electrician | **el / la electricista** (m+f) |
| engineer | **el ingeniero** |
| farmer | **el granjero** |
| fireman | **el bombero** |
| hairdresser | **el peluquero** |
| journalist | **el / la periodista** (m+f) |
| lawyer | **el abogado** |
| lecturer / professor | **el profesor** |
| mechanic | **el mecánico** |

| | |
|---|---|
| *musician* | **el músico** |
| *nurse* | **el enfermero / la enfermera** |
| *plumber* | **el fontanero** |
| *police officer* | **el guardia / policía** (m+f) |
| *postman* | **el cartero** |
| *receptionist* | **el / la recepcionista** (m+f) |
| *scientist* | **el científico** |
| *secretary* | **el secretario / la secretaria** |
| *shop assistant* | **el dependiente / la dependienta** |
| *shop keeper* | **el tendero** |
| *student* | **el / la estudiante** |
| *waiter / waitress* | **el camarero / la camarera** |
| *unemployed* | **desempleado / parado** |
| *retired* | **jubilado** |

---

### Insight

We have included a few obvious feminine forms, and quirky ones like **actor / actriz**, but others are straightforward to work out. The feminine form will usually be similar to the masculine but will end in **-a**, except for words ending in **-e** and a few odd words marked (m+f). which don't change. So, apart from these, with words ending in -o, just change the ending to **-a**; with words ending in **-or**, just add –a: **el arquitecto → la arquitecta, el contable → la contable, el profesor → la profesora.**

---

| | |
|---|---|
| *the staff* | **el personal** |
| *chairman* | **el presidente** |
| *chief executive* | **el director** |
| *managing director* | **el director / gerente** |
| *director* | **el director** |
| *company secretary* | **el administrador de empresa** |
| *departmental head* | **el jefe de departamento** |
| *accountant* | **el contable** |
| *manager* | **el gerente** |

| | |
|---|---|
| business consultant | **el asesor comercial** |
| personal assistant | **el ayudante personal** |
| employer | **el empleador / empresario** |
| employee | **el empleado** |
| sales representative | **el representante / viajante** |
| secretary | **el secretario / la secretaria** |
| caretaker | **el conserje** |
| cleaner | **el limpiador / la limpiadora / el encargado de la limpieza** |
| workman / labourer | **el obrero** |
| trainee | **el aprendiz** |
| work experience | **la experiencia laboral** |

## I would like to work in / I work in / I used to work in

| | |
|---|---|
| I'd like to work as / in... | **Me gustaría trabajar de / en ...** |
| I work as / in | **Trabajo en / de ...** |
| I used to work as / in | **Trabajaba en / de** |
| agriculture | **la agricultura** |
| banking | **la banca** |
| building trade | **la industria de la construcción** |
| catering | **la hostelería** |
| civil service | **la administración pública** |
| commerce | **el comercio** |
| finance | **las finanzas** |
| the hotel industry | **el sector hotelero** |
| insurance | **el seguro** |
| leisure services | **el ocio** |
| manufacturing | **la fabricación** |
| medicine | **la medicina** |
| the media | **los medios de comunicación de masa** |
| the public services | **los servicios públicos** |
| purchasing | **la compra** |
| retail | **la venta al por menor** |
| service industry | **el sector de servicios** |
| show business | **el mundo del espectáculo** |

| | |
|---|---|
| *textiles* | **la industria textil** |
| *tourism* | **el turismo** |
| *transport* | **el transporte** |
| *wholesale* | **la venta al por mayor** |

## Insight

There is not space here for an exhaustive list; if you need other jobs and professions, try www.wordreference.com This on-line dictionary offers not only direct translations, but also a forum in which users can consult native Spanish speakers to help find the correct word.

### Useful verbs

| | |
|---|---|
| *to work / earn my living* | **trabajar / ganarme la vida** |
| *to be out of work* | **estar desempleado / en paro** |
| *to buy / sell* | **comprar / vender** |
| *to import / export* | **importar / exportar** |
| *to manage* | **dirigir, gestionar** |
| *to manufacture* | **fabricar** |

## Insight

• In Spain, many 'state' jobs fall into the category of **funcionario**; for these and the majority of professions, entry and promotion are usually by **oposiciones** – competitive exams; these can take several years to prepare for, and some people will take them several times before getting the type of job they want.
• In many of these state jobs, you have to go where the appropriate government department sends you.
• Spain has had a minimum salary level for many years which is known as the **salario mínimo interprofesional.**
Owing to its very low birth-rate in recent decades, Spain has welcomed large numbers of immigrants to provide much-needed labour, particularly for agriculture and the construction industry.

You can build up your vocabulary by learning a cluster of words:

| | |
|---|---|
| *work* | **el trabajo** |
| *to work* | **trabajar** |
| *hard working* | **trabajador** |
| *worker* | **el trabajador** |
| *worker (f)* | **la trabajadora** |
| *employment* | **el empleo** |
| *unemployment* | **el desempleo** |
| *employer* | **el empleador** |
| *employee* | **el empleado** |
| *to employ* | **emplear** |
| *employed* | **empleado** |
| *unemployed* | **desempleado** |
| *manager* | **gerente** |
| *to manage* | **gestionar** |
| *management* | **gestión** |
| *manageable* | **gestionable** |

_____

## 3.2 Where do you work?

### Core vocabulary

| | |
|---|---|
| *I work in a ...* | **Trabajo en ...** |
| *bank* | **un banco** |
| *building site* | **una obra** |
| *factory* | **una fábrica** |
| *farm* | **una granja** |
| *garage* | **un garaje** |
| *hospital* | **un hospital** |
| *hotel* | **un hotel** |
| *mine* | **una mina** |
| *office* | **una oficina** |
| *post office* | **(una oficina de) correos** |
| *restaurant* | **un restaurante** |
| *school* | **una escuela** |
| *private school* | **un colegio** |

| | |
|---|---|
| *junior school* | **un colegio** |
| *secondary upper school* | **un instituto** |
| *private academy* | **una academia** |
| *service station* | **una estación de servicio** |
| *shopping centre* | **un centro comercial** |
| *studio* | **un estudio** |
| *town hall* | **el ayuntamiento** |
| *workshop* | **un taller** |

## 3.3 The office

| | |
|---|---|
| *the company* | **la compañía / empresa** |
| *headquarters* | **la oficina central** |
| *subsidiary* | **la filial** |
| *firm* | **la firma / empresa** |
| *limited company* | **la sociedad anónima / limitada** |
| *the premises* | **el local** |
| *boardroom* | **la sala de juntas** |
| *canteen* | **la cantina / el comedor** |
| *meeting room* | **la sala de conferencias** |
| *reception* | **la recepción** |
| *entrance* | **la entrada** |
| *exit* | **la salida** |
| *security code* | **el código de seguridad** |
| *pass* | **el pase / permiso** |
| *switchboard* | **la central** |
| *mail* | **el correo** |
| *extension* | **el interno** |

| | |
|---|---|
| **I work in the ... department** | *Trabajo en el departamento de ...* |
| *accounts* | **contabilidad** |
| *administration* | **administración** |
| *advertising* | **publicidad** |
| *after-sales* | **posventa** |
| *catering* | **hostelería** |
| *distribution* | **distribución** |
| *export* | **exportación** |

| import | **importación** |
| facilities management | **gestión de servicios** |
| information technology | **informática** |
| insurance | **seguro** |
| legal | **legal** |
| manufacturing | **fabricación** |
| marketing | **mercadeo / márketing** |
| personnel / human resources | **personal / recursos humanos** |
| property | **propiedades** |
| purchasing | **compras** |
| sales | **ventas** |
| technical | **técnico** |

## Useful verbs

| to buy | **comprar** | compro |
| to manage | **dirigir** | dirijo |
| to manufacture | **fabricar** | fabrico |
| to research | **investigar** | investigo |
| to sell | **vender** | vendo |
| to study | **estudiar** | estudio |
| to travel | **viajar** | viajo |
| to work | **trabajar** | trabajo |

### Useful phrases

| Where do you work? | **¿Dónde trabaja usted?** |
| Which department do you work in? | **¿En qué departamento trabaja usted?** |
| Our head office is based in ... | **Nuestra sede central está en ...** |
| Can I get you a coffee? | **¿Le puedo traer un café?** |
| Would you like to meet ...? | **¿Le gustaría conocer a ...?** |

## 3.4 Conditions of employment

| | |
|---|---|
| *working conditions* | **las condiciones de trabajo** |
| *the working day* | **el día laboral** |
| *the working week* | **la semana laboral** |
| *holidays* | **las vacaciones** |
| *annual holiday* | **las vacaciones anuales** |
| *national holidays* | **las fiestas nacionales** |
| *pay* | **el sueldo** |
| *salary* | **el salario** |
| *income* | **los ingresos** |
| *income tax* | **los impuestos sobre la renta** |
| *VAT* | **el impuesto de valor añadido** |
| *applicant* | **el aspirante / candidato** |
| *application* | **la solicitud** |
| *application form* | **la solicitud** |
| *CV* | **el currículum (vitae)** |
| *contract* | **el contrato** |
| *job interview* | **la entrevista de trabajo** |
| *full-time job* | **el empleo a tiempo completo** |
| *part-time job* | **el empleo a tiempo parcial** |
| *office hours* | **las horas de oficina** |
| *overtime* | **las horas extra(s)** |
| *flexitime* | **el horario flexible** |
| *coffee break* | **el descanso (para tomar café)** |
| *lunch-time* | **la hora del almuerzo** |
| *meeting* | **la reunión** |
| *union* | **el sindicato** |
| *union meeting* | **la reunión sindical** |
| *strike* | **la huelga** |
| *demand* | **la demanda** |
| *leave* | **el permiso** |
| *sick leave* | **el permiso por enfermedad** |
| *sick note* | **el justificante por enfermedad** |
| *compassionate leave* | **el permiso por motives familiares** |
| *dismissal* | **el despedido** |
| *redundancy* | **el desempleo** |
| *bankruptcy* | **la quiebra** |

| laying off | **el despido** |
| standard of living | **el nivel de vida** |
| unemployment rate | **la tasa de paro / desempleo** |

### Useful phrases

| It is stressful / stimulating. | **Es estresante / estimulante.** |
| He / she is very ... | **Es muy ...** |
| efficient. | **eficiente.** |
| organized / disorganized. | **organizado / desorganizado.** |
| hard working / lazy. | **trabajador / perezoso.** |

### Verbs

| to be behind with one's work | **estar atrasado en el trabajo** |
| to catch up | **alcanzar** |
| to be ahead | **ir por delante** |
| to have a deadline | **la fecha tope** |
| to be overworked | **trabajar demasiado** |
| to be stressed | **estar estresado/a** |

---

## 3.5 Writing a letter

### Insight
- Always write your name / address on the back of the envelope, after the abbreviation **Rte:** (**Remitente** *sender*).
- Only write your town / city and the date at the top right of your letter.
- Familiar letters usually begin with **Querido/a.**
- After the person's name, use a colon, **Querido Xavier:**

### Informal letters

| | |
|---|---|
| *Dear Dad / brother / son / grandad* | **Querido papá / hermano / hijo / abuelito** |
| *Dear Mum / sister / daughter / grandma* | **Querida mamá / hermana / hija / abuelita** |
| *Dear José / Manuel / Xavier* | **Querido José / Manuel / Xavier** |
| *Dear friend* | **Querido amigo / amiga** |
| *Till the next (letter)* | **Hasta la próxima ...** |
| *Write soon* | **Escríbe(me) pronto** |
| *Give my regards to your father / parents ...* | **Dale mis recuerdos a tu(s) padre(s) ...** |
| *Give a kiss to your little brother* | **Dale un beso a tu hermanito** |
| *A kiss / hug (= love from...)* | **Un beso / abrazo (de ...)** |

### Formal letters

| | |
|---|---|
| *Dear Don Pablo / Mr Blanco,* | **Querido don Pablo / señor Blanco:** |
| *Dear Doña Lola / Mrs / Miss Morales,* | **Querida doña Lola / señor(it)a Morales:** |
| *Dear Sir / Madam* | **Muy señor mío / señora mía** |
| *Dear ... (very formal)* | **Estimado/a ...** |
| *To whom it may concern* | **A quien corresponda** |
| *Yours sincerely* | **(Le saluda) atentamente** |

---

## 3.6 Using the telephone

### Core vocabulary

| | |
|---|---|
| *telephone* | **el teléfono** |
| *receiver* | **el auricular** |
| *extension* | **la extensión** |
| *mobile* | **el (teléfono) móvil / celular** |
| *telephone number* | **el número de teléfono** |
| *directory* | **la guía telefónica** |

| local call | **la llamada local** |
| long distance call | **la llamada de larga distancia** |
| international call | **la llamada internacional** |

## Useful verbs

| to phone | **llamar por teléfono** |
| to call | **llamar** |
| to call back | **devolver la llamada** |
| to divert a call | **desviar una llamada** |
| to put someone through | **pasar** |
| to look up a number | **buscar** |

## Useful phrases

| Hello! | **¡Díga(me)!** (answering the phone) |
| Hello! | **¡Oíga(me)!** (making a call) |
| Could I speak to ...? | **Póngame con ...** |
| Can I have extension ... please? | **Deme la extensión ..., por favor** |
| Can I have someone who deals with ...? | **Póngame con alguien que se encargue de ...** |
| Who is calling? | **¿Dígame? ¿De parte de quién?** |
| Can you tell me what it is about? | **¿Me puede decir de qué se trata?** |
| Who would you like to speak to? | **¿Con quién quiere usted hablar?** |
| Speaking! | **¡Soy yo!** |
| Can you wait a moment? | **Espere un momento.** |
| I am putting you through. | **Le estoy pasando.** |
| The line is engaged / busy. | **Está comunicando.** |
| The line is free. | **La línea está abierta / libre.** |
| Do you want to hold? | **¿Quiere esperar?** |
| Would you like to leave a message? | **¿Quiere dejar un recado?** |
| Can I take your name and number? | **Deme su nombre y su número.** |
| I haven't got a signal | **No tengo señal.** |
| My battery is running low. | **Mi batería se está agotando.** |
| Can you ring back? | **¿Puede volver a llamar?** |
| Can you text me? | **¿Puede mandarme un texto?** |

## Insight

Text messaging: as in the UK, this has become an extremely popular form of communication. Also as in English, Spanish-speaking people make use of lots of short-hand expressions and abbreviated forms. Certain letters are commonly simplified, all in the name of speed of texting. Here is an example to give you a flavour, but remember that such language use is constantly changing and developing.

**¿Ke tal**

## 3.7 Using the computer

### Core words

| | |
|---|---|
| computer | **el ordenador / la computadora** |
| keyboard | **el teclado** |
| mouse | **el ratón** |
| microphone | **el micrófono** |
| speakers | **los altoparlantes** |
| hard drive | **el disco duro** |
| screen | **la pantalla** |
| laptop | **el ordenador portátil** |
| printer | **la impresora** |
| scanner | **el escáner** |
| e-mail | **el e-mail / emilio / correo electrónico** |
| worldwide web | **el / la web** |
| net | **la red** |
| code | **el código** |
| password | **la contraseña de acceso** |
| programme | **el programa** |
| modem | **el módem** |
| connector | **el conector** |
| battery | **la pila** (dry) **/ batería** (wet) |
| phone jack | **el enchufe de teléfono** |

## Useful verbs

| | |
|---|---|
| *switch on* | **encender** |
| *type in* | **escribir** |
| *log on* | **acceder al sistema** |
| *log off* | **salir del sistema** |
| *save* | **guardar / archivar** |
| *go on line* | **conectar** |
| *send an e-mail* | **mandar un e-mail** |
| *receive mail* | **recibir un e-mail** |
| *download a file* | **descargar un fichero / archivo** |
| *recharge the battery* | **recargar la pila / la batería** |

## Useful phrases

| | |
|---|---|
| *Have you got a ...?* | **¿Tiene un ...?** |
| *My computer isn't working.* | **Mi ordenador no funciona.** |
| *Is there anyone who can help me?* | **¿Hay alguien que pueda ayudarme?** |

# Test yourself

Match the following Spanish words in the left-hand column to the English words in the right-hand one. To see if your answers are correct, go to *Test yourself Answer key* at the end of the book.

| | | | |
|---|---|---|---|
| 1 | el contable | a | *switchboard* |
| 2 | la dependienta | b | *lawyer* |
| 3 | la hostelería | c | *civil servant* |
| 4 | recargar | d | *strike* |
| 5 | el taller | e | *network, internet* |
| 6 | el funcionario | f | *catering* |
| 7 | la red | g | *accountant* |
| 8 | el abogado | h | *workshop* |
| 9 | la central | i | *shop assistant* |
| 10 | la huelga | j | *to recharge* |

# 4

# Education

---

## 4.1 Primary and secondary education

### The school system

### Insight

| age *edad* | school | escuela |
|---|---|---|
| 2–6 | *infant* | parvulario / jardín de infancia |
| 6–14 | *middle* | colegio |
| 14–18/19 | *upper* | instituto |

- A high proportion of Spanish children attend a nursery school.
- Primary and secondary school children follow a national curriculum regulated by the local offices of the Ministry of Education.
- Private sector schools are called colegio regardless of the age of the children. The private sector has more freedom over the curriculum and many are religious schools / institutions.

### Insight

Spanish school students who fail their end-of-year exams have to spend much of the summer studying at revision lessons to prepare for retakes in September; if they fail these exams, they have to repeat the whole year, and may even do so two or three times.

## Core vocabulary

| | |
|---|---|
| headmaster | **el director** |
| deputy head | **el vice-director** |
| primary teacher | **el maestro** |
| secondary teacher | **el profesor** |
| pupil | **el alumno / la alumna** |
| the school secretary | **el secretario / la secretaria** |
| the school nurse | **la enfermera de escuela** |
| the school caretaker | **el conserje** |
| lesson | **la lección / la clase** |
| break | **el recreo** |
| lunch time | **el almuerzo** |
| the bell | **el timbre** |
| the end of lessons | **el fin de la jornada escolar** |
| term | **el trimestre** |
| half-term | **las vacaciones de mediados del trimestre** |
| holidays | **las vacaciones** |

> ## Insight
> Note that school holidays in Spain follow a different pattern: the summer holidays last for three months practically from June to October; however, Christmas and Easter holidays are usually shorter than in the UK, and there are no half-term breaks.

| | |
|---|---|
| school hours | **el horario lectivo / escolar** |
| progress test | **la evaluación** |
| final examination | **la reválida** |
| continuous assessment | **la evaluación continua** |
| the timetable | **el horario** |
| school subjects | **las asignaturas** |
| Art | **el Diseño** |
| Biology | **la Biología** |

| | |
|---|---|
| Chemistry | **la Química** |
| Civics | **la Educación Cívica** |
| English | **el Inglés** |
| French | **el Francés** |
| History | **la Historia** |
| Geography | **la Geografía** |
| German | **el Alemán** |
| Information technology | **la Informática** |
| Maths | **las Matemáticas** |
| Music | **la Música** |
| P.E. | **la Educación Física** |
| Physics | **la Física** |
| Science | **la Ciencia** |
| Spanish | **el Español** |
| Technology | **la Tecnología** |
| the building | **el edificio** |
| the classroom | **el aula** (f) |
| the corridor | **el pasillo** |
| the science laboratory | **el laboratorio de ciencias** |
| the gym | **el gimnasio** |
| the games room | **la sala de juegos** |
| the sports hall | **el polideportivo** |
| the music room | **el aula de música** |
| the library | **la biblioteca** |
| the computer room | **el aula de Informática** |
| the cloakroom | **el guardarropa** |
| the changing rooms | **los vestuarios** |
| the toilets | **los aseos / servicios** |
| the desk | **el pupitre** |
| the blackboard | **la pizarra** |
| the projector | **el proyector** |
| the computer | **el ordenador / la computadora** |
| the white board | **la pizarra blanca** |
| the interactive whiteboard | **la pizarra blanca interactiva** |
| the overhead projector | **el retroproyector** |
| the book | **el libro** |
| the exercise book | **el cuaderno** |
| the pencil case | **el estuche / plumero** |

| the pen | **la pluma** |
| the biro / ballpoint | **el boli / bolígrafo** |
| the pencil | **el lápiz** |
| the eraser | **la goma de borrar** |
| the board-rubber | **el borrador** |
| the calculator | **la calculadora** |
| the protractor | **el transportador** |
| the ruler | **la regla** |
| the report | **el boletín (de notas)** |
| the school bag | **el bolso** |
| the sports kit | **el equipo de deporte** |

## Useful verbs

| to read | **leer** |
| to speak | **hablar** |
| to listen | **escuchar** |
| to talk | **hablar** |
| to discuss | **discutir** |
| to write | **escribir** |
| to copy | **copiar** |
| to take notes | **tomar apuntes / apuntar** |
| to be quiet | **estar / quedar en silencio / callado** |
| to do your homework | **hacer los deberes** |
| to get a good mark | **sacar buena nota** |
| to sit an exam | **pasar un examen** |
| to pass a test | **aprobar una prueba** |
| to fail a test | **fracasar / suspender una prueba** |
| to re-sit | **volver a presentarse / repetir un examen** |
| to repeat a year | **repetir el curso** |

## 4.2 Further and higher education

### Insight

- A very high proportion of young Spanish people go to university.
- There are more girls at Spanish universities than boys.
- University fees and expenses are considerable, and few students get grants.
- Most Spanish students go to their local university and live at home.
- Many Spanish students do a part-time job to help pay for their education.
- For certain specialized degrees, e.g. medicine, students may go away from home.
- Most degrees start with a general, foundation course; many last five years or more.

### Core vocabulary

| | |
|---|---|
| college | **el colegio** |
| technical college | **la escuela politécnica / el instituto de formación profesional** |
| university | **la universidad** |
| faculty | **la facultad** |
| class | **la clase** |
| lecture | **la clase / conferencia** |
| seminar | **el seminario** |
| tutorial | **el seminario** |
| professor | **el catedrático** |
| student | **el estudiante** |
| research student | **el estudiante investigador** |
| graduate | **el licenciado** |
| undergraduate | **el estudiante universitario** |
| apprentice | **el aprendiz** |
| trainee | **el aprendiz** |
| an essay | **un ensayo** |
| an essay (language) | **una redacción** |

| a paper (research paper) | **el ensayo / artículo de investigación** |
| a report | **un reportaje / boletín** |
| a dissertation | **la tesina** |
| a thesis | **la tesis** |

### Useful verbs

| to present a paper | **presentar una ponencia** |
| to do a sandwich course | **combinar los estudios con el trabajo** |
| to study part-time | **estudiar a tiempo parcial** |
| to attend evening class | **asistir a clases nocturnas** |
| to do work experience | **hacer experiencia laboral** |
| to correct | **corregir** |
| to discuss | **discutir** |
| to explain | **explicar** |
| to learn | **aprender** |
| to qualify | **sacar el título** |
| to register / enrol | **matricularse** |
| to study | **estudiar** |
| to teach | **enseñar** |
| to translate | **traducir** |
| to understand | **comprender / entender** |
| to do research | **hacer investigaciones** |

## Insight
### False friends

| **pasar un examen** | to sit an exam (not to pass – as we understand it) |
| **un curso** | a school year (not just a course) |
| **la formación** | training |
| **una carrera** | a university course (as well as a career) |

## Insight

Spanish teachers have a quite different working life to their British counterparts. Here are some major differences:
• Candidates for teaching jobs have to do competitive exams; the one with the best result gets the job.
• Teachers entering the profession (having passed the entrance exam, **oposiciones**) are sent to wherever the Ministry of Education wants to send them; there is no choice.
• Generally speaking teachers have less administrative work than their UK colleagues, and spend less time working.
Pupils often address teachers by their first name, with or without the courtesy title Don / Doña.
e.g. Don José, Doña Blanca

# Test yourself

See how quickly you can unjumble these words from Unit 4.

**a** emaelstro
**b** meltresrite
**c** Clieanaci
**d** eldoradoren
**e** pracio
**f** cancelliedio
**g** carlipex
**h** carnaurera
**i** carrudit
**j** flatculada

When you have unjumbled them, try to write down the English for each word in a set time (say, three minutes). If you need to check your answers, go to the *Test yourself Answer key*.

# 5

# At home

## 5.1 The house

### Core vocabulary

| | |
|---|---|
| *house* | **la casa** |
| *home* | **el hogar** |
| *appartment* | **el apartamento** |
| *flat* | **el piso / apartamento** |
| *studio* | **el estudio** |
| *block of flats* | **el bloque (de pisos)** |

## Insight

For Spanish people, the notion of 'home' is usually quite different from what it means to British people. For a start, for a very large proportion of Spaniards, home is a flat rather than a house, especially in towns and cities, although in villages most people live in two-storey houses. Increasing numbers of what we call 'housing estates' with individual dwellings are being built on the fringes of Spanish towns and cities. Given the more clement climatic conditions, Spaniards spend more time out and about; indeed if you phone someone and they are not at home, you are likely to be told **'Está en calle'**, which seems almost to indicate that for a Spaniard the street is his / her second home.

| the building | el edificio |
| floor / storey | el piso / la planta |
| ground floor | la planta baja |
| first floor | el primer piso |
| second floor | el segundo piso |
| basement | el sótano |
| attic | el desván / la buhardilla |
| stairs | la escalera |
| lift | el ascensor |
| garage | el garaje *(usually in the basement of a block of flats)* |
| garage | la cochera *(a single garage next to / under a house)* |
| cellar | el sótano / la bodega |
| cottage | la casita / la choza |
| farm | la granja |
| detached house | el chalé / chalet |
| villa | la villa / casa de campo |
| council flat | el piso de protección oficial |
| semi-detached house | la casa adosada |
| terraced house | la casa adosada |
| central heating | la calefacción |
| double glazing | el doble acristalamiento |
| gas | el gas |
| electricity | la electricidad |
| oil | el aceite |
| water | el agua |
| services | los servicios públicos |
| telephone | el teléfono |
| mains sewerage | el alcantarillado / la cloaca |
| septic tank | la fosa séptica |
| sound proofing | la insonorización |
| insulation | el aislamiento térmico |
| shutters | las contraventanas |
| burglar alarm | la alarma antirrobo |
| outside | fuera |
| balcony | el balcón |
| roof | el techo / tejado |

| slates | las tejas / pizarras |
| terrace | la terraza |
| conservatory | el invernadero |
| garden | el jardín |
| gate | la puerta / verja |
| path | el sendero |
| lawn | el césped |
| flower bed | el arriate / parterre |
| vegetable garden | la huerta / el huerto |
| greenhouse | el invernadero |
| the situation | la situación / ubicación |
| aspect | el aspecto |
| view | la vista / el panorama |
| swimming pool | la piscina |
| barbecue | la barbacoa |
| tennis court | la pista de tenis |
| stone | la piedra |
| brick | el ladrillo |
| timber | la madera |
| concrete | el hormigón |

## Useful verbs

| to buy | comprar |
| to sell | vender |
| to rent | alquilar |
| to view (a house) | ver |
| to make an appointment | concertar una cita |
| to lock up | cerrar con llave |

## Useful phrases

| it overlooks the bay | tiene vistas a / da a la bahía |
| a central position | una situación central |
| close to all services | cerca de todos los servicios |
| in the town centre | en el centro urbano / del pueblo |

| in the suburbs | **en los suburbios** |
| in the outskirts | **en las afueras** |
| in the country | **en el campo** |

---

## 5.2 Rooms

### Core vocabulary

| room | **la habitación / el cuarto** |
| entrance | **el vestíbulo** |
| kitchen | **la cocina** |
| dining room | **el comedor** |
| sitting room | **el cuarto de estar / el salón /** |
| | **el living** |
| bedroom | **el dormitorio** |
| playroom | **el cuarto de juego** |
| bathroom | **el cuarto de baño** |
| cloakroom (downstairs toilet) | **el lavabo** |
| study / office | **el despacho** |
| shower | **la ducha** |
| hall | **el vestíbulo** |
| landing | **el descansillo** |
| stairs | **la escalera** |
| utility room | **la trascocina** |
| junk room / store room | **el trastero** |
| window | **la ventana** |
| radiator | **el radiador** |
| floor | **el suelo** |
| ceiling | **el techo** |
| door | **la puerta** |
| wall | **la pared** |
| windowsill | **el antepecho (de la ventana),** |
| | **el alféizar** |
| central heating | **la calefacción** |
| water heater | **el calentador de agua** |
| gas | **el gas** |
| electricity | **la electricidad** |

| | |
|---|---|
| oil | **el aceite** |
| double glazing | **el doble acristalamiento** |
| lock | **la cerradura** |
| key | **la llave** |
| plug | **el enchufe** |
| socket | **el enchufe / la toma de corriente** |
| switch | **el interruptor** |
| handle | **el mango** |
| fuse box | **la caja de fusibles** |
| fuse | **el fusible** |
| fuse wire | **el hilo fusible** |
| torch | **la linterna** |

................................................................

## Insight

Notice how, even when Spanish words are not recognizable cognates, they are often quite logical.

e.g. **interruptor** – a switch interrupts the flow of electricity, **fusible** – a fuse melts if overloaded, **contraventana** – is against a window.

................................................................

| | |
|---|---|
| curtains | **las cortinas** |
| blinds | **las persianas** |
| shutters | **las contraventanas** |
| carpet | **la alfombra / la moqueta** (fitted) |
| rug | **el tapete / la alfombrilla** |
| floor tiles | **las baldosas** |
| wall tiles | **los azulejos** |
| flooring | **la solería** |
| wallpaper | **el papel pintado** |
| paint | **la pintura** |
| paintbrush | **la brocha** (decorating) **/ el pincel** (art) |
| ladder | **la escalera de mano** |

## Insight

Generally speaking, the décor of a Spanish home can be quite different from one in the UK, and not just because tastes are different. Fitted carpets are a rarity, and the concept of a 'three-piece suite' is not common. Spanish homeowners are rather less likely to decorate their home themselves, though the concept of DIY is familiar to most: **el bricolaje** – which also refers to a DIY shop.

### Useful verbs

| | |
|---|---|
| *to turn / switch on* | **encender** |
| *to turn / switch off* | **apagar** |
| *to plug in / switch on* | **conectar** |
| *to plug in* | **enchufar** |

### Useful phrases

| | |
|---|---|
| *upstairs* | **arriba** |
| *downstairs* | **abajo** |
| *on the ground floor* | **en la planta baja** |
| *on the first floor* | **en el primer piso** |
| *in the basement* | **en el sótano** |
| *in the attic* | **en la buhardilla / el desván** |
| *Where is the ...?* | **¿Dónde está el / la ... ?** |
| *How does it work?* | **¿Cómo funciona?** |

## 5.3 Furniture

### Core vocabulary

| | |
|---|---|
| *furniture* | **los muebles** |
| *sitting room* | **el salón** |
| *armchair* | **la butaca** |
| *easy chair* | **el sillón** |
| *sofa* | **el sofá** |

| | |
|---|---|
| *coffee table* | **la mesita (para servir el café)** |
| *bookcase* | **la librería / estantería** |
| *lamp* | **la lámpara** |
| *pictures* | **los cuadros** |
| *bedroom* | **el dormitorio** |
| *bed* | **la cama** |
| *bedside table* | **la mesilla de noche** |
| *chair* | **la silla** |
| *wardrobe* | **el armario** |
| *chest of drawers* | **la cómoda** |
| *mirror* | **el espejo** |
| *built-in cupboard* | **el armario empotrado** |
| *shelves* | **los estantes** |
| *bathroom* | **el cuarto de baño** |
| *bath* | **el baño / la bañera** |
| *mirror* | **el espejo** |
| *razor* | **la afeitadora** |
| *shower* | **la ducha** |
| *wash basin* | **el lavabo** |
| *toilet* | **el lavabo / baño / servicio** |
| *toilet (bowl)* | **el retrete / wáter** |
| *taps* | **los grifos** |
| *plug* | **el tapón** |

---

## 5.4 Household goods

### Core vocabulary

### Insight

Note that there are two words for TV: **televisión** is the medium, **televisor** is the actual TV receiver, the TV set. Note also how many of these words are cognates of the English words, albeit sometimes borrowings with quirky spellings to ensure suitable Spanish pronunciation with an approximation to the English sound, e.g. champú, edredón.

| | |
|---|---|
| television | **el televisor** |
| video recorder | **el aparato de vídeo** |
| DVD player | **el lector de disco de vídeo digital, DVD** |
| remote control | **el mando a distancia** |
| stereo | **el estéreo** |
| radio | **la radio** |
| flatscreen television | **el televisor a pantalla plana** |
| bedding | **la ropa de cama** |
| pillow / pillowcase | **la almohada / la funda de almohada** |
| quilt | **el edredón** |
| quilt cover | **la funda de edredón** |
| sheet | **la sábana** |
| fitted sheet | **la sábana de cuatro picos** |
| shampoo | **el champú** |
| conditioner | **el suavizante / acondicionador** |
| hairdryer | **el secador de pelo** |
| soap | **el jabón** |
| towel | **la toalla** |
| deodorant | **el desodorante** |
| toothbrush | **el cepillo de dientes** |
| toothpaste | **la pasta de dientes** |
| vacuum cleaner | **la aspiradora** |
| duster | **el trapo** |
| brush | **el cepillo** |
| dustpan | **el recogedor, la pala** |
| cleaning materials | **los materiales de limpieza** |
| scrubbing brush | **el cepillo de fregar** |
| floor mop | **la fregona** |
| detergent | **el detergente** |

### Useful phrases

| | |
|---|---|
| Where is the ...? | **¿Dónde está el / la ...?** |
| It's ... | **Está ...** |
| on the table | **en / encima de la mesa** |
| under the bed | **debajo de la cama** |

| in the armchair | **en la butaca** |
| in the cupboard / drawer | **en el armario / cajón** |
| Can I have a clean ....? | **¿Me puede dar un/a ... limpio/a?** |
| How does the (television) work? | **¿Cómo funciona (el televisor)?** |

## Insight

Note that sometimes you need to be clear about exactly what you want to say; *to work* is normally **trabajar**, but if you mean a machine of some sort is or is not working, then you need to use **funcionar**. If you really mean '*to make something work*', use **hacer funcionar**.

| e.g. **Trabajo en una oficina** | *I work in an office.* |
| **Mi reloj no funciona** | *My watch isn't working.* |
| **¿Sabes hacer funcionar la tele?** | *Do you know how to work the TV? (to get the TV to work?)* |

### Useful verbs

| to do housework | **hacer las tareas de la casa** |
| to wash | **lavar** |
| to clean | **limpiar** |
| to vacuum | **pasar el aspirador** |
| to make the bed | **hacer la cama** |
| to sweep | **barrer** |
| to scrub / wash up | **fregar** |

## 5.5 In the kitchen

### Core vocabulary

| | |
|---|---|
| *in the kitchen* | **en la cocina** |
| *table* | **la mesa** |
| *chair* | **la silla** |
| *stool* | **el taburete** |
| *drawer* | **el cajón** |
| *cupboard* | **el armario** |
| *shelf* | **el estante** |
| *sink* | **la pila** |
| *fridge* | **la nevera** |
| *dishwasher* | **el lavaplatos / lavavajillas** |
| *washing machine* | **la lavadora** |
| *tumble drier* | **la secadora** |
| *mixer* | **la batidora** |
| *liquidizer* | **la licuadora** |
| *plate* | **el plato** |
| *dinner plate* | **el plato llano** |
| *bowl* | **el tazón / el plato** |
| *salad bowl* | **la fuente** |
| *dish* | **el plato / la fuente** |
| *cup* | **la taza** |
| *saucer* | **el platillo** |
| *mug* | **el tazón** |
| *jug* | **el jarro / la jarra** |
| *teapot* | **la tetera** |
| *sugar bowl* | **la azucarera** |
| *knife* | **el cuchillo** |
| *fork* | **el tenedor** |
| *spoon* | **la cuchara** |
| *teaspoon* | **la cucharita** |
| *soup spoon* | **la cuchara sopera** |
| *dessert spoon* | **la cuchara de postre** |
| *carving knife* | **el cuchillo de trinchar** |
| *bread knife* | **el cuchillo para cortar pan** |
| *vegetable knife* | **el cuchillo para cortar legumbres** |

## Insight

Many of these words are recognizable as cognates, but remember how useful it is to learn new words with some sort of 'association' to help you recall them; here are a few examples:

**cuchillo** is for *cutting*

**tenedor** comes from **tener**, *to have / hold*

**tetera** contains **té**, *tea*

**sal** is part of *salary* (in ancient times soldiers were paid with *salt*, a very precious commodity then)

| | |
|---|---|
| salt | **la sal** |
| pepper | **la pimienta** |
| mustard | **la mostaza** |
| glass | **el vaso** |
| wineglass | **la copa** |
| champagne glass | **la copa de champán** |
| water glass | **el vaso** |
| tumbler | **el vaso** |
| rubbish | **la basura** |
| left-overs | **las sobras** |
| packaging | **el material de envasado** |
| plastic bags | **las bolsas de plástico** |
| kitchen bin / waste bin | **el cubo de la basura** |
| bin liner | **la bolsa de la basura** |
| dustbin | **el cubo de la basura** |
| recycling | **el reciclaje** |
| bottle bank | **el contenedor de vidrio** |
| compost | **el abono orgánico** |

### Useful phrases

| | |
|---|---|
| *I like / dislike cooking.* | **(No) me gusta cocinar.** |
| *I'll do the washing up.* | **Voy a lavar los platos.** |

> ## Insight
> You may remember that many verb expressions in fact
> consist of two verbs: an 'auxiliary' verb and a main verb in
> the infinitive form. This is because the first verb is already in
> the appropriate form for the person and tense, so no need
> to repeat this in the second verb; as in English, the infinitive
> gives all the information needed, i.e. just 'what' action is
> involved.

### Useful verbs

In recipes, instructions are usually given using the infinitive form of
the verb.

| Cooking terms | *Los términos de cocina* |
|---|---|
| *mix* | **mezclar** |
| *beat* | **batir** |
| *roast* | **asar** |
| *toast* | **tostar** |
| *bake* | **cocer (al horno)** |
| *boil* | **hervir** |
| *steam* | **cocer al vapor** |
| *grill* | **asar a la parrilla** |
| *barbecue* | **asar a la parrilla** |
| *peel* | **pelar** |
| *cut* | **cortar** |
| *slice* | **cortar en lonchas / tajadas / rodajas / trozos** |
| *chop* | **picar** |

## 5.6 Outside

### Core vocabulary

| | |
|---|---|
| garage | **la cochera** |
| shed | **el cobertizo** |
| footpath | **el sendero / la vereda** |
| gate | **la verja** |
| security code | **el código de (la) seguridad** |
| in the garden | **en el jardín** |
| flower bed | **el arriate / parterre** |
| lawn | **el césped** |
| flower | **la flor** |
| plant | **la planta** |
| bush / shrub | **el arbusto** |
| tree | **el árbol** |
| grass | **la hierba** |
| weeds | **las malas hierbas** |
| herbs | **las hierbas finas** |
| bulb | **el bulbo** |

| | |
|---|---|
| **Trees** | *Los árboles* |
| beech | **la haya** |
| chestnut | **el castaño** |
| elm | **el olmo** |
| hazel | **el avellano** |
| holly | **el acebo** |
| oak | **el roble** |
| sycamore | **el sicomoro** |
| willow | **el sauce** |
| poplar | **el álamo / chopo** |
| strawberry tree | **el madroño** (part of symbol of Madrid) |

| | |
|---|---|
| **Flowers** | ***Las flores*** |
| *carnation* | **el clavel** |
| *daffodil* | **el narciso** |
| *rose* | **la rosa** |
| *sweet pea* | **el guisante de olor / clarín** |
| *tulip* | **el tulipán** |
| *mimosa* | **la mimosa** |
| *orange-blossom* | **el azahar** |

| | |
|---|---|
| **Garden tools** | ***Las herramientas de jardinería*** |
| *fork* | **la horca / horquilla** |
| *hoe* | **la azada** |
| *rake* | **el rastrillo** |
| *spade* | **la pala** |
| *trowel* | **el desplantador** |
| *lawnmower* | **el cortacésped** |
| *wheelbarrow* | **la carretilla** |
| *garden tractor* | **el tractor de jardín** |
| *garden cultivator / rotavator* | **la cultivadora** |
| *hose* | **la manguera** |
| *sprinkler* | **el aspersor** |
| *watering can* | **la regadera** |
| *weedkiller* | **el herbicida** |
| *fertilizer* | **el fertilizante** |

## Insight

You might observe that the gender of these words is quite random and upredictable... you just have to learn them with **el / la** as appropriate!

| | |
|---|---|
| **Insects and pests** | ***Los insectos y los animales dañinos*** |
| *ant* | **la hormiga** |
| *bee* | **la abeja** |
| *greenfly* | **el pulgón** |

| housefly | **la mosca** |
| mosquito | **el mosquito** |
| spider | **la araña** |
| wasp | **la avispa** |

## Insight

In section 2.1 you met diminutives. Here is a classic example of how the diminutive form alters the meaning of a word – a mosquito is like a fly, but smaller! You will probably also find augmentatives, which do the opposite.

| **Garden furniture** | ***Los muebles de jardín*** |
| barbecue | **la parrilla** |
| table | **la mesa** |
| deck chair | **la tumbona** |
| lounger | **la tumbona** |
| bench | **el banco** |
| swing | **el columpio** |
| slide | **el tobogán** |

### Useful phrases

| It needs to be weeded. | **Hace falta desherbarlo.** |
| It needs to be watered. | **Hace falta regarlo.** |
| The grass needs to be cut. | **Hace falta cortar el césped / la hierba.** |
| They are ripe / not ripe. | **(No) están maduros/as.** |
| I like / dislike gardening. | **(No) me gusta la jardinería.** |
| He / she has green fingers. | **Se le dan muy bien las plantas.** |
| I am allergic to ... | **Soy alérgico/a a ...** |
| I have been stung! | **¡Me ha picado!** |

## Insight

Note how **hace falta** is followed by the infinitive, just like the expressions in 5.5.

### Useful verbs

| | |
|---|---|
| to dig | **cavar** |
| to plant | **plantar** |
| to grow | **cultivar** *(what a gardener does)* |
| to weed | **desherbar** |
| to water | **regar** |
| to pick | **(re)coger** |
| to cut the grass | **cortar la hierba** |

## 5.7 Tools and DIY

### Core vocabulary

| | |
|---|---|
| DIY | **el bricolaje** |
| tools | **las herramientas** |
| drill | **el taladro** |
| (drill) bits | **las brocas** |
| hammer | **el martillo** |
| pincers | **las pinzas** |
| pliers | **los alicates** |
| saw | **la sierra** |
| chain saw | **la sierra de cadena** |
| screwdriver | **el destornillador** |
| spanner | **la llave de tuercas** |
| staple gun | **la grapadora** |
| tape measure | **la cinta métrica** |
| nail | **el clavo** |
| bolt | **el tornillo** |
| nut | **la tuerca** |
| staple | **la grapa** |
| brush | **el cepillo** |
| paint brush | **la brocha** |
| scissors | **las tijeras** |
| sandpaper | **el papel de lija** |
| ladder | **la escalera de mano** |
| scaffold | **el andamio** |

| tiles (roof) | **las tejas** |
| slates | **las pizarras** |
| windowpane | **el cristal / vidrio** |
| window frame | **el marco de ventana** |
| sliding window | **la ventana corrediza** |
| shutters | **las contraventanas** |

| **Plumbing and electricity** | *Las tuberías y la electricidad* |
| pipe | **el tubo / caño** |
| tap | **el grifo** |
| wire | **el alambre** |
| fuse | **el fusible** |
| plug | **el enchufe** |
| socket | **el enchufe** |

## Insight

Note how the same word – **enchufe** – is used for both *plug* and *socket*. In fact it also has a colloquial use, loosely meaning 'string-pulling' (using contacts or influence to obtain a favour or a job).

### Useful phrases

| Can you fix it? | **¿Puedes / puede usted arreglarlo?** |
| Yes I can! | **¡Claro que sí!** |
| to fix something to a wall | **clavar / fijar algo en la pared** |
| to fix /mend | **arreglar / reparar** |

### Useful verbs

| to screw | **atornillar** |
| to unscrew | **destornillar** |
| to hammer | **clavar / martillar** |
| to nail | **clavar** |
| to drill | **taladrar / perforar** |
| to fasten | **sujetar** |

| to cut | **cortar** |
| to rub down (sandpaper) | **lijar** |
| to paint | **pintar** |
| to plane | **cepillar** |
| to glue | **pegar** |
| to solder | **soldar** |
| to weld | **soldar** |

## Insight

Note how all of the above verbs are **-ar** verbs. This is not just because **-ar** verbs are the biggest by far of the three families of verbs, but also because verbs derived from a noun or another part of speech (as many of the above words), or on words 'imported' from other languages are always **-ar** verbs: a useful tip to remember. Thus, e.g. **tornillo** = *screw* → **atornillar, clavo** = *nail* → **clavar, corte** = *cut* → **cortar.**

# Test yourself

Here are 25 words that fit into five different groups of words. Put five words under each of the correct group headings.

| Group 1 | Group 2 | Group 3 | Group 4 | Group 5 |
|---|---|---|---|---|
| La casa | Las habitaciones | Los muebles | En la cocina | En el jardín |
| *The house* | *Rooms* | *Furniture* | *In the kitchen* | *In the garden* |

el bulbo
el sótano
el césped
el despacho
el vestíbulo
la nevera
la flor
la ventana
la calefacción
el dormitorio
la cama
el armario
la lavadora
el tazón
la secadora
la pila
el comedor
las malas hierbas
el roble
la butaca
la lámpara
el espejo
la escalera
el balcón
el hogar

There is an *Answer key* at the end of the book.

# 6

# Entertaining and food

## 6.1 Parties and celebrations

### Core vocabulary

| | |
|---|---|
| *Congratulations!* | **¡Felicitaciones! / ¡Enhorabuena!** |
| *a party* | **una fiesta** |
| *a birthday* | **un cumpleaños** |
| *an anniversary* | **un aniversario** |
| *an engagement* | **un compromiso / noviazgo** |
| *a wedding* | **una boda** |
| *a celebration* | **una celebración / un festejo** |
| *silver wedding* | **las bodas de plata** |
| *golden wedding* | **las bodas de oro** |
| *an invitation* | **una invitación** |
| *a reply* | **una respuesta** |
| *an acceptance* | **una aceptación** |
| *a refusal* | **una denegación** |
| *an excuse* | **una excusa** |
| *a thank you letter* | **una carta de gratitud** |
| *a cake* | **un pastel / una tarta** |
| *champagne* | **champán** |
| *a toast* | **un brindis** |
| *a present* | **un regalo** |
| *Cheers!* | **¡Salud!** |

## Insight

Notice how many of the above words are cognates, some because they are borrowings into Spanish (**champán**), borrowings from Spanish (**fiesta**), or simply from the same original source, usually Latin (**invitación, excusa, tarta**). Then of course there are derivatives, based on other words you probably already know, such as **cumpleaños** (**cumple** + **años** = completes years!). So, what about the other words which offer no such clues, such as **boda**, or **brindis**? Well, this would be a good time to make a special effort to learn them, such as with a suitable picture of a wedding or a glass of **champán**!

### Useful phrases

| | |
|---|---|
| *Let's have a party.* | **Vamos a dar una fiesta.** |
| *Let's dance.* | **Vamos a bailar. / Bailemos.** |
| *I would like to propose a toast.* | **Quisiera proponer un brindis.** |
| *I would like to thank our hosts.* | **Quisiera darles las gracias a nuestros huéspedes.** |
| *I've got a hangover.* | **Tengo una resaca.** |

### Useful verbs

| | |
|---|---|
| *to party* | **irse de juerga** |
| *to eat* | **comer** |
| *to drink* | **beber** |
| *to toast (the bride)* | **proponer un brindis por la novia** |
| *to enjoy oneself* | **divertirse** |
| *to overindulge* | **excederse** |
| *to have too much to drink* | **abusar del alcohol** |
| *to get drunk* | **emborracharse** |
| *to feel sick* | **marearse** |

## Insight

Notice that some of the above verbs are reflexive yet, apart from **divertirse**, are not reflexive in English and don't really seem typical of verbs one would expect to be reflexive! It simply is the case that lots of expressions in Spanish use the reflexive forms of verbs; in one or two cases one can begin to understand why. For example, **emborrachar** means to make somebody drunk, such as **'el coñac te emborracha facilmente'** = *'Cognac gets you drunk easily'*. So, if *you* drink too much, you are getting yourself drunk... Which is more typical of a reflexive!

## 6.2 Mealtimes

## Insight

- Breakfast (**el desayuno**) is light – it usually comprises coffee, fruit juice, bread and jam, a pastry, biscuits or toast; children often have chocolate spread on bread or toast; cereals and milk are becoming increasingly popular.
- Many people go out from work to a bar mid-morning for coffee and a bun or **churros** – these are thin, crispy, finger-doughnuts, dunked in coffee or hot chocolate. Surprisingly in relation to British habits, some adults may have a brandy or liquor with their coffee during the mid-morning break in a bar, typically **un carajillo**, a dash of liquor or brandy in their coffee!
- Lunch (**el almuerzo**) is the main meal of the day; any time from about 1 to 3 p.m.; it usually comprises two or three courses, perhaps beginning with a starter or fish, then the main course with vegetables or salad served separately, and often fruit for dessert. The meal is often accompanied by wine, especially at weekends, and may be followed by a **siesta** if time permits.

- **La merienda** is a teatime snack often eaten by children and may consist of a cake or chocolate with a drink.
- Dinner (**la cena**) is served any time from about 8 p.m. to midnight. It is usually a lighter meal than lunch, unless it is a special occasion.

## Core vocabulary

| | |
|---|---|
| meals | **las comidas** |
| mealtimes | **las horas de las comidas** |
| breakfast | **el desayuno** |
| elevenses | **el tentempié de las once** |
| lunch | **el almuerzo / la comida** |
| afternoon tea | **la merienda** |
| dinner | **la cena** |
| supper | **la cena** |
| the menu | **la carta** |
| starter | **la entrada / el primer plato** |
| soup | **la sopa** |
| fish | **el pescado** |
| main course | **el plato principal** |
| dessert | **el postre** |
| cheese | **el queso** |
| coffee | **el café** |

## Insight

- wine is drunk at many meals, but always balanced with mineral water
- Spanish people often eat with a fork in the right hand, and bread in the left hand
- mealtimes are a family occasion, to be enjoyed, and definitely not to be rushed
- to help you remember the vocabulary, try planning your meals in Spanish for a few weeks; you could even prepare menus in Spanish for the family!

| Drinks | *Las bebidas* |
|---|---|
| soft drink | **el refresco** |
| orange juice | **el zumo / jugo de naranja** |
| water | **el agua** |
| mineral water | **el agua mineral** |
| fizzy | **con gas** |
| still | **sin gas** |
| aperitif | **el aperitivo** |
| cocktail | **el cóctel** |
| sherry | **el jerez** |
| gin and tonic | **el gin-tonic** |
| red wine | **el vino tinto** |
| white wine | **el vino blanco** |
| champagne | **el champán** |
| beer | **la cerveza** |
| cider | **la sidra** |
| brandy | **el coñac** |
| liqueur | **el licor** |

Here are a few examples of popular Spanish dishes to give you a taster!

| Starters | *Entradas* |
|---|---|
| cold meats | **los fiambres** |
| hors d'oeuvres | **los entremeses** |
| Spanish omelette | **la tortilla española** |
| plain omelette | **la tortilla francesa** |
| macaroni with tomato sauce | **los macarrones con tomate** |
| green salad | **la ensalada verde** |
| mixed salad | **la ensalada mixta** |
| Russian salad | **la ensaladilla rusa** |

| Soups | *Sopas* |
|---|---|
| noodle soup | **la sopa de fideos** |
| fish soup | **la sopa de pescado** |
| garlic soup | **la sopa de ajo** |
| consommé | **el consomé** |
| chilled vegetable soup | **el gazpacho** |

| Stews | *Cocidos* |
|---|---|
| chickpea stew | **el cocido de garbanzos** |
| lentil stew | **el potaje de lentejas** |
| Asturian bean stew | **la fabada asturiana** |

| **Fish and seafood** | *Pescados y mariscos* |
|---|---|
| hake | **la merluza** |
| tuna | **el atún** |
| sardines | **las sardinas** |
| squid | **los calamares** |
| mussels | **los mejillones** |
| anchovies | **los boquerones / las anchoas** |

| **Meat** | *La carne* |
|---|---|
| steak | **el bistec** |
| veal fillet | **el filete de ternera** |
| pork chop | **la chuleta de cerdo** |
| roast chicken | **el pollo asado** |
| stewed lamb | **el estofado de cordero** |

| **Vegetables** | *Los vegetales* |
|---|---|
| green vegetables | **las verduras** |
| peas | **los guisantes** |
| green beans | **las judías verdes** |
| beans | **las habas** |
| cauliflower | **la coliflor** |
| aubergine | **la berenjena** |
| pepper | **el pimiento** |
| lettuce | **la lechuga** |
| tomato | **el tomate** |
| cucumber | **el pepino** |
| mixed salad | **la ensalada mixta** |
| potatoes | **las patatas** (**papas** in Latin America) |
| chips / crisps | **las patatas fritas** |
| rice | **el arroz** |
| pasta | **las pastas** |
| spaghetti | **los espaguetis** |

| **Desserts** | *Los postres* |
|---|---|
| *frozen tart* | **la tarta helada** |
| *fruit salad* | **la macedonia de fruta** |
| *yoghurt* | **el yogur** |
| *caramel custard* | **el flan** |
| *peaches in syrup* | **el melocotón en almíbar** |
| *cream* | **la nata** |
| *seasonal fruit* | **fruta del tiempo** |
| *ice cream* | **el helado** |

| **Flavours of ice cream** | *Los sabores* |
|---|---|
| *coconut* | **el coco** |
| *pistachio* | **el pistacho** |
| *strawberry* | **la fresa** |
| *raspberry* | **la frambuesa** |
| *vanilla* | **la vainilla** |
| *lemon* | **el limón** |
| *chocolate* | **el chocolate** |

| **Coffee** | *El café* |
|---|---|
| *espresso* | **el café exprés** |
| *cappuccino* | **el capuchino** |
| *coffee with milk* | **el café con leche** |
| *coffee without milk* | **el café solo** |
| *with sugar* | **con azúcar** |
| *with sweetener* | **con edulcorante** |
| *without sugar* | **sin azúcar** |
| *decaffeinated coffee* | **el café descafeinado** |

| Tea | *El té* |
| --- | --- |
| *Indian tea* | **el té indio** |
| *China tea* | **el té chino** |
| *herbal tea* | **la infusión de hierbas** |
| *fruit tea* | **la infusión de fruta** |
| *with milk* | **con leche** |
| *with lemon* | **con limón** |
| *with sugar* | **con azúcar** |

## Insight

Note how many of these expressions are 'built up', using **con** or **de** to link the two elements, as in **el café con leche** and **la infusión de fruta**; whilst this is more complex than in English, where we can just stick two nouns together, it is at least very logical, so easy to get used to.

### Useful phrases

| *I have a special diet.* | **Estoy a una dieta especial.** |
| --- | --- |
| *I am allergic to ...* | **Soy alérgico/a a ...** |
| *I don't eat ...* | **No como ...** |
| *I can't eat ...* | **No puedo comer ...** |
| *I am a vegetarian.* | **Soy vegetariano.** |
| *I am a vegan.* | **Soy vegetariano estricto.** |
| *I have to have a gluten-free diet.* | **Sigo una dieta sin gluten.** |
| *I am diabetic.* | **Soy diabético/a.** |

### Useful verbs

| *to like / dislike* | **(no) gustar** |
| --- | --- |
| *to love, like a lot* | **encantar** (works like *gustar*) |
| *to eat* | **comer** |
| *to drink* | **beber** |
| *to prefer* | **preferir** |
| *to love* | **amar** |

## 6.3 Breakfast

### Core vocabulary

| | |
|---|---|
| cereals | **los cereales** |
| wheat | **el trigo** |
| oats | **la avena** |
| barley | **la cebada** |
| rye | **el centeno** |
| bran | **el salvado** |
| cornflakes | **los copos de maíz** |
| muesli | **el muesli** |
| milk | **la leche** |
| semi-skimmed milk | **la leche semi-desnatada** |
| fat-free milk | **la leche desnatada** |
| soya milk | **la leche de soja** |
| goat's milk | **la leche de cabra** |
| cream | **la nata** |
| yoghurt | **el yogur** |
| bacon | **el bacón** |
| egg(s) | **el / los huevo(s)** |
| scrambled | **revuelto(s)** |
| poached | **escalfado(s)** |
| boiled | **pasado(s) por agua** |
| hard boiled | **duro(s)** |
| fried | **frito(s)** |
| sunny side up | **frito(s) sólo por un lado** |
| sausages | **las salchichas** |
| hash browns | **croquetas de patata y cebolla** |

| | |
|---|---|
| mushrooms | **los champiñones** |
| tomatoes | **los tomates** |
| fried | **fritos** |
| grilled | **a la parrilla** |
| tinned | **en lata** |
| baked beans | **judías en salsa de tomate** |
| pancake | **la tortita** |
| maple syrup | **el jarabe de arce** |
| ham | **el jamón** |
| salami | **el salami** |
| cheese | **el queso** |
| bread | **el pan** |
| white | **blanco** |
| brown | **moreno** |
| granary | **con granos enteros** |
| wholemeal | **integral** |
| sliced | **en rebanadas** |
| organic | **orgánico** |
| rolls | **los panecillos** |
| croissants | **los croissants / el cruasán** |
| danish pastries | **los bollos de hojaldre daneses** |
| butter | **la mantequilla** |
| margarine | **la margarina** |
| low-fat spread | **la margarina con poca materia grasa** |
| jam | **la mermelada** |
| marmalade | **la mermelada de naranja** |
| honey | **la miel** |
| peanut butter | **la mantequilla de cacahuete** |
| drinks | **las bebidas** |
| tea | **el té** |
| coffee | **el café** |
| milk | **la leche** |
| cold milk | **la leche fría** |
| hot milk | **la leche caliente** |
| hot chocolate | **el chocolate caliente** |
| fruit juice | **el zumo de fruta** |
| orange juice | **el zumo de naranja** |

| | |
|---|---|
| *freshly squeezed orange juice* | **el zumo de naranja recién exprimido** |

**Useful phrases**

| | |
|---|---|
| *I don't eat breakfast.* | **No tomo el desayuno.** |
| *I only eat ...* | **Sólo como ...** |
| *I don't drink milk ...* | **No bebo (la) leche ...** |
| *I have my breakfast at ...* | **Desayuno a las ...** |

## Insight

One way to help yourself learn food vocabulary is to try to associate the taste with the word – a good excuse to try lots of different dishes on a Spanish menu! But in Spain you won't usually find typically English things like marmalade, and you will be lucky to find a really good cuppa the way you drink it at home!

Equally, it can be difficult eating in Spain if you have special dietary requirements. Vegetarians are not well catered for, in that few restaurants will have specifically vegetarian dishes. However, good fresh vegetables and salads are aplenty. However, be aware that if you order **una ensalada mixta**, it will often have in it tuna, ham or other ingredients you don't expect.

The next section is particularly important in Spain, where few people drink without some sort of food snack, usually referred to as **tapas**. Sometimes these are complimentary, but many bars and cafés have a good selection of **tapas**. Spanish people will often order a selection of them to share as a meal.

## 6.4 Snacks

### Core vocabulary

| | |
|---|---|
| *snack* | **el tentempié, tapas** |
| *a (ham)burger* | **una hamburguesa** |
| *cheeseburger* | **una hamburguesa con queso** |
| *fishburger* | **una hamburguesa de pescado** |
| *portion* | **la ración** |
| *portion on a stick* | **el pincho** |
| *salad* | **una ensalada** |
| *green salad* | **una ensalada verde** |
| *tomato salad* | **una ensalada con tomate** |
| *mixed salad* | **una ensalada mixta** |
| *potato salad* | **una ensaladilla de patatas** |
| *Russian salad* | **una ensaladilla rusa** |
| *Spanish omelette* | **la tortilla española** |
| *croquettes* | **las croquetas** |
| *olives* | **las aceitunas** |
| *anchovies* | **los boquerones** |
| *serrano ham* | **el jamón serrano** |
| *yoghurt* | **el yogur** |
| *biscuit / cookie* | **la galleta** |
| *chocolate biscuit* | **la galleta de chocolate** |
| *piece of cake* | **el trozo de pastel** |
| *bun* | **el bollo** |
| *sweets* | **los caramelos** |
| *sandwich* (English style) | **el sándwich** |
| *in brown bread* | **en pan moreno** |
| *in white bread* | **en pan blanco** |
| *in a roll* | **en un panecillo** |
| *sandwich* (Spanish style) | **el bocadillo** |
| *with mayonnaise / salad dressing* | **con mayonesa / aliño** |
| *without mayonnaise / salad dressing* | **sin mayonesa / aliño** |

## Useful phrases

| | |
|---|---|
| Can I offer you a cup of coffee? | **¿Te apetece un café?** |
| How do you take it? | **¿Cómo lo prefieres?** |
| With milk or without milk? | **¿Con leche o sin leche?** |
| Do you take sugar? | **¿Lo tomas con azúcar?** |
| Have you got a sweetener? | **¿Tienes un edulcorante?** |
| Would you like a biscuit? | **¿Te gustaría una galleta?** |
| Yes please. | **Sí, por favor.** |
| No thank you. | **No, gracias.** |
| I am on a diet. | **Estoy a dieta.** |
| I don't take ... | **No tomo / como / bebo ...** |
| It's too hot / cold / spicy. | **Es demasiado caliente / frío / picante.** |
| It isn't cooked properly. | **No está bien guisado.** |
| It is delicious! | **Es / está muy delicioso / rico.** |

> ### Insight
> Practise these phrases by having a dialogue with a member of
> your family or a friend, or with an imaginary guest.

## 6.5 Fruit and vegetables

### Useful vocabulary

| Fruit | *La fruta* |
|---|---|
| apple | **la manzana** |
| cooking apple | **la manzana para cocer** |
| dessert apple | **la manzana para repostería** |
| apricot | **el albaricoque** |
| banana | **el plátano** |
| grapes | **las uvas** |
| cherries | **las cerezas** |
| melon | **el melón** |
| watermelon | **la sandía** |

| peach | el melocotón |
|---|---|
| pear | la pera |
| plum | la ciruela |
| raspberry | la frambuesa |
| rhubarb | el ruibarbo |
| strawberry | la fresa |

| **Salad** | *La ensalada* |
|---|---|
| cucumber | el pepino |
| lettuce | la lechuga |
| olives | las aceitunas |
| radish | el rábano |
| onion | la cebolla |
| tomatoes | los tomates |
| tuna | el atún |
| hard-boiled egg | el huevo duro |

| **Vegetables** | *Las legumbres / los vegetales / las verduras* |
|---|---|
| beans | las habas |
| green beans | las judías verdes |
| broccoli | el brécol |
| cabbage | la col |
| carrot | la zanahoria |
| cauliflower | la coliflor |
| aubergine | la berenjena |
| courgette | el calabacín |
| pepper | el pimiento |
| garlic | el ajo |
| leek | el puerro |
| lettuce | la lechuga |
| mushroom | el champiñón |
| onion | la cebolla |
| potato | la patata |
| sweetcorn | el maíz |
| turnip | el nabo |

| | |
|---|---|
| swede | **el nabo sueco** |
| pumpkin | **la calabaza** |
| shallots | **los chalotes** |
| spinach | **las espinacas** |
| watercress | **el berro** |

| | |
|---|---|
| **Pulses** | *Las leguminosas* |
| chick-peas | **los garbanzos** |
| lentils | **las lentejas** |
| beans | **las habas, judías, alubias** |
| | (depending on type) |
| green beans | **las judías verdes** |
| chillibeans | **los frijoles** |

## Insight

You might find it surprising that many regions of Spain, especially in the north, have their own special stews based usually on pulses. Try **cocido de lentejas** or **fabada asturiana**... just the thing on a cold winter's night!

| | |
|---|---|
| **Citrus fruits** | *Las frutas cítricas* |
| grapefruit | **el pomelo** |
| lemon | **el limón** |
| lime | **la lima** |
| orange | **la naranja** |

| | |
|---|---|
| **Berries** | *Las bayas* |
| blackberry | **la mora** |
| blueberry / bilberry / cranberry | **el arándano** |
| gooseberry | **la grosella** |
| blackcurrant | **la grosella negra** |
| redcurrant | **la grosella roja** |

**Exotic fruits**

| | |
|---|---|
| avocado | **el aguacate** |
| coconut | **el coco** |
| date | **el dátil** |
| fig | **el higo** |
| kiwi fruit | **el kiwi** |
| mango | **el mango** |
| passion fruit | **la granadilla** |
| pineapple | **la piña** |

*Las frutas exóticas*

**Nuts**

| | |
|---|---|
| almond | **la almendra** |
| brazil | **la nuez del Brasil** |
| cashew | **el anacardo** |
| hazel | **la avellana** |
| peanut | **el cacahuete** |
| pistachio | **el pistacho** |
| walnut | **la nuez** |

*Las nueces*

---

## 6.6 Fish and meat

**Seafood**

| | |
|---|---|
| fish* | **el pez, el pescado** |
| anchovy | **las anchoas** |
| cod | **el bacalao** |
| eel | **la anguila** |
| haddock | **el eglefino** |
| hake | **la merluza** |
| herring | **el arenque** |
| jellyfish | **la medusa** |
| mackerel | **la caballa** |
| octopus | **el pulpo** |
| plaice | **la platija** |
| red mullet | **el salmonete** |
| sardine | **la sardina** |
| sea bream | **el besugo** |

*Pescados y mariscos*

| sea bass | la lubina / el robalo |
| skate | la raya |
| sole | el lenguado |
| squid | el calamar |
| tuna | el atún |
| whiting | la pescadilla |
| turbot | el rodaballo |

| **Shellfish** | *Los mariscos* |
| crab | el cangrejo |
| langoustine | el langostino |
| lobster | la langosta |
| mussels | los mejillones |
| oyster | la ostra |
| prawn | la gamba |

| **Fresh water fish** | *El pez de agua fresca* |
| trout | la trucha |
| salmon | el salmón |
| perch | la perca |
| pike | el lucio |

## Insight

* There are two words for fish: **el pez** – live *fish*, and **el pescado** – 'fished' fish, ready to buy / cook / eat!

Fish and seafood are extremely popular in Spain, and you will find them fresh anywhere in Spain, no matter how far from the sea. So, try it. But beware, the English translations on a Spanish menu often leave a lot to be desired, so don't be put off! (The author once saw in a fish restaurant in Málaga three types of fish translated as: fish, little fish, more little fish. The translator was obviously not trying very hard!)

| **Meat** | *La carne* |
| --- | --- |
| beef | **la vaca / la ternera /** |
| | **la carne de res** |
| lamb | **el cordero** |
| pork | **el cerdo** |
| veal | **la ternera** |
| ham | **el jamón** |
| serrano ham | **el jamón serrano** |
| cooked ham | **el jamón de York** |
| liver | **el hígado** |
| kidneys | **los riñones** |
| (cooked) sausage | **el embutido** |
| hard, spicy pork sausage | **el chorizo** |
| black pudding | **la morcilla** |
| long pork sausage | **la longaniza** |
| tripe | **los callos** |

| **Poultry** | *Las aves* |
| --- | --- |
| chicken | **el pollo** |
| turkey | **el pavo** |
| duck | **el pato** |
| goose | **el ganso** |

| **Game** | *La caza* |
| --- | --- |
| grouse | **el urogallo** |
| hare | **la liebre** |
| partridge | **la perdiz** |
| pheasant | **el faisán** |
| pigeon | **el pichón** |
| rabbit | **el conejo** |
| venison | **la carne de venado** |
| wild boar | **el jabalí** |

## 6.7 Using a recipe

### Core vocabulary

| | |
|---|---|
| *making a cake* | **hacer un pastel** |
| *ingredients* | **los ingredientes** |
| *flour* | **la harina** |
|   *plain flour* |   **la harina sin levadura** |
|   *self-raising flour* |   **la harina con levadura** |
|   *raising agent (baking powder)* |   **la levadura en polvo** |
| *cornflour* | **la harina de maíz** |
| *potato flower* | **la harina de patata** |
| *sugar* | **el azúcar** |
| *butter* | **la mantequilla** |
| *salt* | **la sal** |
| *vanilla / almond essence* | **la esencia de vainilla / almendra** |
| *grated chocolate* | **el chocolate rallado** |
| *melted chocolate* | **el chocolate fundido** |
| *grated lemon rind* | **la ralladura de limón** |
| *the juice of an orange* | **el zumo de una naranja** |
| *chopped nuts* | **las nueces picadas** |
| *weighing scales* | **la balanza** |
| *mixing bowl* | **el cuenco grande** |
| *wooden spoon* | **la cuchara de palo** |
| *mixer* | **la batidora** |
| *grater* | **el rallador** |
| *sieve* | **el colador / la criba** |
| *baking tin* | **el molde (para el horno)** |
| *oven* | **el horno** |

| | |
|---|---|
| *oven gloves* | **los guantes para el horno** |
| *saucepan* | **la cacerola** |
| *casserole* | **la cacerola / cazuela** |
| *frying pan* | **la sartén** |
| *lid* | **la tapa** |
| *handle* | **la manga** |
| *silver foil* | **el papel de aluminio** |
| *cling film* | **el film adhesivo** |
| *grease-proof paper* | **el papel encerado** |
| *plastic bags* | **las bolsas de plástico** |
| *plastic containers* | **las recipientes de plástico** |

### Useful phrases

| | |
|---|---|
| *make a cake* | **hacer un pastel** |
| *make soup* | **hacer la sopa** |
| *prepare the vegetables* | **preparar las verduras** |
| *peel the carrots* | **pelar las zanahorias** |
| *chop the leeks* | **picar los puerros** |
| *melt the butter* | **fundir la mantequilla** |
| *add the flour* | **añadir la harina** |
| *stir the mixture* | **agitar la mezcla** |
| *pour in the stock* | **echar / verter el caldo** |

## Insight

One thing that makes recipes in Spanish easier to understand is that they usually use the verbs in the infinitive form.

### Useful verbs

| | |
|---|---|
| *heat* | **calentar** |
| *cook* | **cocinar** |
| *roast* | **asar** |
| *bake* | **cocer (en el horno)** |
| *fry* | **freír** |
| *boil* | **hervir** |
| *poach (egg)* | **escalfar** |
| *poach (fish)* | **cocer a fuego lento** |
| *steam* | **cocer al vapor** |

# Test yourself

Pick out the three words that are to do with food and mealtimes.

1 a las comidas, b la boda, c la merienda, d la cena, e la respuesta
2 a el brindis, b la carta, c la sopa, d la resaca, e la entrada
3 a el pescado, b el queso, c las entradas, d el champán, e la fiesta
4 a la excusa, b el postre, c el fusible, d el desayuno, e el consomé
5 a las habas, b el pimiento, c la campana, d la coliflor, e la mezcla
6 a las pastas, b los padres, c los postres, d el ordenador, e la nata
7 a las páginas, b el cazador, c la trucha, d el arroz, e la anguila
8 a la sobrina, b las salchichas, c los mariscos, d las gambas,
  e la red
9 a calentar, b freír, c reparar, d callarse, e hervir
10 a un muchacho, b la miel, c el helado, d un cumpleaños, e el flan

You may want to check your answers in the *Test yourself Answer key* at the end of the book.

# In the town

## 7.1 The town plan and the sights

### Core vocabulary

| About the town | En la ciudad |
|---|---|
| bank | el banco |
| bus station | la estación de autobuses |
| car park | el aparcamiento / estacionamiento |
| cinema | el cine |
| council offices | las oficinas municipales |
| football ground | el estadio / campo de fútbol |
| hospital | el hospital |
| hotel | el hotel |
| law courts | el tribunal de justicia |
| library | la biblioteca |
| market | el mercado |
| museum | el museo |
| police station | la comisaría |
| post office | (la oficina de) Correos |
| station | la estación |
| swimming pool | la piscina |
| tourist office | la oficina de (información y) turismo |
| town hall | el ayuntamiento |

| region | la región |
| district | el distrito |
| built-up area | la zona urbanizada |
| town | el pueblo |
| suburbs | los suburbios |
| town centre | el centro de la ciudad |
| industrial zone | la zona industrial |
| opening times | las horas de apertura |
| open | abierto/a |
| closed | cerrado/a |
| holidays | las vacaciones |
| bank holiday | el día festivo |
| annual holiday | la fiesta anual |

## Insight

Notice how relatively reliable Spanish is when it comes to gender: words ending in **-o** are almost always masculine; almost all of those ending in **-a** are feminine, and those which end in **-ión** and **-dad** are all feminine.

## The sights — *Los lugares de interés*

| bridge | el puente |
| castle | el castillo |
| cathedral | la catedral |
| church | la iglesia |
| fountain | la fuente |
| monument | el monumento |
| museum | el museo |
| old town | el casco viejo |
| opera house | el teatro de la ópera |
| park | el parque |
| river | el río |
| square | la plaza |
| statue | la estatua |
| theatre | el teatro |

## Insight

In this short section there are examples of some Spanish 'spelling quirks':

**th** → **t** as in **teatro, catedral**

**o** → **ue** as in **puente** (like French **pont**), **fuente** (like *font* or *fountain*)

**c** → **qu** as in **parque**, where the **c** changes to **qu** to preserve the hard **-c-** sound before **-e**

and of course the **-o** which so often converts an English spelling into Spanish: **museo, monumento**

### Useful verbs

| | |
|---|---|
| *to meet* | **reunirse / encontrar** |
| *to look for* | **buscar** |
| *to be situated* | **estar situado/a** |

### Useful phrases

| | |
|---|---|
| *Let's meet at the café Goya.* | **Nos quedamos en el café Goya** |
| *Where is it...?* | **¿Dónde está ...?** |
| *It is in the centre* | **Está en el centro** |
| *on the main street* | **en la calle principal** |
| *near the post office* | **cerca de Correos** |
| *opposite the bank* | **enfrente del banco** |
| *on the market place* | **en la plaza del mercado** |
| *beside the river* | **a orillas del río** |

## 7.2 Getting around town

### Core vocabulary

| | |
|---|---|
| road | **la carretera** *(between towns)* |
| road / street | **la calle** *(in towns)* |
| avenue | **la avenida** |
| pavement | **la acera** |
| gutter | **la cuneta** |
| pedestrian crossing | **el paso de peatones** |
| pedestrian zone | **la zona peatonal** |
| traffic lights | **el semáforo** |
| crossing lights | **las luces del paso de peatones** |
| subway (foot passage) | **el paso subterráneo** |
| the bus stop | **la parada de autobuses** |
| the subway / tube station | **la estación de metro** |

| **How do I get into town?** | *¿Por dónde / cómo puedo ir a la ciudad?* |
|---|---|
| by car | **en coche** |
| by bus | **en autobús** |
| by tram | **en tranvía** |
| by underground / tube / subway / metro | **en metro** |
| on foot | **a pie / andando** |

| **Parking the car** | *Aparcar el coche* |
|---|---|
| car park | **el aparcamiento** |
| multistorey car park | **el aparcamiento de varias plantas** |

| underground car park | el parking subterráneo |
| full | completo |
| spaces | espacios (libres) |
| entrance | la entrada |
| ticket machine | la máquina de billetes |
| change | el cambio / suelto |
| credit card | la tarjeta de crédito |
| ticket | el billete / la entrada |
| exit | la salida |
| barrier | la barrera |
| traffic warden | el guardia de tráfico |

## Useful phrases

| Use the crossing. | Usar el paso de peatones. |
| Don't cross. | ¡No cruce(s)! |
| There's a car coming. | Llega un coche. |
| Excuse me ... | Diga / Dígame / Oiga / Oígame |
| Can you tell me ...? | ¿Me puede decir ...? |
| How do I get to the station | ¿Por dónde se va a la estación? |
| Where is the nearest car park? | ¿Dónde está el aparcamiento más cercano? |
| When is the next bus? | ¿A qué hora pasa el próximo autobús? |
| It is forbidden ... | Prohibido ... |
|   to cross the road here. |   cruzar la calle aquí. |
|   to drop litter. |   dejar caer basura / papeles. |
|   to park. |   aparcar. |

## Useful verbs

| to walk | andar / ir andando |
| to cross | cruzar |
| to turn left / right | girar a / tomar la izquierda / derecha |
| to go straight on | seguir todo recto / derecho |
| to run | correr |

| to drive | **llevar el coche a ...** |
| to catch the bus | **coger el autobús** |
| to miss the bus | **perder el autobús** |

## 7.3 Shops and shopping

### Core vocabulary

| **Shops** | *Las tiendas* |
|---|---|
| bakery | **la panadería** |
| butcher | **la carnicería** |
| cake shop | **la pastelería** |
| chemist's | **la farmacia** |
| clothes shop | **la boutique / la tienda de ropa** |
| confectioner's | **la confitería** |
| department store | **el almacén / los almacenes** |
| dry-cleaner's | **la tintorería** |
| flower shop | **la floristería / florería** |
| hairdresser | **el peluquero** |
| health food store | **la tienda de alimentos dietéticos** |
| hypermarket | **el hipermercado** |
| market | **el mercado** |
| newsagent's | **el tienda de periódicos** |
| optician | **la óptica** |
| shoe shop | **la zapatería** |
| shopping centre | **el centro comercial** |
| sports shop | **la tienda de deportes** |
| supermarket | **el supermercado** |
| travel agent | **la agencia de viajes** |

### Insight

Note how many of these shop-names are derivatives, i.e. derived from the name of the product and / or the name of the person who works there. Thus we have word families such as:

**pan → panadero → panadería** (*bread, baker, baker's*)
**pelo → peluca → peluquero > peluquería** (*hair, wig, hairdresser, hairdresser's*)

| Store guide | *La guía del almacén* |
|---|---|
| escalator | **la escalera mecánica** |
| lift | **el ascensor** |
| ground floor | **la planta baja** |
| first floor | **el primer piso** |
| bedding | **la ropa de cama** |
| fashion | **la moda** |
| sportswear | **la ropa deportiva** |
| casual wear | **la ropa de sport / ropa informal** |
| leather goods | **los artículos de cuero** |
| television and electrical goods | **la tienda de televisión y electrodomésticos** |
| sales person | **el dependiente / la dependienta** |
| cash desk | **la caja** |
| changing room | **el vestuario** |
| customer, client | **el cliente** |
| price | **el precio** |
| deposit | **el depósito** |
| discount | **el descuento** |
| reductions / sales | **rebajas** |
| reduced prices | **precios reducidos** |
| clearance / closing-down sale | **liquidación** |
| bargain offers | **ofertas** |
| bargains | **gangas** |

## Insight

Try to learn these by visualizing them in an imaginary department store, or better still by experiencing them in a store in Spain, such as **El Corte Inglés**. Just look on the internet!

### Useful phrases

| How much does it cost? | **¿Cuánto cuesta?** |
|---|---|
| How are you paying? | **¿Cómo va(s) a pagar?** |
| Are you paying cash? | **¿Paga(s) al contado?** |
| Do you have the right change? | **¿Tiene(s) la cantidad correcta?** |

| Will you wrap it as a gift? | ¿Lo puede(s) envolver en papel de regalo? |
| out of stock | agotado |

---

### Insight

Note that there are different words in Spanish for 'change', each with a different meaning:

- **las monedas** – *small / loose change,* (**moneda** also means *coin*)

- **el cambio** – change in the sense of exchange, what you do when you change currency

- **la vuelta** – the change you are given if you pay with a banknote.

---

#### Useful verbs

| to buy | comprar |
| to sell | vender |
| to look for | buscar |
| to pay | pagar |
| to prefer | preferir |
| to go shopping | ir de compras |
| to order | pedir / encargar |
| to deliver | entregar |
| to window shop | mirar escaparates |

---

## 7.4 At the supermarket

#### Core vocabulary

| food department | la sección de comestibles |
| fruit and vegetables | fruta y verduras |
| dairy products | productos lácteos |

| | |
|---|---|
| *frozen foods* | **productos congelados** |
| *cleaning materials* | **productos de limpieza** |
| *electrical goods* | **electrodomésticos** |
| *household appliances* | **electrodomésticos** |
| *wines and spirits* | **vinos y licores** |
| *drinks* | **bebidas** |
| *photographic shop* | **la tienda de material fotográfico** |
| *dry-cleaning* | **la tintorería** |
| *flower shop* | **la floristería** |
| *card shop* | **la tienda de tarjetas** |
| *shopping list* | **la lista de compras** |
| *assistant* | **el dependiente / la dependienta** |
| *basket* | **la cesta** |
| *trolley* | **el carrito** |
| *cash machine* | **el cajero automático** |
| *checkout* | **la caja** |

## Insight

Notice how some of these expressions use adjectives (**lácteos, congelados**), and others use nouns after **de**. You could try learning and remembering them in the context of your regular supermarket, saying them to yourself as you come across each aisle or section.

### Useful verbs

| | |
|---|---|
| *to weigh* | **pesar** |
| *to look for* | **buscar** |
| *to find* | **encontrar** |
| *to deliver* | **entregar** |

## Insight

Which of these is the one radical-changing verb? It is difficult to predict if you don't know! In fact it is **encontrar**; it is a good idea always to learn these verbs by memorizing the infinitive form and alongside it the first person singular of the present tense, e.g. **encontrar → encuentro**.

## Useful phrases

| | |
|---|---|
| *Where is / are the ... ?* | **¿Dónde está(n) ...?** |
| *on the .... aisle* | **en el pasillo ...** |
| *on the shelf* | **en el estante** |
| *on the row with the ...* | **en el pasillo con el / la ...** |
| *at the far end* | **al otro extremo** |
| *on the left / right-hand side* | **a mano derecha / izquierda** |
| *What time do you shut?* | **¿A qué hora cierra(n)?** |
| *Are you open on a Sunday?* | **¿Abren los domingos?** |

---

## 7.5   At the post office and the bank

### Core vocabulary

| | |
|---|---|
| *letter box* | **el buzón** |
| *post (letters and parcels in general)* | **Correos** |
| *letter* | **la carta** |
| *packet* | **el paquete** |
| *parcel* | **el paquete** |
| *postcard* | **la (tarjeta) postal** |
| *writing paper* | **el papel de escribir** |
| *envelope* | **el sobre** |
| *pen* | **la pluma** |
| *biro / ballpoint* | **el bolígrafo** |
| *form* | **el formulario / impreso** |
| *stamp* | **el sello** |
| *postman* | **el cartero** |
| *phone card* | **la tarjeta telefónica** |
| *printed matter* | **impresos** |
| *recorded delivery* | **el servicio de entrega con acuse de recibo** |
| *overnight delivery* | **la entrega / el reparto de la noche a la mañana** |
| *air mail* | **(correo) por avión / correo aéreo** |
| *money* | **el dinero** |
| *cash* | **el (dinero en) efectivo** |

| coins | las monedas |
| notes | los billetes (de banco) |
| cheque book | el talonario (de cheques) |
| credit card | la tarjeta de crédito |
| cash machine | el cajero automático |
| a cash transfer | una transferencia bancaria |
| the date | la fecha |
| the amount | la cantidad |
| signature | la firma |
| the bank code | el número de agencia del banco |
| the credit card number | el número de tarjeta de crédito |
| the expiry date | la fecha de vencimiento |
| balance | el saldo |
| loan | el préstamo |
| mortgage | la hipoteca |

## Insight

Once again in this section there are examples of some Spanish 'spelling quirks':

• **-qu-** for a hard -c- sound in **pa*qu*ete**, and also as in **sa*qu*e** in the next section

• **-f-** instead of *-ph-* as in **bolígra*f*o** and **telé*f*onica**

• and the common Spanish suffix **-dad** which usually equates to English **-ty**, as in **cantidad**, *quantity*. Though it might sound odd, note that in Spanish **-dad** words are always feminine!

### Useful phrases

| insert your card | introduzca la tarjeta |
| type in your number | teclee su número |
| wait | espere |
| remove your card | saque su tarjeta |
| take your money | coja su dinero |

| fill in the form | **rellene el formulario** |
| go to the counter / cash desk | **vaya a la caja** |
| Where do I have to sign? | **¿Dónde tengo que firmar?** |
| How much does it cost to send this to ...? | **¿Cuánto cuesta / vale para mandar esto a...?** |
| by air mail | **por avión** |

## Useful verbs

| to cash | **cobrar** |
| to deposit | **ingresar** |
| to transfer | **transferir** |
| to sign | **firmar** |
| to fill in | **rellenar** |

# Test yourself

Match the sentence-halves together.

1 ¿Por dónde puedo      **a** izquierda.
2 ¿A qué hora      **b** a las diez.
3 ¿Abren      **c** del banco.
4 ¿Dónde tengo      **d** aparcar aquí.
5 ¿Dónde está      **e** mandar una carta a Francia?
6 Prohibido      **f** los domingos?
7 Está a mano      **g** el aparcamiento?
8 Esperamos un reparto      **h** que firmar?
9 Está enfrente      **i** sale el próximo autobús?
10 ¿Cuánto cuesta para      **j** ir a la ciudad?

If you need to check your answers, go to *Test yourself Answer key* after Unit 16.

# In the country

• Spain occupies most of the Iberian Peninsula, with Portugal taking up the remainder. It is situated in a strategically important position at the mouth of the Mediterranean, and is the closest point in Europe to Africa.

• Spain is a high tableland – it has an average height second only to Switzerland in Europe – tilted in such a way that much of the highest land is in the north and east, and the lowest in the south and west; several high but flattish areas are known as **mesetas**. This is criss-crossed by mountain ranges – **sierras** – and rivers, mainly orientated from east to west.

## Insight

Notice how many geographical terms are in fact Spanish words, such as **sierra, cordillera, ría meseta, caldera**. Many of these feature in place names not only in Spanish-speaking countries but also in the US; indeed many US geographical names we take for granted are Spanish in origin, e.g. Los Angeles, Sacramento, Nevada, Florida, San Francisco, Amarillo, El Alamo, reminding us that the Spanish were the first to explore, conquer and settle the southern, central and western areas of the US.

• In its geography and climate, Spain is a land of great variety and contrasts: the north and north-west have a wet, moderate Atlantic climate; the centre has a continental climate – extremes of very hot, dry summers and very cold winters; the east and south-east have a Mediterranean climate – mild, wet winters and hot, dry summers; the far south also has a Mediterranean climate, but with warmer winters and higher temperatures overall. All of this is varied by local micro-climates, principally because of the many mountain ranges: even the mountains in the far south – the Sierra Nevada – are snow-capped for much of the year (hence the name!)

- Spain used to be a largely agricultural country, and several crops are still very important, notably production of olive oil (Spain is the world's greatest producer), wine, fruit and vegetables. Much of its territory, however, is wild or semi-wild, being so mountainous; large areas are covered with forest, and some lower areas are so dry as to be almost desert-like except where irrigation enables agricultural activity.

- In the 20th century, Spain developed industry, notably in the north and north-east; after the Spanish Civil War of 1936–9, the growth of mass tourism helped to fund a tremendous economic recovery which pulled Spain back into line with the other main countries of western Europe; this in its turn facilitated Spain gaining membership of the European Union in 1986, and involvement in NATO. Spain is now one of the most visited countries in the world, known for its pleasant climate and quality of life. Then of course there are the prosperous immigrants, 'expats' from the UK and other northern European countries who seek a pleasant life under the Spanish sky.

---

## 8.1 The countryside

### Core vocabulary

| In the countryside | *En el campo* |
|---|---|
| *field* | **el campo** |
| *meadow* | **el prado** |

| | |
|---|---|
| *footpath* | **el sendero** |
| *hill* | **la colina** |
| *mountain* | **la montaña** |

## Insight

Note **el monte**, which can mean *mountain, woodland, scrubland*

| | |
|---|---|
| *stream* | **el arroyo** |
| *river* | **el río** |
| *lake* | **el lago** |
| *valley* | **el valle** |
| *grass* | **la hierba** |
| *plant* | **la planta** |
| *wild flower* | **la flor silvestre** |
| *moss* | **el musgo** |
| *fungi* | **los hongos** |
| *fern* | **el helecho** |
| *bush* | **el arbusto** |
| *tree* | **el árbol** |
| *wood* | **el bosque** |
| *forest* | **la selva** |
| *hedge* | **el seto** |
| *fence* | **la valla** |
| *ditch* | **la zanja** |
| *gate* | **la verja** |
| *spring* | **la fuente / el manantial** |
| *pond* | **el charco / estanque** |
| *bridge* | **el puente** |
| *waterfall* | **la cascada** |
| *weir* | **la presa / encañizada** |
| *watermill* | **el molino de agua** |
| *reservoir* | **el embalse** |
| *dam* | **la presa** |
| *flood* | **la inundación** |

| copse | **el bosquecillo** |
| beech | **la haya** |
| chestnut | **el castaño** |
| elm | **el olmo** |
| oak | **el roble** |
| sycamore | **el sicomoro** |
| willow | **el sauce** |

### Useful verbs

| to go for a walk | **dar un paseo / ir de paseo / pasearse** |
| to go swimming | **bañarse (nadar = *to swim*)** |
| to go hiking | **ir de excursión a pie** |
| to ride a bike | **montar en bicicleta** |
| to go fishing | **ir de pesca** |
| to flood (a river) | **desbordarse** |

## Insight

For visual references and associations for some of these, try looking them up on Spanish Wikipedia for photographs! Try this with **el sauce llorón** and see if you can work out its English equivalent.

## 8.2 In the mountains

### Core vocabulary

| hill | **la colina** |
| mountain | **la montaña** |
| mountain range | **la sierra** |
| mountain pass | **el puerto** |
| mountain pass (through a gorge) | **el desfiladero** |
| mountain path | **el sendero de montaña** |

| | |
|---|---|
| *mountain railway* | **el funicular / ferrocarril de montaña** |
| *mountain hut / refuge* | **el albergue de montaña** |
| *cable car* | **el teleférico** |
| *summit* | **la cumbre** |
| *the weather* | **el tiempo** |
| *cloudy* | **nuboso / nublado** |
| *rainy* | **lluvioso** |
| *sunny* | **soleado** |
| *dry* | **seco** |
| *windy* | **de mucho viento / ventoso** |

## Insight

As always, try to associate words with their derivatives or core forms, such as:

**nuboso → la nube**
**lluvioso → la lluvia**
**soleado → el sol**

Try also to work out the derivation of words like **teleférico, ferrocarril** – they are very logical!

| | |
|---|---|
| *easy* | **fácil** |
| *moderate difficulty* | **dificultad moderada** |
| *difficult* | **difícil** |
| *extreme* | **dificultad extrema** |
| *peak* | **el pico** |
| *rock face* | **la pared de roca** |
| *slope* | **la vertiente** |
| *gorge* | **el cañón / barranco** |
| *cave* | **la cueva** |
| *equipment* | **el equipo / las herramientas** |
| *rope* | **la cuerda** |
| *harness* | **el arnés** |
| *carabiner* | **el mosquetón** |
| *rucksack* | **la mochila** |
| *torch* | **la linterna** |

| | |
|---|---|
| *stove* | **la cocina / estufa** |
| *dried food* | **los alimentos secos** |
| *waterproofs* | **los impermeables** |
| *pen knife* | **la navaja** |
| *water bottle* | **la cantimplora** |
| *sleeping bag* | **el saco de dormir** |
| *tent* | **la tienda de campaña** |

## Insight

You will certainly have spotted the cognates in spite of spelling changes; it always helps to be flexible and imaginative and to think of synonyms in English! For example:

**la linterna** – *lantern – torch*
**la cuerda** – *cord – rope*

### Useful phrases

| | |
|---|---|
| *What is the forecast?* | **¿Cuál es el pronóstico del tiempo?** |
| *How difficult is it?* | **¿Qué nivel de dificultad tiene?** |
| *How long does it take?* | **¿Cuánto tiempo hace falta para hacerlo?** |

### Useful verbs

| | |
|---|---|
| *to climb* | **escalar** |
| *to abseil* | **hacer rapel** |
| *to bivouac* | **vivaquear** |
| *to hike* | **ir de excursión a pie / dar una caminata** |
| *to rock climb* | **escalar en rocas** |
| *to boulder* | **escalar en cantos rodados** |
| *to ice climb* | **escalar en hielo** |

## 8.3 At the seaside

### Core vocabulary

| | |
|---|---|
| seaside | **la playa / la orilla del mar** |
| sea | **el mar** |
| ocean | **el océano** |
| wave | **la ola** |
| harbour | **el puerto** |
| port | **el puerto** |
| jetty | **el muelle / embarcadero** |
| pier | **el embarcadero / muelle** |
| quay | **el muelle** |
| beach | **la playa** |
| sand | **la arena** |
| sand dune | **la duna** |
| cliff | **el acantilado / risco** |
| shell | **la concha** |
| pebbles | **los guijarros** |
| rock | **la roca** |
| island | **la isla** |
| reef | **el arrecife** |
| surf | **las olas rompientes** |
| shore | **la orilla** |
| estuary | **el estuario** |
| cape | **el cabo** |
| promontory | **el promontorio** |
| peninsula | **la península** |
| boat | **el barco** |
| rowing boat | **la barca de remos / el bote de remo** |
| yacht | **el velero / barco de vela** |
| sailing dinghy | **el bote** |
| rubber dinghy | **la lancha neumática** |
| motor boat | **la lancha motora** |
| ferry | **la barca (de pasaje)** |
| car ferry | **el ferry / transbordador** |
| cruiser | **el crucero** |

| | |
|---|---|
| liner | **el transatlántico** |
| pilot (harbour) | **el práctico** |
| sailing | **la vela / navegación a vela** |
| navigation | **la navegación** |
| port | **babor** |
| starboard | **estribor** |
| buoy | **la boya** |
| lighthouse | **el faro** |
| mast | **el mástil** |
| sail | **la vela** |
| rudder | **el timón** |
| anchor | **el ancla** (f) |
| satellite positioning | **el posicionamiento / la ubicación por satélite** |
| automatic pilot | **el piloto automático** |
| ropes | **los cabos** |
| high tide | **la marea alta** |
| low tide | **la marea baja** |
| sea level | **el nivel del mar** |
| calm | **en calma / tranquilo** |
| choppy | **agitado** |
| rough | **agitado / encrespado** |
| sandy | **arenoso** |
| rocky | **rocoso** |
| rough | **desigual** |
| smooth | **liso** |

## Insight

You will notice how a couple of these last few adjectives are derivatives of words already introduced:

**roca → rocoso; arena → arenoso**

Spanish often forms adjectives based on nouns like this.

Once again you will have spotted the cognates which actually link to synonyms or other words with similar meanings in English! For example:

**el puerto** – *port – harbour*
**la arena** – *sandy area – arena*
**la lancha** – *launch – small boat*

Note also that **el *Cabo* de Trafalgar** in south-western Spain, off which a certain famous naval battle took place, has given its name to a famous site in London!

### Useful phrases

| | |
|---|---|
| *When is high tide?* | **¿Cuándo llega la marea alta?** |
| *Where can I moor?* | **¿Dónde puedo amarrar / atracar?** |

### Useful verbs

| | |
|---|---|
| *to row* | **remar** |
| *to sail* | **navegar (a vela)** |
| *to motor* | **navegar a motor** |
| *to cast off* | **soltar las amarras** |
| *to tie up* | **amarrar** |

## 8.4 Working in the country

### Insight

Agriculture has always been important in Spain and remains so, though the proportion of the population who work the land has fallen dramatically in the last few decades owing to mechanization and the drift of young people to the cities. Indeed, many immigrants have provided much-needed labour (**mano de obra**) in agricultural areas, especially in southern Spain.
Many regions of Spain have their own types of *farmhouse*: look up the following on Spanish Wikipedia to discover where to find them in Spain: **la masía, el caserío, la barraca.**

## Core vocabulary

| | |
|---|---|
| agriculture | **la agricultura** |
| bee keeping | **la apicultura** |
| game keeping | **el oficio del guardabosques** |
| horticulture | **la horticultura** |
| wine growing | **la vinicultura** |
| forestry | **la silvicultura** |
| farm | **la granja** |
| market garden | **el huerto / la huerta** |
| farmhouse | **el caserío** |
| barn | **el granero** |
| stables | **la cuadra** |
| cattle shed | **el establo** |
| cattle | **el ganado** |
| cow / heifer / bull / calf | **la vaca / la vaquilla / el toro / el ternero** |
| sheep or ewe / ram / lamb | **la oveja / el carnero / el cordero** |
| pig or boar / sow / piglet | **el cerdo / la puerca / el cerdito** or **lechón** |
| (billy)goat / nanny / kid | **el chivo** or **macho cabrío / la cabra / el cabrito** |
| poultry | **las aves (de corral)** |
| chickens / hens | **las gallinas / el pollo** |
| duck / drake / ducklings | **la pata / el pato / los patitos** |
| goose / goslings | **el ganso / los ansarinos** |
| turkey | **el pavo** |
| pheasant | **el faisán** |
| sheep dog | **el perro pastor** |
| guard dog | **el perro guardián** |
| dog / bitch / puppy | **el perro / la perra / el cachorro** or **perrito** |

Much has been said and written about the Spanish attitude towards animals, and this is not the place for a debate. However, it is appropriate to say that for most Spaniards animals are there to be of use, to provide them with food or a living, which is why Spaniards have not developed the sentimental attachment to animals which typifies the British attitude. However, the increasing popularity of family pets is changing this, and the concern for animal rights is growing.

| Crops | *Los cultivos / productos agrícolas* |
|---|---|
| cereals | los cereales |
| grain | el grano |
| barley | la cebada |
| oats | la avena |
| rice | el arroz |
| rye | el centeno |
| wheat | el trigo |
| hay | el heno |
| straw | la paja |
| bee keeper | el apicultor |
| farmer | el granjero |
| farm worker | el jornalero / obrero agrícola |
| horticulturist | el horticultor |
| vet | el veterinario |
| wine grower | el viñador |
| vineyard | el viñedo |
| vines | las viñas |
| grapes | las uvas |
| fruit growing | la fruticultura |
| olives | las aceitunas |
| cultivating | el cultivo |
| planting | la plantación |
| spreading fertilizer | la fertilización / distribución de abonos |
| weeding | desherbar |
| harvesting | la cosecha |

| packaging | el embalaje / envasado |
| farm equipment | las herramientas agrícolas |
| tractor | el tractor |
| trailer | el remolque |
| plough | el arado |
| (combine) harvester | la cosechadora |

## Useful phrases

| Beware of the dog / bull! | ¡Cuidado con el perro / toro! |
| Please shut the gate. | Por favor, cierre la barrera. |
| electric fence | la valla electrificada |
| No entry. | Se prohíbe la entrada. |

## Insight

Why not draw these signs as a way of learning them; you might even place them as appropriate around your house!

## Useful verbs

| to feed | dar de comer a |
| to milk | ordeñar |
| to breed | criar |
| to sow | sembrar |
| to fertilize | abonar / fertilizar |
| to weed | desherbar |
| to pick | (re)coger / cosechar |
| to harvest | cosechar |
| to take to market | llevar al mercado |
| to grow (= cultivate) | cultivar |
| to grow (= what a plant does) | crecer |

## Insight

This last pair of verbs provides a good illustration of the difference between *transitive* and *intransitive* verbs (usually abbreviated as *tr.* and *intr.* in dicitionaries).

The action described by a *transitive* verb *transits* from the *subject* or perpetrator to the *object* or victim; transitive verbs *always* have an object. So, **'El jardinero cultiva sus plantas aquí'**. – *'The gardener grows his plants here'*.

The action described by an *intransitive* verb only has a *subject* and no object; in fact the effect of the action only affects the *subject* himself / herself / itself. Hence **'Las plantas crecen bien aquí'** – *'The plants grow well here'*.

It is sometimes the case that a single English verb has two equivalents in Spanish, one transitive and one intransitive according to the meaning, so it is always useful to attach *tr.* or *intr.* to new verbs when you learn them.

# Test yourself

How quickly can you match together these halves of words from this unit?

| | | | |
|---|---|---|---|
| **1** | el send | **a** | ontorio |
| **2** | el ar | **b** | ranco |
| **3** | la co | **c** | meables |
| **4** | la ver | **d** | busto |
| **5** | el bar | **e** | char |
| **6** | los imper | **f** | lina |
| **7** | esca | **g** | cultura |
| **8** | el prom | **h** | ero |
| **9** | la fruti | **i** | tiente |
| **10** | cose | **j** | lar |

Answers in *Test yourself Answer key* after Unit 16.

# 9

## Hobbies and sports

### 9.1 Hobbies

**Core vocabulary**

| **Hobbies** | *Los pasatiempos* |
|---|---|
| acting | **la interpretación** |
| archaeology | **la arqueología** |
| astronomy | **la astronomía** |
| cooking | **cocinar** |
| dancing | **bailar** |
|   modern |     **hacer baile moderno** |
|   ballroom |     **hacer el baile de salón** |
| DIY | **el bricolaje** |
| drawing | **dibujar** |
| gardening | **trabajar en el jardín** |
| going out (socially) | **salir (con amigos)** |
| history | **la historia** |
| listening to music | **escuchar música** |
| meeting people | **conocer a gente** |
| painting | **pintar** |
| photography | **la fotografía / sacar fotos** |
| pottery | **hacer cerámica** |
| reading | **leer / la lectura** |
| sewing | **coser / hacer costura** |
| singing | **cantar** |

| | |
|---|---|
| sport | **el deporte / hacer deporte** |
| *visiting historical sites* | **visitar sitios históricos** |
| *watching films* | **ver películas** |
| *watching television* | **ver la tele(visión)** |
| *writing* | **escribir** |

| **Outdoor pursuits** | *Actividades al aire libre* |
|---|---|
| *birdwatching* | **observar aves** |
| *fishing* | **pescar / la pesca** |
| *sailing* | **hacer vela** |
| *horse riding* | **montar a caballo** |
| *hunting* | **cazar / la caza** |
| *rambling* | **el excursionismo a pie** |
| *shooting* | **(hacer) el tiro** |
| *walking* | **pasearse / dar paseos** |

## Insight

A very important point to remember is that if you wish to express e.g. *I like reading, We love riding* or *She is interested in sailing*, the 'verbal noun' in Spanish is the infinitive. So, the infinitive is used after expressions like the following:

**Me gusta** *leer.*
**Nos encanta** *montar* **a caballo.**
**Le interesa** *hacer* **vela.**

### Indoor games

| | |
|---|---|
| *chess* | **el ajedrez** |
| *cards* | **los naipes** |
| *bridge* | **el bridge** |
| *party games* | **juegos de fiesta** |
| *happy families* | **el juego de las familias** |
| *bingo* | **el bingo** |
| *jigsaw puzzles* | **puzzles / rompecabezas** |
| *dominoes* | **el dominó** |
| *draughts* | **las damas** |

| billiards | **el billar** |
| snooker | **el snooker** |
| table football | **el futbolín** |
| crossword | **el crucigrama** |

| **Music** | *La música* |
| making music | **tocar música** |
| playing in an orchestra | **tocar en una orquesta** |
| singing in a group | **cantar en un grupo** |
| playing an instrument | **tocar un instrumento** |
| piano | **el piano** |
| guitar | **la guitarra** |
| violin | **el violín** |
| trumpet | **la trompeta** |
| drums | **la batería** |

## Insight

Notice how, as in English, the definite article is used to express e.g. *I play the piano* – **Toco el piano**

Note also the 'unexpected' cognate: **la batería**. What else could it be?!

### Useful verbs

| to attend | **asistir a** |
| to be a member of ... | **ser socio / miembro de ...** |
| to be interested in ... | **tener interés en ...** |
| (I am interested in ... ) | **me interesa ...** |
| to be keen on | **ser aficionado/a a** |
| to enjoy | **gustar (me gusta ...** *I enjoy ...***)** |
| to meet | **encontrar / conocer** (to get to know) |
| to spend my time | **pasar el tiempo** |
| to play | **jugar a** |

## Insight

Notice how the Spanish meaning and use of words sometimes overlaps with different words in English, that they occupy different 'areas of meaning': **encontrar** = *to find*, **conocer** = *to meet* (to meet for the first time, know a person), **saber** = *to know* (to know a fact), **reunir** = *to meet, to get together*.

| | |
|---|---|
| **Nos encontramos en la calle una semana después.** | *We met in the street a week later.* |
| **Ayer mis padres conocieron a mi novio.** | *Yesterday, my parents met my boyfriend.* |
| **Sé un poco de ajedrez.** | *I know (= can play) a little bit of chess.* |
| **Nos vamos a reunir más tarde.** | *We are going to meet later.* |

### Useful phrases

| | |
|---|---|
| *What do you do in your free time?* | **¿Qué hace(s) en tu tiempo libre?** |
| *Do you like ...?* | **¿Te / le gusta ...?** |
| *I like meeting people.* | **Me gusta conocer a gente.** |
| *I do (painting).* | **Pinto / Hago pintura.** |
| *I belong to a club.* | **Soy socio de un club.** |
| *We meet every ...* | **Nos reunimos cada ...** |
| *It's interesting.* | **Es interesante.** |
| *It's fantastic.* | **Es fantástico.** |
| *It's boring.* | **Es aburrido.** |

---

## 9.2 Sports

| | |
|---|---|
| *ball games* | **los juegos de pelota / balón** |
| *football* | **el fútbol** |
|   *footballer* | **el futbolista** |
|   *ball* | **el balón** |
|   *team* | **el equipo** |
|   *goal* | **el gol** |
|   *match* | **el partido** |

| | |
|---|---|
| *football ground* | **el campo de fútbol / el estadio** (stadium) |
| *score* | **el tanto** |
| *rugby* | **el rugby** |
| *player* | **el jugador** |
| *manager* | **el mánager** |
| *to shoot* | **chutar** |
| *pitch* | **el campo de rugby** |
| *to score a try* | **marcar un ensayo** |
| *basketball* | **el baloncesto** |
| *basket* | **la canasta** |
| *volleyball* | **el voleibol** |
| *net* | **la red** |
| *handball* | **el balonmano** |
| *hockey* | **el hockey** |
| *hockey stick* | **el palo de hockey** |
| *golf* | **el golf** |
| *golf club* | **el palo de golf** |
| *golf course* | **el campo de golf** |
| *green* | **el green** |
| *hole* | **el hoyo** |
| *bunker* | **el búnker** |

Note that the vast majority of sports are masculine.

## Insight

An important point with this group of words, as elsewhere, is the need for clarity of thought when you think of a particular word you wish to translate: and not just, for example, *ball* = **el balón** = *large ball*, as in football (reminds us of the English word *balloon*), as opposed to *ball* = *la pelota* = *small ball* as for tennis.

Several words have more than one application, so need to be chosen carefully according to context: e.g.

*match* as in game of x = **el partido** BUT **la cerilla** as in match to light a fire or cigarette

*club* as in tool used in golf = **el palo** BUT **el club** as in golf club meaning a group of members

*goal* as in point scored in e.g. football = **el gol** BUT **el objetivo** when it means goal, purpose

Note also how **marcar** has several meanings: *to score a goal, to set hair, to mark*

Since many sports were invented in Britain, it is hardly surprising to find that many English sporting words are used in Spanish, some with adapted spellings (e.g. **chutar**) and others unchanged.

| Racket sports | *Juegos de raqueta* |
|---|---|
| *tennis* | **el tenis** |
|   *tennis racquet* |   **la raqueta de tenis** |
|   *tennis court* |   **la pista de tenis** |
|   *tennis ball* |   **la pelota de tenis** |
|   *tennis player* |   **el jugador de tenis / tenista** |
| *badminton* | **el badminton** |
|   *net* |   **la red** |
|   *shuttlecock* |   **el volante** |
| *squash* | **el squash** |
|   *squash racquet* |   **la raqueta de squash** |
|   *squash court* |   **la cancha de squash** |

## Insight

Note the two different words for *court* (tennis and squash/badminton): **la cancha** implies an indoor court, whilst **la pista** implies an outside facility; indeed it is also used for track and runway (at an airport).

| Martial arts | Las artes marciales |
|---|---|
| judo | el judo |
| karate | el karate |
| taekwando | el tae-kwondo |
| wrestling | la lucha libre |

| Athletics | El atletismo |
|---|---|
| running | correr |
| cross country | el cross |
| jumping | (las pruebas de) salto |
| hurdles | las vallas |
| track | la pista |

| Keep fit | El ejercicio (para mantenerse en forma) |
|---|---|
| aerobics | el aeróbic(o) |
| gymnastics | la gimnasia |
| jogging | el footing / jogging |
| weightlifting | el levantamiento de pesas |
| weight training | el entrenamiento con pesas |
| yoga | el yoga |

## Insight

It is curious that Spanish sometimes uses borrowed English words correctly (**el jogging**) and other times 'invents' a term we would not use in English (**el footing**)!

### Useful verbs

| to win | ganar |
|---|---|
| to lose | perder |
| to draw | empatar |
| to box | boxear |
| to do | hacer |
| to jog | hacer footing |
| to run | correr |

Contrary to popular belief, football is the national sport in Spain (bullfighting is a festival – **la fiesta nacional**). Basketball, handball and cycling are other popular sports for participants and spectators. In the Basque country **pelota** is played in every district and village – this is a sort of very fast, outdoor racket game with some general similarities to squash. Spain's climate favours outdoor games such as golf and tennis, and many Spaniards enjoy skiing in the snow-covered mountain areas, as well as swimming, water sports and other outdoor activities. Village squares and parks are often the venue for **petanca,** a Spanish version of *boules*.

---

## 9.3 More sports

| **Water sports** | ***Los deportes acuáticos*** |
|---|---|
| *canoeing* | **el piragüismo** |
|   *canoe* |   **la piragua** |
|   *paddle* |   **la pala** |
| *diving (deep sea)* | **el buceo (de altura)** |
|   *wet suit* |   **el traje isotérmico** |
|   *dry suit* |   **el traje seco** |
|   *gas bottles* |   **los tanques de gas** |
|   *mask* |   **la mascarilla** |
|   *flippers* |   **las aletas** |
|   *snorkel* |   **el tubo de respiración** |
| *rowing* | **el remo** |
|   *boat* |   **el barco** |
|   *oars* |   **los remos** |
| *sailing* | **la vela** |
|   *sail* |   **la vela** |
| *surfing* | **el surf** |
|   *surf board* |   **la plancha de surf** |
| *windsurfing* | **el windsurf** |
|   *windsurfer* |   **el surfista** |
| *yachting* | **la navegación a vela** |
|   *yacht* |   **el velero** |
|   *dinghy* |   **el bote** |

| | |
|---|---|
| swimming | **la natación** |
| breast stroke | **la braza de pecho** |
| front crawl | **el crol** |
| butterfly | **la braza de mariposa** |
| backstroke | **la espalda** |
| diving | **el salto de trampolín** |
| swimming pool | **la piscina** |
| length | **el largo** |
| diving board | **el trampolín** |
| swimming costume | **el traje de baño** |
| goggles | **los anteojos / las gafas de submarinismo** |

## Insight

Notice the spelling approximations to English pronunciation in **el crol** and **el trampolín**; also try 'breaking up' **los anteojos** – they go in front of your eyes!

| | |
|---|---|
| archery | **el tiro con arco** |
| bow | **el arco** |
| arrow | **la flecha** |
| target | **el blanco / la diana** |
| boxing | **el boxeo** |
| cycling | **el ciclismo** |
| racing bike | **la bicicleta de carreras** |
| mountain bike | **la bicicleta de montaña** |
| bike | **la bicicleta** |
| handlebars | **los manillares** |
| saddle | **la silla** |
| fencing | **la esgrima** |
| foil | **el florete** |
| horse riding | **la equitación** |
| saddle | **la silla de montar** |
| bridle | **la brida / el freno** |
| stirrups | **el estribo** |
| roller skating | **el patinaje sobre ruedas** |

| | |
|---|---|
| skates | **los patines** |
| skateboarding | **el monopatinaje** |
| skateboard | **el monopatín** |
| climbing | **el montañismo** |
| mountaineering | **el alpinismo** |
| rock climbing | **la escalada en rocas** |
| pot holing / caving | **la espeleología** |
| climbing boots | **las botas de montañismo** |
| rope | **la cuerda** |
| carabiner | **el mosquetón** |
| rucksack | **la mochila** |
| skiing | **el esquí** |
| skis | **los esquís** |
| poles | **los bastones** |
| piste | **la pista** |
| snowboarding, snowboard | **el snowboard** |
| sledging, sledge | **el trineo** |
| tobogganning, toboggan | **el tobogán** |
| ice skating | **el patinaje sobre hielo** |
| skates | **los patines** |
| ice rink | **la pista de patinaje sobre hielo** |

## Insight

Most suffixes added to nouns or verbs to describe the actions are instantly recognizable, others take a bit more effort to recognize because they aren't the same as in the English equivalent. You should soon get used to them!

*mountain – mountain**eering** = **ismo** – el montañ**ismo***

*skate – skat**ing** = **aje** – el patin**aje***

Notice also the similar endings **-ión** and **-eo**, both giving the idea of the action.

### Useful phrases

| | |
|---|---|
| *I enjoy doing ...* | **Me encanta ...** |
| *I am good at ...* | **Soy fuerte en... / Mi fuerte es ...** |
| *I am not good at ...* | **No soy fuerte en... / ... no es mi fuerte** |

## Insight

**fuerte** normally means *strong*, but here it has the idiomatic meaning *'good at...'*. Notice, of course the connection with *fort, fortress, fortitude*, once you remember the common Spanish spelling change **o → ue**.

# Test yourself

Delete the repeated letters to work out what these words are. Then write the English.

1  xhxaxcxerx xbxaxixlxex xmxoxdxexrxnxox
2  ddidbdudjdadrd
3  fvfefrf flfaf ftfeflfef
4  erlr rcrrrurcrirgrrrarmra
5  shehrh hahfhihchihohnhahdhoh ha
6  lelsl lflalnltlálslltlilclol
7  mpaprpcpapr pupnp pepnpspapyo
8  ecl lcevcanctacmicenctoc dce pcecscas
9  lwaw pwlwawnwcwhwaw wdwew wswuwrwfw
10 memlm mtmombmomgmámnm

You may want to check your answers in the *Answer key*, after Unit 16.

# Clothing

## 10.1 Garments and styles

### Core vocabulary

| Ladies' fashion | *La moda femenina* |
|---|---|
| blouse | **la blusa** |
| cardigan | **la rebeca / chaqueta de punto** |
| clothes | **los vestidos / la ropa** |
| dress | **el vestido** |
|   evening dress |   **el traje de noche** |
|   sundress |   **el vestido de playa** |
| jacket | **la chaqueta** |
|   long jacket |   **la chaqueta larga** |
|   short jacket |   **la chaqueta corta** |
| jersey | **el jersey / el suéter** |
| shorts | **el short / pantalón corto** |
| skirt | **la falda** |
| suit | **el traje** |
| trouser suit | **el traje pantalón** |
| trousers | **el pantalón** |
| lingerie | **la ropa interior femenina** |
| bra | **el sostén / sujetador** |
| knickers | **las braguitas** |

| | |
|---|---|
| slip | la enagua / combinación |
| stockings | las medias |
| tights | los pantis |
| nightie | el camisón de noche |
| pyjamas | el pijama |
| negligee | el negligé / salto de cama |
| | |
| **Men's fashion** | *La moda masculina* |
| blazer | la chaqueta de sport / blazer |
| dinner jacket | el esmoquin / smóking |
| jacket | la chaqueta / americana |
| jeans | los vaqueros / tejanos / bluejeans |
| jumper | el jersey / el suéter |
| pullover | el jersey / el suéter |
| shirt | la camisa |
| shorts | el short / el pantalón corto |
| socks | los calcetines |
| suit | el traje |
| sweatshirt | la sudadera |
| T-shirt | la camiseta |
| tie | la corbata |
| trousers | el pantalón |
|   belt |   el cinturón |
|   braces |   los tirantes |
| waistcoat | el chaleco |
| boxers | los calzones |
| shorts | el short / los calzones |
| vest | la camiseta |
| pyjamas | el pijama |
| coat | el abrigo |
| raincoat | el impermeable |
| jacket | la chaqueta |
| hat | el sombrero |
| scarf | la bufanda |
| gloves | los guantes |

## Insight

The striking thing about this section is how many of these words should be easy to learn because they offer interesting associations. First there are words borrowed from English unchanged, such as **blazer**. Then there are those like **blusa** which are close to the English words, but with changes to simplify the spelling. There are words also borrowed from English like **chaqueta** which have more major spelling changes to preserve a sound close to the English (*j* in Spanish has a totally different sound). Some words are interesting for reasons of logic: **sudadera** actually means *sweater*, being derived from **sudar** – *to sweat*; and what item of clothing could **impermeable** mean if not *raincoat*?! Finally, a pair of words which demonstrate how they have come into Spanish: *jersey* has the English spelling, but is pronounced something like *hersei*. By contrast, **suéter** doesn't look much like the English word *sweater*, but if you pronounce it aloud in Spanish you will produce the English sound almost exactly. Why? Probably because *jersey* entered Spanish on labels on the item itself, perhaps in Marks and Spencers in Madrid (there was a branch there once). One can imagine that the word *sweater* was heard being used by British tourists caught out by colder weather than expected in Spain ('*I think I'll put my sweater on!*'), and then imitated, the Spanish spelling following when Spanish people wrote it down.

### Useful verbs

| | |
|---|---|
| to wear | **llevar (puesto)** |
| to fit | **quedar bien** |
| to suit | **quedar bien / sentar bien** |

### Useful phrases

| | |
|---|---|
| Does it fit / suit me? | **¿Me queda bien? / ¿Me sienta bien?** |
| I will be wearing ... | **Llevaré puesto ...** |
| a dark suit. | **un traje oscuro.** |

| a coat and hat. | un sombrero y un abrigo. |
| a sweatshirt, jeans and trainers | una sudadera, vaqueros y zapatillas |
| What will you be wearing? | ¿Qué llevará(s) puesto? |
| What size are you? | ¿Qué talla tiene(s) / usa(s)? |
| It is too short (for me). | Es demasiado corto / me queda corto. |
| It is too short. | Es demasiado corto / le queda corto. |
| too wide | demasiado ancho |
| too long | demasiado largo |
| too tight | demasiado estrecho |
| Have you got anything bigger / smaller? | ¿Tiene(s) algo más grande / pequeño? |
| in a different colour? | en otro color? |
| It suits you / it doesn't suit you. | (No) Te / le queda bien. |
| They suit you / they don't suit you. | (No) Te / le quedan bien. |
| menswear department | la sección de moda masculina |
| ladieswear department | la sección de moda femenina |
| childrenswear department | la sección de moda juvenil |

## Insight

Once again, we have lots of associations to point out! Here are four examples: can you find others?

**vaca** means *cow*, so **vaquero** is a *cowboy* – and what do cowboys wear? Denim jeans, of course!

**zapato** is *shoe*, so the diminutive form **zapatillas** is used for light shoes such as trainers – and slippers!

**talla** comes from **tallar** (to cut), related to English *tailor*, and even Italian *tagliatelle* (pasta cut into strips)

**estrecho** also means *straits*, as in **el Estrecho de Gibraltar**, which sort of fits – or doesn't!

## Useful verbs

Many verbs to do with clothing are reflexive verbs (see Toolbox, Reflexive verbs).

| | |
|---|---|
| to get dressed | **vestirse** |
| I get dressed | **me visto** |
| to get undressed | **desnudarse** |
| I get undressed | **me desnudo** |
| to put on one's shirt | **ponerse la camisa** |
| I put on my shirt | **me pongo la camisa** |
| to take off one's shirt | **quitarse la camisa** |
| I take off my shirt | **me quito la camisa** |

## Insight

Note that all of these verbs are reflexive – quite logical really, as all of the actions described are actions you do to yourself!

## 10.2 The garment

| | |
|---|---|
| measurements | **las medidas** |
| tape measure | **la cinta métrica** |
| length | **el largo** |
| width | **el ancho** |
| size | **la talla** |
| collar | **el collar** |
| neck | **el cuello** |
| shoulders | **los hombros** |
| sleeves | **las mangas** |
| chest | **el pecho** |
| waist | **la cintura** |
| cuffs | **los puños** |
| hips | **(la talla de) cadera** |
| inside leg | **(la medida de) la entrepierna** |
| materials | **las telas / los tejidos** |
| fabric | **la tela / el tejido** |

| | |
|---|---|
| cotton | el algodón |
| fur | la piel |
| artificial fur | la piel artificial |
| jersey | el tejido de punto |
| leather | la piel / el cuero |
| linen | el lino |
| satin | el satén / raso |
| silk | la seda |
| suede | el ante |
| synthetic fibre | la fibra sintética |
| tweed | el tweed |
| velvet | el terciopelo |
| wool | la lana |
| floral | de flores / floreado |
| multi-colour | multicolor |
| patterned | estampado |
| pleated | con tablas / plisado |
| plain (one colour) | de un solo color |
| self colour | de color uniforme / unicolor |
| spotted | de lunares |
| striped | a rayas |
| button | el botón |
| fastener | el corchete |
| needle | la aguja |
| ribbon | la cinta |
| scissors | las tijeras |
| sewing machine | la máquina de coser |
| thread | el algodón / el hilo |
| velcro | el velcro |
| zip | la cremallera |
| detergent | el detergente |
| detergent for wool | el detergente para lana |
| fabric softener | el suavizante |
| soap powder | el detergente en polvo |

## Insight

Some explanations which will help you to remember some of these words:

- **medidas** comes from **medir** – *to measure*, so literally means measures / measurements
- there is obviously a link between **cinta** (*tape, band*) and **cintura** (*waist*)
- *collar* and **cuello** are clearly related; note the **o > ue** when the stress is on this syllable
- **puño** also means *fist*, where you would expect to find the cuff part of the shirt?
- **entrepierna** means *'between the legs'*, which is logical for *'inside leg measurement'*
- **tejido** comes from **tejer** – *to weave*, so **tejido** means *woven*
- **el algodón** – this comes from the Arabic original, so like many Arabic words absorbed into Spanish begins with *al-* meaning *the*, so it really means *the the* cotton!
- **punto** means *knitting*, hence **el tejido de punto** – *knitted cloth*
- **estampado** means *'printed'* (as in *stamp*), a logical expression for *'patterned'*
- **suave** means *soft*, so gives us **suavizante** – *fabric softener*

### Useful verbs

| | |
|---|---|
| *to wash* | **lavar** |
| *to dry* | **secar** |
| *to dry-clean* | **lavar en seco** |
| *to iron* | **planchar** |
| *to mend* | **remendar** |
| *to darn* | **zurcir** |

### Useful phrases

| | |
|---|---|
| *I have lost a button.* | **Se me ha caído un botón.** |

| | |
|---|---|
| Can I get this laundered / dry-cleaned / pressed (ironed)? | ¿Puedo hacer lavar / lavar en seco / planchar esto? |
| How long will it take? | ¿Cuánto tiempo hace falta para hacerlo? |
| Can you remove this stain? | ¿Puede(s) quitar esta mancha? |
| Can you sew this button on? | ¿Puede(s) coser este botón? |
| Can you take it in? | ¿Puede(s) achicarlo/la? |
| Can you shorten it? | ¿Puede(s) acortarlo/la? |
| This garment must be dry-cleaned. | Esta prenda tiene que lavarse en seco. |
| This garment can be machine washed. | Esta prenda puede lavarse a máquina. |
| Hand-wash only. | Esta prenda sólo se debe lavar a mano. |
| Don't use bleach. | No use(s) lejía. |
| made in ... | confeccionado en ... |

## Insight

In this section there are some examples of slightly odd usage, for example:

**Se me ha caído el botón** literally means 'the button has fallen to me'

**¿Puedo hacer lavar esto?** means 'can I make this wash?'

Don't be put off – just learn to use them!

## 10.3 Special occasions

### Core vocabulary

| **Going to work** | *Al trabajo* |
|---|---|
| uniform | **el uniforme** |
| apron | **el delantal** |
| overall | **el mono** |

| It's raining | Llueve / está lloviendo |
|---|---|
| rain coat | **el impermeable** |
| rain hat | **el sombrero impermeable** |
| rubber boots | **las botas de agua / goma** |
| umbrella | **el paraguas** |
| waterproof trousers | **el pantalón impermeable** |

| It's cold | Hace frío |
|---|---|
| anorak | **el ánorak** |
| gloves | **los guantes** |
| thick socks | **los calcetines gruesos** |
| woolly hat | **el sombrero de lana** |

| On the beach | En la playa |
|---|---|
| bikini | **el bikini** |
| flip flops | **las chancletas** |
| flippers | **las aletas** |
| goggles | **las gafas de bucear / gafas submarinas** |
| snorkel | **el esnórquel** |
| suntan cream | **el bronceador** |
| swimming costume | **el traje de baño** |
| trunks | **el bañador** |

| To spend a night on the town | Salir de juerga |
|---|---|
| casual dress | **la ropa informal** |
| evening dress | **el traje de noche** (women) **traje de etiqueta** (men) |
| formal dress | **la ropa de etiqueta** |
| high heels | **los tacones altos** |
| smart clothes | **la ropa elegante** |

| Playing the game | Jugando a los deportes |
|---|---|
| baseball hat | **el sombrero de béisbol** |
| polo shirt | **el polo** |
| shorts | **el short / pantalón corto** |
| socks | **los calcetines** |
| T-shirt | **la camiseta / el niki** |

| | |
|---|---|
| *trainers* | **las zapatillas (de deporte)** |
| *sweatshirt* | **la sudadera** |
| | |
| **Jewellery** | *La joyería* |
| *bracelet* | **la pulsera** |
| *brooch* | **el prendedor / broche** |
| *earrings* | **los pendientes** |
| *necklace* | **el collar** |
| *ring* | **el anillo** |
| *watch* | **el reloj** |
| *gold* | **el oro** |
| *silver* | **la plata** |
| *platinum* | **el platino** |
| *diamond* | **el diamante** |
| *emerald* | **la esmeralda** |
| *ruby* | **el rubí** |
| *sapphire* | **el zafiro** |
| *semi-precious stone* | **la piedra semipreciosa** |

## Insight

This time a challenge: can you find the words explained by the following:

1) related to **delante** – *in front*
2) it is useful *against waters!*
3) your socks are *gross!*
4) they look like small *wings* (**alas**)
5) helps to bronze you...

In addition, the following are examples of Spanish spelling quirks:

**esnórquel** – **e-** in front of s+consonant
**beisbol** – Spanish spelling to mimick English sound

You will have spotted several other associations for yourself, a very useful learning technique.

The words in the final group here, precious stones and metals, are mostly similar to English anyway.

### Useful verbs

| | |
|---|---|
| to wear | **llevar (puesto)** |

### Useful phrases

| | |
|---|---|
| he / she always looks ... | **él / ella siempre parece ...** |
| casual | **informal** |
| fashionable | **de moda** |
| smart | **elegante** |
| unfashionable | **pasado de moda** |
| untidy | **descuidado** |

---

## 10.4 Footwear

### Core vocabulary

| | |
|---|---|
| **The shoe shop** | *La zapatería* |
| footwear | **el calzado** |
| hosiery | **la calcetería** |
| socks | **los calcetines** |
| stockings | **las medias** |
| tights | **los pantis** |
| boots | **las botas** |
| clogs | **los zuecos / chanclos** |
| flip flops | **las chancletas** |
| moccasins | **los mocasines** |
| sandals | **las sandalias** |
| shoes | **los zapatos** |
| slip ons | **los zapatos sin cordones** |
| slippers | **las zapatillas** |
| tennis shoes | **las zapatillas de tenis** |
| trainers | **las zapatillas (de deporte)** |
| wellington / rubber boots | **las botas de agua / goma** |
| ballet shoes | **las zapatillas de ballet** |
| climbing boots | **las botas de alpinismo / escalada** |
| cycling shoes | **las zapatillas de ciclismo** |

| dancing shoes | los zapatos de baile |
| diving boots | las botas de buceo |
| flippers | las aletas |
| ski boots | las botas de esquí |
| snowboard boots | las botas de snow(board) |
| steel-tipped boots | las botas con punteras de acero |
| walking boots | las botas para andar |
| leather | el cuero |
| rubber | la goma |
| synthetics | la fibra sintética |
| high-heeled shoes | los zapatos de tacón alto |
| flat shoes | los zapatos planos |
| shoe polish | el betún |
| shoe cleaner | la crema para zapatos |
| shoe stretcher | el ensanchador para zapatos |
| chiropody | la podología / pedicura |
| massage | el masaje |
| reflexology | la reflexología / reflejoterapia |
| foot | el pie |
| toe | el dedo del pie |
| ankle | el tobillo |
| sole (of foot) | la planta |
| sole (of shoe) | la suela |
| toe nail | la uña del dedo del pie |
| arch of the foot | el puente del pie |

## Insight

Most of these words and expressions are very logical 'composites', but here are a couple of associations worth remembering:

- **calzar** is basically 'to cover the feet'; several words derive from this.
- the base words **zapato** – *shoe* – and **bota** produce lots of names of footwear.

The final group of words describing parts of the foot might best be learnt by means of a labelled sketch – if you are artistic, try to produce one!

## Useful verbs

| | |
|---|---|
| to try shoes on | **probarse unos zapatos** |
| to put on your shoes | **ponerse los zapatos** |
| to take off your shoes | **quitarse los zapatos** |
| to get blisters | **ampollarse** |

## Insight

Note that, once again, these verbs are all reflexive.

## Useful phrases

| | |
|---|---|
| bare foot | **descalzo** |
| I have got sore feet. | **Me duelen los pies.** |
| I have got blisters. | **Tengo ampollas en los pies.** |
| Have you got a plaster? | **¿Tiene(s) un esparadrapo / una tirita?** |
| Please remove your shoes in the house. | **Por favor, quítate / quítese los zapatos en la casa.** |
| What shoe size are you? | **¿Qué número (de zapato) calzas / gastas?** |
| These shoes are comfortable / uncomfortable. | **Estos zapatos (no) son cómodos.** |

## Insight

Notice the two words based on **calzar**: **descalzo** and **calzas** as in **¿Qué número calzas?**

# Test yourself

To decipher these words, write down the letter in the alphabet that comes before each letter in them (if you see a *w*, change it to *v*; an *a* means *z*). Then write the English words.

abcdefghijklmnopqrstuvwxyz

1 wftujep
2 tptutfo
3 wbrvfspt
4 jnqfsnfbcmf
5 hvbouft
6 tvebefsb
7 abqbujmmbt
8 bodip
9 dsfnbmmfsb
10 eftdbmap

# Travel

## 11.1 Travel

### Core vocabulary

| | |
|---|---|
| *itinerary* | **el itinerario** |
| *journey* | **el viaje** |
| *map* | **el mapa** |
| *route* | **la ruta** |
| *travel* | **los viajes** |
| *overland* | **por tierra** |
| *by air* | **por avión** |
| *by sea* | **por mar** |
| *by rail* | **por ferrocarril** |
| *by train* | **en tren** |
| *by coach* | **en autocar** |
| *by car* | **en coche** |
| *by hire car* | **en un coche de alquiler** |
| *by boat* | **en barco** |
| *by ferry* | **en ferry** |
| *by bike* | **en bicicleta** |
| *on horseback* | **a caballo** |
| *on foot* | **a pie / andando** |
| *timetable* | **el horario** |
| *ticket* | **el billete** |
| *booking* | **la reserva** |

| | |
|---|---|
| reservation | **la reserva** |
| on-line booking | **la reserva por internet / on-line** |
| arrival | **la llegada** |
| departure | **la salida** |

## Insight

You will be only too aware by now of the need to learn the gender with each noun; one word here looks as though it should be feminine, but is actually masculine – **el mapa**; the fact that it is unusual should make it stand out as different... and therefore easy to learn and remember! The words for modes of travel are given without the gender – **en tren**, etc. Note that all are masculine except **bicicleta**. You should also note that **andando** is not a noun but a verb form: it means *walking*. Finally, the last two are also verb-based: they are noun forms of the past participles of the verbs **llegar** – *to arrive* and **salir** – *to leave*.

### Useful verbs

| | |
|---|---|
| to travel | **viajar** |
| to go | **ir** |
| to sail | **navegar** |
| to fly | **volar** |
| to drive | **viajar en coche** |
| to tour | **viajar / ir de gira** |
| to arrive | **llegar** |
| to leave (transport) | **salir** |
| to leave (person) | **irse / marcharse** |

### Useful phrases

| | |
|---|---|
| Can you help me please? | **¿Me puede ayudar? / Ayúdeme por favor.** |
| I'm lost. | **Me he perdido.** |
| How do I get to ...? | **¿Cómo puedo ir a ...?** |
| What is the best way to go to ...? | **¿Cuál es la mejor ruta para ...?** |

| Is it far? | ¿Está lejos? |
| How far is it? | ¿A qué distancia está? |
| How long does it take? | ¿Cuánto tiempo se lleva para ir allí? |

---

---

## 11.2 Travel by train

### Core vocabulary

| station | la estación |
| station master | el jefe de estación |
| booking office | el despacho de billetes |
| timetable | el horario |
| ticket | el billete |
| single ticket | el billete de ida |
| return ticket | el billete de ida y vuelta |

| **Types of ticket** | *Tipos de billete* |
| child | **de niño** |
| adult | **de adulto / mayor** |
| family | **familiar** |

| | |
|---|---|
| senior / pensioners | de jubilados / pensionistas |
| group | de grupo |
| arrivals | llegadas |
| departures | salidas |
| indicator board | el tablero de anuncios |
| information | la información |
| waiting room | la sala de espera |
| platform | el andén |
| subway | el paso subterráneo |
| stairs | la escalera |
| lift | el ascensor |
| line | la línea |
| | |
| train | el tren |
| express | el rápido |
| Intercity | el Intercity |
| local / slow | el tren de cercanías |
| underground | el metro |
| | |
| coach | el vagón |
| non-smoking | de no fumadores |
| first class | de primera clase |
| buffet | el vagón restaurante |
| personnel | el personal |
| guard | el jefe de tren |
| ticket inspector | el revisor |
| train driver | el maquinista |
| passenger | el pasajero |
| traveller | el viajero |
| level crossing | el paso a nivel |
| railway track | la vía (férrea) |
| signals | los semáforos (de ferrocarril) |
| | |
| luggage | el equipaje |
| suitcase | la maleta |
| left luggage | la consigna |

### Useful verbs

| | |
|---|---|
| *to book a ticket* | **reservar un billete** |
| *to make a reservation* | **hacer una reserva** |

### Useful phrases

| | |
|---|---|
| *Do I have to change?* | **¿Tengo que cambiar?** |
| *Is the train on time?* | **¿El tren, llega puntual?** |
| *How late is the train?* | **¿Qué retraso lleva el tren?** |
| *Will I miss the connection?* | **¿Perderé el enlace?** |
| *Is there a car park at the station?* | **¿Hay un aparcamiento en la estación?** |
| *Which platform does it leave from?* | **¿De qué andén sale?** |
| *Is this the train for ...?* | **¿Este es el tren para ...?** |
| *This is my place.* | **Este es mi asiento.** |
| *I have a reservation.* | **Tengo (una) reserva.** |
| *How often does it run?* | **¿Con cuánta frecuencia circula ...?** |
| *Which line do I need for ...?* | **¿Qué línea tengo que tomar para ...?** |

## 11.3 Travel by plane

### Core vocabulary

| | |
|---|---|
| airport | **el aeropuerto** |
| car park | **el aparcamiento** |
| departures | **(las) salidas** |
| check-in desk | **el mostrador de facturación** |
| luggage search | **registro de equipaje** |
| security check | **control de seguridad** |
| departure lounge | **sala de embarque** |
| executive lounge | **sala para ejecutivos** |
| information | **información** |
| announcements | **anuncios / avisos** |

### Insight

Of course the best way to remember most words and expressions in this section is in context, from having experienced them travelling to and from Spain. If you travel with a Spanish airline, even better, as you will see and hear more Spanish. **¡Buen viaje!**

| | |
|---|---|
| economy | **clase económica / turista** |
| business | **clase preferente** |
| first | **primera clase** |
| ticket | **el billete** |
| passport | **el pasaporte** |
| visa | **el visado** |
| green card | **la tarjeta verde** |
| flight | **el vuelo** |
| gate | **la puerta** |
| delay | **el retraso** |
| plane | **el avión** |
| row | **la fila** |
| seat | **el asiento** |
| window seat | **el asiento junto a la ventanilla** |
| aisle seat | **el asiento de pasillo** |

| | |
|---|---|
| seat belt | **el cinturón de seguridad** |
| life jacket | **el chaleco salvavidas** |
| emergency exit | **la salida de emergencia** |
| toilet | **el lavabo** |
| Can I have ...? | **¿Me da ...? ¿Puede darme ...?** |
| earphones | **unos auriculares** |
| a blanket | **una manta** |
| a pillow | **una almohada** |
| a glass of water | **un vaso de agua** |
| arrivals | **llegadas** |
| baggage reclaim | **recogida de equipaje** |
| customs | **la aduana** |
| duty | **derechos de Aduana** |
| pilot | **el piloto** |
| steward | **el auxiliar de vuelo** |
| stewardess | **la azafata** |

### Useful verbs

| | |
|---|---|
| to leave / depart | **salir** |
| to take off | **despegar** |
| to fly | **volar** |
| to land | **aterrizar** |
| to arrive | **llegar** |
| to navigate | **navegar** |
| to put the seat back | **echar el asiento hacia atrás** |
| to put the seat upright | **poner el asiento hacia delante** |
| to stow the table | **guardar la mesilla plegable** |
| to experience turbulence | **entrar en un área de turbulencias** |

## Insight

A few comments here to help you learn and remember:
**aterrizar** is derived from **tierra** – *land*, and **despegar** literally
means *to come unstuck*! Notice also the adverbial idea in
**hacia atrás** and **hacia delante**; and finally that **guardar** gives
the idea of putting something away safely.

## Useful phrases

| | |
|---|---|
| *The plane is delayed.* | **El avión lleva un retraso.** |
| *Your flight leaves from gate ...* | **Su vuelo sale de la puerta número ...** |
| *Please will you return to your seats and fasten your seatbelts.* | **Por favor, vuelvan a sus asientos y pónganse los cinturones de seguridad.** |
| *We are flying at an altitude of ...* | **Volamos a una altura de ...** |
| *And a speed of ...* | **Y a una velocidad de ...** |
| *My luggage is missing.* | **Falta mi equipaje.** |

### Insight

Once again, actual experience will help you to remember these – but hopefully not the last one!

---

## 11.4 Travel by car

| | |
|---|---|
| *car* | **el coche** |
| *estate car* | **el coche familiar / la ranchera** |
| *four-wheel drive* | **con tracción a las cuatro ruedas** |
| *off-road car* | **coche todoterreno** |
| *sports car* | **el coche deportivo** |
| *convertible* | **el coche descapotable** |
| *hatchback* | **el hatchback** |
| *automatic* | **automático** |
| *it has ...* | **tiene ...** |
| *2/4 doors* | **2/4 puertas** |
| *16 valves* | **16 válvulas** |

### Insight

Of course it makes sense to learn the terms relating to your own car, but you might need other words in the context of hire cars.

| | |
|---|---|
| pedals | **los pedales** |
| accelerator | **el acelerador** |
| brake | **el freno** |
| clutch | **el embrague** |

## Insight

Just as when learning to drive it helps to learn A B C for accelerator, brake, clutch, try A F E…

| | |
|---|---|
| windscreen | **el parabrisas** |
| gears | **las velocidades / las marchas** |
| gear lever | **la palanca de cambios** |
| the steering wheel | **el volante** |
| the handbrake | **el freno de mano** |
| the indicators | **los intermitentes** |
| the lights | **las luces** |
| headlamps | **los faros** |
| side lights | **las luces laterales** |
| on full | **las luces largas** |
| on dip | **las luces cortas** |
| the speedometer | **el velocímetro** |
| the mileometer | **el cuentakilómetros** |
| the petrol gauge | **el indicador del nivel de gasolina** |

## Insight

Many of these words and expressions are very logical, such as **velocidades** for *gears*, **luces laterales** for *sidelights*, **cuentakilómetros** for *mileometer* and so on. Notice how this last one consists of a verb idea '**cuenta…**' (*it counts…*) and a plural noun … '**kilómetros**' (*…kilometres*).

| **The interior** | *El interior* |
|---|---|
| seats | **los asientos** |
| safety belt | **el cinturón de seguridad** |
| leg room | **el sitio para las piernas** |

| glove compartment | la guantera |
| visor / sunshield | la visera |
| door mirror | el retrovisor |
| rearview mirror | el espejo retrovisor |
| heating | la calefacción |
| air conditioning | el aire acondicionado |
| wheel | la rueda / llanta |
| tyre | el neumático |
| valve | la válvula |
| tyre pressure | la presión de los neumáticos |
| jack | el gato |
| spare wheel | la rueda de repuesto |
| | |
| **The exterior** | *El exterior* |
| boot | el maletero |
| bumper | el parachoques |
| number plate | la matrícula |
| foglights | los faros antiniebla |
| rear lights | las luces traseras |
| exhaust | el escape |
| battery | la batería |
| radiator | el radiador |
| ignition | el encendido |
| spark plug | la bujía |
| oil pressure | la presión del aceite |
| fan belt | la correa del ventilador |
| windscreen wiper | el limpiaparabrisas |
| windscreen washer | el lavaparabrisas |
| warning light | la señal luminosa |
| gears | las marchas / velocidades |

## Insight

Try a labelled diagram of a car to help you to learn these…
Note also the logic of **escape** and **encendido** *(lights up)*. Then
there two more examples of composite words made up of a
verb and a plural noun: **limpiaparabrisas** and **lavaparabrisas**.

## Useful verbs

| | |
|---|---|
| to drive | **conducir / llevar el coche** |
| to put your lights on | **poner las luces** |
| to turn your lights off | **apagar las luces** |
| to put your indicator on | **poner el intermitente** |
| to give way | **ceder el paso** |
| to overtake | **adelantar** |

---

### Insight

**ceder** reminds us of *cede*, to give way, and **adelantar** = *to go in front*

---

## 11.5 The road

### Core vocabulary

| | |
|---|---|
| a road | **una carretera** |
| a country road | **un camino de campo / rural** |
| a main road | **una carretera principal** |
| a toll road | **carretera de peaje** |
| a one-way road | **una carretera de sentido único / dirección única** |
| a dual carriageway | **una autovía / carretera de doble calzada** |
| motorway | **una autopista** |
| motorway lane | **un carril de la autopista** |
| inside lane | **el carril de la derecha** |
| outside lane | **el carril de la izquierda** |
| central reservation | **la mediana** |
| access road | **la vía de acceso** |

A good way to learn these is with the key to a Spanish map if you have one or can obtain one.

• Many motorways in Spain are toll roads. It is a good idea to have enough change ready when you get to a **peaje**, but in any case, you can always pay with a credit card.

• Note that an **autovía** is a near motorway-standard dual carriageway, with no tolls.

| | |
|---|---|
| *the road surface is ...* | **la calzada / el firme es ...** |
| *good / bad* | **buena / mala** |
| *smooth / uneven* | **igual / desigual** |
| *bumpy* | **lleno de baches** |
| *intersection* | **el enlace, cruce** |
| *crossroad* | **la encrucijada** |
| *T-junction* | **el cruce en T** |
| *roundabout* | **el cruce giratorio / la glorieta / la rotonda** |
| *bridge* | **el puente** |
| *toll bridge* | **el puente de peaje** |
| *level crossing* | **el paso a nivel** |
| *traffic lights* | **los semáforos** |

## Insight

Note that Spanish traffic lights go straight from red to green, with no red + amber phase.

| | |
|---|---|
| *road works* | **las obras** |
| *emergency traffic lights* | **los semáforos de emergencia** |
| *the diversion* | **la desviación / el desvío** |
| *road signs* | **las señales de tráfico** |
| *crawler lane* | **el carril para vehículos lentos** |

| | |
|---|---|
| hard shoulder | **el arcén** |
| speed limit | **el límite de velocidad** |
| speed camera | **la cámara electrónica de velocidad** |

| | |
|---|---|
| traffic police | **la policía de tráfico** |
| driving licence | **el permiso de conducir** |
| insurance | **el seguro** |
| fine | **la multa** |
| garage (for repairs / service) | **el taller** |
| petrol | **la gasolina** |
| services | **el área** *(f)* **de servicio** |
| petrol station | **la estación de servicio / la gasolinera** |

| | |
|---|---|
| diesel | **el diesel** |
| air | **el aire** |
| water | **el agua** |
| oil | **el aceite** |
| oil change | **el cambio de aceite** |
| emergency services | **los servicios de emergencia / urgencia** |
| breakdown | **la avería** |

## Useful verbs

| | |
|---|---|
| *to speed* | **conducir por encima del límite de velocidad permitida** |
| *to accelerate* | **acelerar** |
| *to slow down* | **reducir la velocidad** |
| *to brake* | **frenar** |
| *to break down* | **averiarse** |

## Useful phrases

| | |
|---|---|
| *I have broken down.* | **Mi coche está averiado.** |
| *The car is overheating.* | **Se sobrecalienta el coche.** |
| *The engine has stopped.* | **El motor ha dejado de funcionar / andar.** |
| *I have a puncture.* | **Tengo un pinchazo.** |

# Test yourself

Look at these groups of words and write 'TRAINS', 'BOATS', 'PLANES' or 'AUTOMOBILES' for each group. Then write down the English for the words.

1 el andén, la estación, el horario, el rápido, el vagón
2 el registro de equipaje, la sala de embarque, el avión, el vuelo, el asiento
3 el coche, el todoterreno, las luces, el parabrisas, el cuentakilómetros
4 el acelerador, el volante, los faros, los neumáticos, la gasolina
5 el chaleco salvavidas, los auriculares, despegar, la azafata, la turbulencia
6 el maquinista, la vía, el revisor, la consigna, el paso a nivel
7 el ferrocarril, el jefe de tren, el vagón restaurante, el pasajero, el intercity
8 navegar, el ferry, el barco, el pasajero, el chaleco salvavidas
9 la fila, la salida de emergencia, el piloto, el aeropuerto, la puerta
10 el espejo retrovisor, el maletero, la matrícula, la batería, el encendido

# Tourism

## 12.1 Where to go

### Core vocabulary

| | |
|---|---|
| tourism industry | la industria turística, el turismo |
| travel agency | la agencia de viajes |
| a brochure | un folleto |
| the tourist | el / la turista |
| excursion | una excursión |
| tour | una gira |
| coach trip | una excursión en autocar |
| guided visit | una visita con guía |
| cruise | un crucero |
| holiday resort | el lugar de veraneo |
| seaside | la playa / orilla del mar |
| sea, sand and sun | el mar, la arena y el sol |
| mountains and lakes | montañas y lagos |
| countryside | el campo / paisaje |
| adventure holiday | las vacaciones de aventura |
| winter sports | los deportes de invierno |
| outdoor pursuits | las actividades al aire libre |
| peak season holidays | vacaciones durante períodos de máxima demanda |
| national holiday | la fiesta nacional |
| to go on holiday | ir de vacaciones |
| to go on summer holiday | veranear |

## Insight

- If you travel around Spain, especially by road, you will almost certainly at some stage come across a town or village in **fiesta**: every place has its patron saint, on whose feast-day there will be celebrations – usually consisting of music, dancing, food and drink, as well as a (usually religious) procession. Many areas have their own specialities.
- Cataluña has many **fiestas** celebrating the national dance, the **sardana**, which is also danced on Sunday mornings in front of Barcelona cathedral.
- Valencia has an annual festival based on the ancient water laws, and another in March called **Las Fallas** at which huge effigies are burned.
- The region south of Valencia celebrates the victories of Christians against Moors – **Moros y Cristianos** – with mock battles and processions.
- Andalucía has many colourful **fiestas** such as **Las Cruces de mayo** in Granada, and the **Fiesta de abril** in Sevilla.
- Madrid celebrates the feast of **San Isidro** with a festival of bullfighting, while Pamplona has the annual bull-running through the streets to celebrate **San Fermín** in July.

All over Spain, national festivals are celebrated such as the following:

- **Semana Santa** – a week of often sombre religious processions leading up to Easter
- **el día de la Hispanidad** celebrated on the day of **La Virgen del Pilar** on October 12 – Spain's national day
- **el día de los Reyes** celebrating the Epiphany and the three kings (Magi) on January 6; there are processions on the evening of January 5 in which the kings throw sweets to the children, and that night children leave their shoes on the balcony, to be filled with presents by the **Reyes Magos**.

## 12.2 What to take

### Core vocabulary

| | |
|---|---|
| luggage | el equipaje |
| suitcase | la maleta |
| travel bag | el bolso de viaje |
| overnight bag | el bolso de viaje |
| rucksack | la mochila |
| hand luggage | el equipaje de mano |
| passport | el pasaporte |
| visa | el visado |
| tickets | los billetes |
| insurance | el seguro |
| driving licence | el permiso de conducir |
| credit card | la tarjeta de crédito |
| currency | la moneda |
| travellers cheques | los cheques de viaje / viajero |
| emergency phone number | número de teléfono de urgencia / emergencia |
| laptop | el ordenador portátil |
| mobile phone | el (teléfono) móvil |
| sponge bag | la esponjera |
| toilet bag | el neceser, la bolsa de aseo |
| soap | el jabón |
| toothbrush | el cepillo de dientes |
| toothpaste | la pasta de dientes |
| razor | la maquinilla de afeitar |
| electric razor | la máquina de afeitar |
| nail scissors | las tijeras para las uñas |
| tweezers | las pinzas |
| shampoo | el champú |
| conditioner | el suavizante / acondicionador |
| hairbrush | el cepillo para el pelo / cabello |
| comb | el peine |
| face cream | la crema para la cara |
| hand cream | la crema para las manos |
| cleanser | la crema limpiadora |

| | |
|---|---|
| moisturiser | **la crema hidratante** |
| sun cream | **el bronceador** |
| waterproof sun cream | **el bronceador resistente al agua** |
| aftersun cream | **la crema para después de tomar el sol** |
| sunblock | **el filtro solar** |
| wardrobe | **el armario** |
| coat hanger | **la percha** |
| iron | **la plancha** |

### Useful verbs

| | |
|---|---|
| to pack | **hacer la(s) maleta(s)** |
| to unpack | **deshacer la(s) maleta(s)** |
| to fold | **plegar** |
| to hang up | **colgar** |
| to wash | **lavar** |
| to dry clean | **lavar en seco** |
| to mend | **remendar / zurcir** |
| to press / iron | **planchar** |

## Insight

The obvious learning method here is to have a labelled drawing of the most important of these items, or better still to have labels attached to them with their Spanish names!

Note also the expressions which are quite logically constructed with the word **para** to link the two parts, describing what the products are used for.

Finally notice **plancha**, which literally means *plank* ... hence its use here for a device for flattening clothes!

## Useful phrases

| | |
|---|---|
| *I have lost my luggage.* | **He perdido mi equipaje.** |
| *I can't find ...* | **No encuentro ...** |
| *Have you got a ...?* | **¿Tiene(s) (usted) un(a) ...?** |
| *Where can I get a ...?* | **¿Dónde puedo obtener / comprar / encontrar un(a) ...?** |
| *Where is the nearest ...?* | **¿Dónde está el / la .... más cerca de aquí?** |

## Insight

Just a couple of points here:

You may have spotted the logic of **hacer la maleta** and **deshacer la maleta** – almost too logical if one considers the 'making up' of the full item of luggage!

Notice also **remendar** – *to mend* and **plegar** – *to fold*, related to the English word pleat...

---

## 12.3 Where to stay

### Core vocabulary

| | |
|---|---|
| **Accommodation** | *El alojamiento* |
| *two-star hotel* | **un hotel de dos estrellas** |
| *three-star hotel* | **un hotel de tres estrellas** |
| *luxury hotel* | **un hotel de lujo** |
| *inn* | **la taberna / posada / el mesón** |
| *bed and breakfast* | **pensión con desayuno\*** |
| *holiday house / home* | **la casa para ocupar durante las vacaciones** |
| *youth hostel* | **el albergue juvenil** |
| *campsite* | **el camping** |
| *caravan site* | **el camping para caravanas** |

| | |
|---|---|
| entrance | **la entrada** |
| reception | **la recepción** |
| night porter | **el guardia nocturno** |
| manager | **el director / gerente** |
| staff | **el personal** |
| porter | **el portero** |
| bill | **la cuenta** |
| single room | **una habitación individual / sencilla** |
| room with a double bed | **una habitación doble (con cama) de matrimonio** |
| twin-bedded room | **una habitación doble (con dos camas)** |
| family room | **una habitación familiar** |
| with shower | **con ducha** |
| with bathroom | **con baño** |
| with toilet | **con wáter / retrete** |
| with phone | **con teléfono** |
| with television | **con televisor** |
| with internet connection | **con conexión de Internet, con wifi** |
| with a balcony | **con balcón** |
| with a sea view | **con vista al mar** |
| with air conditioning | **con aire acondicionado** |
| reception | **la recepción** |
| stairs | **la escalera** |
| lift | **el ascensor** |
| restaurant | **el restaurante** |
| fitness room | **el gimnasio** |
| pool | **la piscina** |
| hot tub | **el jacuzzi** |

### Useful phrases

| | |
|---|---|
| *Have you got ...?* | **¿Tiene(n) ...?** |
| *anything bigger / smaller* | **algo más grande / pequeño** |
| *anything cheaper / better* | **algo más barato / mejor** |
| *anything quieter* | **algo más tranquilo** |
| *a non-smoking room* | **una habitación para no fumadores** |
| *It is too noisy.* | **Es demasiado ruidoso.** |
| *The shower doesn't work.* | **No funciona la ducha.** |
| *There is no hot water.* | **No hay agua caliente.** |
| *There is no plug in the sink.* | **No hay tapón en el lavabo.** |

**Insight**

Try learning and practising these expressions by imagining and jotting down scenarios using them.

## 12.4 Camping and caravanning

### Core vocabulary

| | |
|---|---|
| *camp site* | **el camping** |
| *caravan* | **la caravana** |
| *camper van* | **la autocaravana** |
| *trailer* | **el remolque** |
| *tent* | **la tienda (de campaña / cámping)** |
| *frame tent* | **la tienda familiar** |
| *site* | **el sitio** |
| *a flat site* | **un sitio plano** |
| *a shady site* | **un sitio sombreado** |

**Insight**

Try to find pictures of these to label and learn; you'll find suitable pictures in Spanish Wikipedia, in a camping catalogue ... or you could trawl using www.google.es

| | |
|---|---|
| **Tent** | *La tienda (de campaña)* |
| *tent peg* | **la estaca (de tienda)** |
| *tent pole* | **el palo** |
| *guy rope* | **la cuerda (de la tienda)** |
| *groundsheet* | **el aislante / suelo de tienda** |
| *sleeping bag* | **el saco de dormir** |
| *torch* | **la linterna** |
| *blanket* | **la manta** |
| *gas cooker* | **la cocina de gas portátil / el cámping gas** |
| *gas bottle* | **el butano / la bomba de gas** |
| | |
| **Facilities** | *Las instalaciones* |
| *electricity* | **la electricidad / la luz** |
| *power socket* | **la toma de corriente / el enchufe** |
| *water* | **el agua** *(f)* |
| *running water* | **el agua corriente** |
| *drinking water* | **el agua potable** |
| *water tap* | **el grifo de agua** |
| *tap water* | **el agua del grifo** |

## Insight

Try learning these with appropriate associations, perhaps visualizing times when you have experienced each.

| | |
|---|---|
| *washrooms* | **los servicios / los aseos** |
| *toilet* | **el aseo / el servicio** |
| *shower* | **la ducha** |
| *wash basin* | **el lavabo** |
| *hair dryers* | **los secadores de pelo** |
| *cooking area* | **la cocina** |
| *gas rings* | **el fuego de gas** |
| *washing-up sinks* | **las pilas para lavar platos** |
| *washing machines* | **las lavadoras** |
| *clothes driers* | **las secadoras** |
| *drying area* | **la zona para tender ropa** |
| *restaurant* | **el restaurante** |

| | |
|---|---|
| *bar* | **el bar** |
| *shop* | **la tienda** |
| *swimming pool* | **la piscina** |
| *paddling pool* | **la piscina para niños** |
| *children's play area* | **la zona de recreo para niños** |
| *swings* | **los columpios** |
| *slide* | **el tobogán** |
| *roundabout* | **el carrusel** |

## Insight

Learn the following verbs using visual images to associate the verb with the actions.

Note that all of these are **-ar** verbs – members of by far the largest of the three verb families.

You will have seen the logic of **montar / desmontar** – always useful to learn a pair of related verbs.

The verb **enchufar** also means *to plug in*, and **el enchufe** means *plug* or *socket*. It also has a figurative meaning rather like English 'string-pulling', i.e. using influence…

### Useful verbs

| | |
|---|---|
| *to tow* | **remolcar** |
| *to park* | **aparcar** |
| *to put up* | **montar** |
| *to take down* | **desmontar** |
| *to hook up (connect)* | **enchufar / conectar** |
| *to get wet* | **mojarse** |
| *to wash / do the washing* | **lavar la ropa** |
| *to dry* | **secar** |

## Useful phrases

| | |
|---|---|
| Can you help me? | **¿Me puede ayudar?** |
| I don't understand how the ... works. | **No entiendo cómo funciona el / la ...** |
| Where is the ...? | **¿Dónde está el / la ...?** |
| Is there electricity / water / shade...? | **¿Hay electricidad / agua / sombra?** |
| Do you have ...? | **¿Tiene(s) (usted) ...?** |
| When is the shop open? | **¿A qué hora se abre la tienda?** |
| Where can I get ...? | **¿Dónde puedo conseguir / obtener ...?** |

---

## Insight

Practise and learn these by writing examples out in full.

---

## 12.5 What are you going to do?

| We want to go ... | Queremos ir a ... |
|---|---|
| swimming | **la natación** |
| diving | **el salto de trampolín, el buceo** |
| water skiing | **el esquí acuático** |
| surfing | **el surf** |
| walking | **el excursionismo** |
| hiking | **el excursionismo (a pie)** |
| climbing | **el montañismo / alpinismo** |
| gliding | **el planeo / vuelo sin motor** |
| paragliding | **el parapente** |
| hang-gliding | **el vuelo con ala delta** |
| do sport | **hacer el deporte** |
| play tennis | **jugar al tenis** |
| play volleyball | **jugar al voleibol** |
| go bike riding | **hacer ciclismo** |

| We want to see ... | Queremos ver ... |
|---|---|
| the sights | **los sitios de interés** |
| monuments | **los monumentos** |
| castles | **los castillos** |
| archeological sites | **los sitios arqueológicos** |
| ancient monuments | **los monumentos antiguos** |
| historic buildings | **los edificios históricos** |
| the scenery | **el paisaje** |
| animals | **los animales** |

| We want ... | Queremos ... |
|---|---|
| to have a good time | **pasarlo bien / divertirnos*** |
| to have a rest | **descansar(nos)*** |
| to relax | **relajar(nos)*** |
| sun, sea and sand | **sol, mar y arena** |
| to do nothing | **no hacer nada** |
| to be waited on | **ser atendidos** |
| to find some sun | **encontrar el sol** |

| In winter I like to go ... | *En el invierno me gusta hacer ...* |
|---|---|
| skiing | **el esquí** |
| snowboarding | **el snowboard** |
| sledging | **el trineo** |
| ice skating | **el patinaje sobre hielo** |
| ice climbing | **escalar en hielo** |

## Insight

Note here how most of these expressions use gerunds in English, whilst in Spanish most are conveyed by a noun except for the last, which is rendered in Spanish by a verb in the infinitive form.

### Useful phrases

| What is there to see / do? | **¿Qué hay para ver / hacer?** |
|---|---|
| Is it suitable for ...? | **¿Es apto para ...?** |
| older people | **las personas mayores / ancianos** |
| younger people | **(los) jóvenes** |
| children | **(los) niños** |

## 12.6 On the beach

## Insight

Easy to know what is the best way to learn the following: visualize them by imagining yourself relaxing on the beach ... just what you need on a cold, grey winter's day!

### Core vocabulary

| sea | **el mar** |
|---|---|
| coast | **la costa** |
| beach | **la playa** |

| | |
|---|---|
| *bay* | **la bahía** |
| *shore* | **la orilla** |
| *sand* | **la arena** |
| *rocks* | **las rocas** |
| *rock pools* | **las charcas entre rocas** |
| *seashells* | **las conchas** |
| *tide* | **la marea** |
| *waves* | **las olas** |
| *private / public beach* | **la playa privada / pública** |
| *beach bar* | **la chiringuito** |
| *wind break* | **el cotavientos** |

## Insight

These last two are a bit 'different': therefore they need a bit of effort. The word **chiringuito** is very idiomatic, whilst there are some obvious associations in **cotavientos**.

| | |
|---|---|
| *shelter* | **el refugio** |
| *parasol* | **la sombrilla / el parasol** |
| *lounger* | **la tumbona** |
| *deck chair* | **la tumbona** |
| *air mattress* | **el colchón inflable** |
| *shower* | **la ducha** |
| *towel* | **la toalla** |
| *swimming costume* | **el traje de baño** |
| *trunks* | **el bañador** |
| *bikini* | **el bikini** |
| *suntan lotion* | **el bronceador** |
| *total screen / sunblock* | **el filtro solar** |
| *sunglasses* | **las gafas de sol** |
| *rubber ring* | **el flotador** |
| *arm bands* | **los brazaletes** |
| *sandcastle* | **el castillo de arena** |
| *bucket* | **el cubito** |
| *spade* | **la pala** |
| *kite* | **la cometa** |

| snorkel | **el esnórquel** |
| flippers | **las aletas** |
| wet suit | **el traje isotérmico** |
| dry suit | **el traje seco** |
| inflatable | **inflable / hinchable** |
| hand / foot pump | **la bomba de mano / pie** |
| surf board | **la tabla / plancha de surf** |
| wind surfer | **el windsurfista** |
| jetski | **la moto acuática** |
| waterski | **el esquí acuático** |
| fish (live) | **el pez** |
| fish (caught/dead) | **el pescado** |
| shells | **las conchas** |
| octopus | **el pulpo** |
| squid | **el calamar** |
| mussels | **el mejillón** |
| scallops | **las veneras** |
| shrimps | **los camarones** |
| jellyfish | **la medusa** |

### Useful verbs

| to snorkel | **hacer el esnórquel** |
| to sunbathe | **tomar el sol** |
| to relax | **relajar(se)** *(reflexive)* |

| to play | **jugar** |
| to dig | **cavar** |
| to dive | **tirarse (al agua)** |
| to sting | **picar** |
| to waterski | **hacer el esquí acuático** |

## Insight

Try to illustrate these to support your learning effort by drawing stick-men performing the actions; you could model them on the figures often seen on roadsigns.

### Useful phrases

| *The tide is in / out.* | **La marea está alta / baja.** |
| *It is safe for bathing / swimming.* | **Es seguro para bañarse / nadar.** |
| *I have been stung by a jellyfish.* | **Me ha picado una medusa.** |
| *He / She is out of her depth.* | **Él / ella no hace fondo / pie.** |
| *He / She can't swim.* | **Él / ella no sabe nadar.** |
| *He / She needs help.* | **Necesita ayuda.** |
| *Help!* | **¡Socorro!** |

## Insight

You could try writing a short narrative using some of these verbs!

---

## 12.7 At sea

### Core vocabulary

| canoe | **la piragua** |
| jetski | **la moto acuática** |
| motor boat | **la lancha a motor** |
| outboard (motor) | **(el motor) fuera bordo** |
| RIB (rigid inflatable boat) | **el zodiac** |
| rubber dinghy | **la lancha neumática** |

| | |
|---|---|
| rowing boat | **la barca de remos** |
| sailing dinghy | **el bote de vela** |
| surf board | **la plancha de surf** |
| waterski | **el esquí acuático** |
| windsurfer | **el windsurfista** |
| yacht | **el velero** |
| emergency services | **los servicios de urgencia / emergencia** |
| lifeboat (from shore) | **la lancha de socorro** |
| lifeboat (from ship) | **el bote salvavidas** |
| lifejacket | **el chaleco salvavidas** |
| lifeguard | **el salvavidas** |
| flare | **la bengala** |

## Insight

Words like **bengala** need a special effort if you are to learn them, as there are no obvious associations. However, notice the verb + plural noun combination: **salvavidas**, with the verb first and the noun afterwards, in the plural form.

| | |
|---|---|
| weather forecast | **el pronóstico del tiempo** |
| the sea is ... | **el mar está ...** |
| calm | **en calma / tranquilo** |
| rough | **agitado** |
| wind force | **la fuerza del viento** |
| gale force wind | **el viento huracanado** |
| rain | **la lluvia** |
| poor / good visibility | **poca / buena visibilidad** |
| fog | **la niebla** |
| equipment | **el equipo** |
| compass | **la brújula** |
| sails | **las velas** |
| hull | **el casco** |
| cabin | **el camarote** |
| berth | **la litera** |
| wheel | **el timón** |

| | |
|---|---|
| harbour | **el puerto** |
| port | **el puerto** |
| lighthouse | **el faro** |
| port | **(a) babor** |
| starboard | **(a) estribor** |
| mooring | **el amarradero** |
| buoy | **la boya** |
| chain | **la cadena** |
| anchor | **el ancla** (f) |

## Insight

Note how **e**stribor is a bit like starboard, but needs an **e-** in front of the sound s+consonant for Spanish people to be able to pronounce it; did you notice the same with **esnórquel**?

### Useful verbs

| | |
|---|---|
| to sail | **navegar** |
| to navigate | **navegar** |
| to steer | **gobernar** |
| to tie up / moor | **amarrar** |
| to anchor | **anclar** |
| to rescue | **rescatar** |
| to be rescued | **ser rescatado/a ...** |

## Insight

Did you notice that most of these are **-ar** verbs? This proves yet again that this is the largest family of verbs in Spanish.

## 12.8 The great outdoors

### Core vocabulary

| | |
|---|---|
| rucksack | **la mochila** |
| sleeping bag | **el saco de dormir** |
| ground mat / mattress | **el colchón inflable** |
| torch | **la linterna** |
| penknife | **la navaja** |
| compass | **la brújula** |
| map | **el mapa** |
| water bottle | **la cantimplora** |
| camping stove | **la cocina de gas portátil /** **el cámping gas** |
| matches | **los fósforos / las cerillas** |
| lighter | **el encendedor / la mechera** |
| gas container | **el butano / la bomba de gas** |
| billycan (for cooking on stove) | **el cazo** |
| bowl | **el plato** |
| knife / fork / spoon | **el cuchillo / el tenedor /** **la cuchara** |
| plate | **el plato** |
| mug | **el tazón** |
| emergency rations | **las raciones de reserva** |
| dried food | **los comestibles secos** |
| dried fruit | **las frutas pasas** |
| nuts | **las nueces** |
| chocolate | **el chocolate** |

## Insight

Once again, you could try composing a narrative using as many of these as possible.

| | |
|---|---|
| transceiver (for snow rescue) | **el transceptor / el transmisor-** **receptor** |
| mobile phone | **el teléfono móvil** |
| batteries | **las pilas** |

| charger | **el cargador** |
| plug | **el enchufe** |
| waterproofs | **la ropa impermeable** |
| spare clothing | **la ropa de reserva** |
| rope | **la cuerda** |
| climbing harness | **el arnés de montañismo** |
| climbing gear | **el equipo de montañismo** |
| crampons | **los garfios** |
| boots | **las botas** |
| ice axe | **la piqueta (de alpinista)** |
| sore feet | **los pies doloridos / lastimados** |
| spare socks | **calcetines de reserva** |
| blisters | **las ampollas** |
| plasters | **los esparadrapos / las tiritas** |
| antiseptic cream | **la crema antiséptica** |
| insect repellent | **el repelente contra insectos** |
| antihistamine cream (for insect bites) | **la crema antihistamínica** |

### Insight

cargador is another example of a noun ending in '-ador';
enchufe has other meanings in different contexts. You could
try pairing these remedies off with the complaints you'd use
them for.

### Useful phrases

| Have you got ...? | ¿Tiene(s) ...? |
| Have you got something for ...? | ¿Tiene(s) algo para ...? |
| I have been stung by a wasp / bee | Me ha picado una avispa / una abeja. |
| a mosquito | un mosquito |
| I have been bitten by ... | Me ha mordido ... |
| a mosquito | un mosquito |
| a snake | una serpiente |
| a dog | un perro |

# Test yourself

Look at the Spanish for each of these English words or phrases and pick a, b or c as appropriate to complete each expression.

1 HOLIDAY RESORT: el lugar de
  **a** veraneo      **b** paisaje      **c** mochila
2 DRIVING LICENCE: el permiso de
  **a** jabón      **b** seguro      **c** conducir
3 TO PACK: hacer las
  **a** perchas      **b** pinzas      **c** maletas
4 I'VE LOST MY LUGGAGE: he perdido mi
  **a** portero      **b** equipaje      **c** armario
5 THREE STAR HOTEL: Un hotel de tres
  **a** escaleras      **b** estrellas      **c** duchas
6 A SINGLE ROOM: una habitación
  **a** sencilla      **b** familiar      **c** barata
7 A TENT: una tienda de
  **a** campo      **b** caravana      **c** campaña
8 ICE SKATING: el patinaje sobre
  **a** ruedas      **b** hielo      **c** nieve
9 WEATHER FORECAST: el pronóstico del
  **a** tiempo      **b** clima      **c** viento
10 HAVE YOU GOT SOMETHING FOR BLISTERS?
  ¿Tiene algo para
  **a** los pies      **b** las ampollas      **c** los calcetines?

# 13

## The body and health

### 13.1 The face

#### Core vocabulary

| | |
|---|---|
| head | **la cabeza** |
| face | **la cara** |
| hair | **el pelo / cabello** |
| forehead | **la frente** |
| ears | **las orejas** |
| eyes | **los ojos** |
| eyelids | **los párpados** |
| eyebrows | **las cejas** |
| eyelashes | **las pestañas** |
| nose | **la nariz** |
| cheeks | **las mejillas** |
| chin | **la barbilla** |
| mouth | **la boca** |
| lips | **los labios** |
| tongue | **la lengua** |
| teeth | **los dientes** |
| neck | **el cuello** |

## Insight

There are several useful associations based on spelling similarities check out:

**cabeza** – *capital* (*head town*); **frente** – the *front* part of your head; **ojos** – bin*oculars* (telescope for both).

**nariz** – *nasal*; **barbilla** – where the beard is (which a *barb*er may trim for you); **lengua** – *langua*ge (what you create with your tongue – cf mother tongue); **dientes** – dental, dentist; **cuello** – which you cover with a *collar* (note the **o > ue** spelling change)

| Toiletries | *Artículos de tocador* |
|---|---|
| shampoo | **el champú** |
| conditioner | **el acondicionador / suavizante** |
| face cream | **la crema facial** |
| moisturiser | **la crema hidratante** |
| face pack | **la mascarilla facial** |
| lip salve | **el protector labial** |
| shaving cream | **la crema de afeitar** |
| shaving brush | **la brocha de afeitar** |
| razor | **la navaja** |
| electric razor | **la máquina de afeitar** |
| after-shave lotion | **la loción para después del afeitado** |
| make-up | **el maquillaje** |
| mascara | **el rímel** |
| lipstick | **la barra de labios** |
| eye shadow | **la sombra de ojos** |
| powder | **los polvos** |

## Insight

There are lots of available associations here: all of the expressions from '**crema**…' down to '**loción**…' are logical. **Maquillaje** is like the French word *maquillage*; **rímel** is a brand-name which has come to be used for any similar product, and **barra de labios** and **sombra de ojos** are again logical.

## Useful phrases

| | |
|---|---|
| He has a beard | **Tiene / Lleva una barba** |
| moustache | **(el) bigote** |
| He / she wears glasses | **Él / Ella lleva gafas** |
| contact lenses | **las lentes de contacto** |
| I am short-sighted | **Soy miope** |
| long-sighted | **présbita** |
| I have a headache | **Me duele la cabeza / Tengo dolor de cabeza** |
| toothache | **el dolor de dientes** |
| earache | **el dolor de oído(s)** |
| a nose bleed | **una hemorragia nasal** |
| My eyes are sore | **Me duelen los ojos** |
| to have a facial | **hacer un tratamiento facial** |
| to have your hair done | **arreglarse el pelo** |
| to have a nose job | **operarse la nariz** |
| to have plastic surgery | **hacerse la cirugía plástica / cosmética** |
| to have wrinkles | **tener arrugas** |
| to have a nice smile | **tener una sonrisa bonita** |

## Insight

Note how **llevar** is used for '*to wear*'. You should also have noticed how **me duele** works like *me* **gusta, me encanta**, etc. Notice the structure of **el dolor de dientes / de oídos**. This will help you to remember these words and expressions. You could try to visualize many of these as a way of having an image with which to jog your memory.

## Useful verbs

| | |
|---|---|
| to hear | **oír** |
| to see | **ver** |
| to smell | **oler** |
| to taste | **gustar** |
| to wink | **guiñar** |

| | |
|---|---|
| to sleep | **dormir** |
| to smile | **sonreír** |
| to laugh | **reír** |
| to talk | **hablar** |
| to shout | **gritar** |
| to cry | **llorar** |
| to snore | **roncar** |
| to hiccup | **hipar** |
| to cough | **toser** |

## Insight

Of course, it is always worthwhile learning how to conjugate these verbs rather than just learning the infinitives as vocabulary items. Notice how the last few are onomatopaeic words: they sound like the words they describe!

## 13.2 The body

| | |
|---|---|
| shoulder | **el hombro** |
| back | **la espalda** |
| arms | **el brazo** |
| elbow | **el codo** |
| wrist | **la muñeca** |
| hands | **la mano** |
| finger | **el dedo** |
| thumb | **el pulgar** |
| fingernail | **la uña** |
| body | **el cuerpo** |
| chest | **el pecho** |
| breasts | **los pechos** |
| nipples | **los pezones** |
| waist | **la cintura / el talle** |
| hips | **las caderas** |

| | |
|---|---|
| abdomen | **el abdomen** |
| bottom | **el trasero** |
| the sexual organs | **los órganos sexuales** |
| the penis | **el pene** |
| the balls | **los cojones** |
| the vagina | **la vagina** |
| legs | **las piernas** |
| thighs | **los muslos** |
| knees | **las rodillas** |
| calves | **las pantorrillas** |
| ankle | **el tobillo** |
| foot | **el pie** |
| toes | **los dedos del pie** |
| arch | **el puente** |
| heel | **el tacón** |
| the back | **el dorso** |
| the front | **la parte delantera** |
| the side | **el lado** |

## Insight

Several of these words have other meanings which might help you remember them:

**muñeca** also means *doll*, especially 'glove puppet'; **mano** is obviously related to 'manual' and **pulgar** is the finger you might use to squash a flea (**pulga**). Notice also the scope of meaning of **cuerpo** – not just corpse! Then of course there are lots of cognates.

| **Internal organs** | *Los órganos internos* |
|---|---|
| brain | **el cerebro** |
| stomach | **el estómago** |
| throat | **la garganta** |
| lungs | **los pulmones** |
| kidneys | **los riñones** |
| heart | **el corazón** |

| blood | **la sangre** |
| the veins | **las venas** |
| the arteries | **las arterias** |
| intestines | **los intestinos** |
| skeleton | **el esqueleto** |
| bones | **los huesos** |
| joints | **las coyunturas** |
| nervous system | **el sistema nervioso** |
| nerves | **los nervios** |
| circulation | **la circulación** |
| breathing | **la respiración** |
| digestion | **la digestión** |

## Insight

Once again, lots of cognates. Note also **estómago** – so typical of Spanish words beginning with **esp-/ est- / esc-** which you have seen before ... and what about **esqueleto**?

### Useful verbs

| to feel | **sentir(se)** *(reflexive)* |
| to touch | **tocar** |
| to stroke | **acariciar** |
| to massage | **dar un masaje** |
| to hold | **agarrar** |
| to embrace | **abrazar(se)** |
| to kiss | **besar** |
| to make love | **hacer el amor** |
| to kick | **dar patadas (a)** |
| to walk | **andar / ir andando** |
| to run | **correr** |
| to jump | **saltar** |

## 13.3 I need to see a doctor

### Core vocabulary

| | |
|---|---|
| *doctor* | **el médico** |
| *appointment* | **la cita** |
| *surgery* | **la consulta** |
| *immunization* | **la inmunización** |
| *innoculation* | **la inoculación** |
| *a health certificate* | **un certificado de salud** |
| *an examination* | **un reconocimiento** |

| **Ailments** | *Las enfermedades* |
|---|---|
| *a cold* | **un resfriado** |
| *flu (influenza)* | **la gripe** |
| *measles* | **el sarampión** |
| *mumps* | **las paperas** |
| *German measles* | **la rubeola** |
| *tonsillitis* | **la amigdalitis** |
| *a cough* | **una tos** |
| *sore throat* | **un dolor de garganta** |
| *indigestion* | **la indigestión** |
| *hypertension* | **la hipertensión** |
| *constipation* | **la estreñimiento** |

| | |
|---|---|
| diarrhoea | **la diarrea** |
| polio | **la polio(mielitis)** |
| hepatitis | **la hepatitis** |
| rabies | **la rabia** |
| typhoid | **la tifoidea** |
| cholera | **la cólera** |
| yellow fever | **la fiebre amarilla** |
| malaria | **la malaria** |
| cancer | **el cáncer** |
| multiple sclerosis | **la esclerosis múltiple** |
| medicine | **la medicina** |
| pills | **las pastillas** |
| pain relief | **el alivio contra el dolor** |
| vitamin supplements | **los suplementos vitamínicos** |
| cure | **la cura** |
| homeopathic remedy | **el remedio homeopático** |
| exercise | **el ejercicio** |
| physiotherapy | **la fisioterapia** |
| rest | **el descanso** |
| sleep | **el sueño** |
| go to bed | **va / vaya a la cama / acuéstate / acuéstese** (reflexive) |
| sleep | **duerme / duerma** |
| take more exercise | **toma / tome / haz / haga más ejercicio** |
| eat less | **come / coma menos** |
| avoid | **evita / evite ...** |

## Insight

Lots of cognates here, as medicine and other sciences borrow much of their vocabulary from Latin which is the origin of most Spanish vocabulary. You should notice the spelling changes in **diarrea, tifoidea, cólera, esclerósis, fioterapia** and so on, all of those changes you have seen before, and are logical when you allow for the Spanish style of spelling. Notice also the 'radical change' in **acuéstese / acuéstate** and **duerme / duerma.**

## Useful phrases

| | |
|---|---|
| I have a pain ... | **Me duele / Tengo (un) dolor de ...** |
| It hurts / They hurt | **Me duele / Me duelen** |
| I don't feel well. | **No me siento bien.** |
| I can't sleep / eat / walk. | **No puedo dormir / comer / andar.** |
| I want to go to the toilet. | **Quiero ir al lavabo / a los aseos / servicios.** |
| I feel sick. | **Me siento enfermo / tengo náuseas.** |
| I feel dizzy. | **Me siento mareado.** |
| I have got spots. | **Tengo granos en la piel.** |
| I have been bitten / stung. | **Se me ha picado.** |
| I have stomach ache. | **Tengo dolor de estómago.** |
|   heart burn |   **la acidez** |
|   indigestion |   **la indigestión** |
|   high / low blood pressure |   **la tensión (de sangre) alta / baja** |
| My foot / hand / leg hurts. | **Me duele el pie / la mano / la pierna.** |
| I am allergic to ... | **Soy alérgico a ...** |
|   penicillin |   **la penicilina** |
|   nuts |   **las nueces** |
|   animals |   **los animales** |
| I have hay fever. | **Tengo fiebre del heno.** |
|   asthma |   **el asma** |
| He needs an inhaler. | **Él necesita un inhalador.** |
| She is handicapped. | **Ella es minusválida.** |
|   paraplegic |   **parapléjico/a** |
| an injection / a jab for | **una inyección para ...** |
| I have broken my leg / ankle / wrist ... | **me he roto la pierna / el tobillo / la muñeca** |
| plaster | **la escayola** |
| crutches | **las muletas** |
| walking stick | **el bastón** |
| wheel chair | **la silla de ruedas** |

## 13.4 At the hospital

### Core vocabulary

| | |
|---|---|
| hospital | **el hospital** |
| department | **el departamento** |
| emergency | **la emergencia / urgencia** |
| doctor | **el médico** |
| nurse | **la enfermera / el enfermero** |
| ward | **la sala** |
| bed | **la cama** |
| anaesthetic | **el anestésico** |
| surgery (medical procedure) | **la cirugía** |
| surgery (place) | **la clínica / consulta** |
| operation | **la operación / intervención quirúrgica** |
| operating theatre | **el quirófano / la sala de operaciones** |
| a blood transfusion | **una transfusión de sangre** |
| a blood donor | **un donador de sangre** |
| my blood type | **mi grupo sanguíneo** |
| an x-ray | **una radiografía** |
| radiation | **la radiación** |

## 13.5 Contraception

| | |
|---|---|
| *family planning* | **la planificación familiar** |
| *contraception* | **la anticoncepción** |
| *condom* | **el preservativo** |
| *the coil* | **el espiral** |
| *the pill* | **la píldora** |
| *the morning-after pill* | **la píldora del día después** |
| *vasectomy* | **la vasectomía** |

**Insight**

Once again, you could just learn those you need.

# Test yourself

Sort the AILMENTS from the BODY PARTS. Then write the English for each word.

1 los párpados
2 las rodillas
3 la gripe
4 las paperas
5 los pulmones
6 el dolor de estómago
7 el resfriado
8 los muslos
9 las mejillas
10 el sarampión

# 14

## The world

### 14.1 Countries

#### Core vocabulary

| | |
|---|---|
| world | **el mundo** |
| earth | **la tierra** |
| globe | **el globo** |
| atlas | **el atlas** |
| country | **el país** |

| **The continents and major regions** | *Los continentes* |
|---|---|
| Africa | **África** |
| North America | **América del Norte** |
| South America | **América del Sur** |
| Asia | **Asia** |
| Australia | **Australia** |
| Europe | **Europa** |
| Antarctica | **Antárctica, Antártida** |
| America | **América** |
| Arctic | **el Ártico** |
| Middle East | **el Oriente Medio** |
| Far East | **el Lejano Oriente / Extremo Oriente** |

| Pacific Rim | (los países de) la Costa del Pacífico |
|---|---|
| Indo-China | Indochina |
| India | India |
| China | China |
| Japan | el Japón |
| Indonesia | Indonesia |
| Australasia | Australasia |
| New Zealand | Nueva Zelanda / Zelandia |
| the Pacific Islands | las Islas del Pacífico |

## Insight

Obviously, the best way to learn these names of countries is on a map! You could try to find some of them, perhaps continent by continent, on Wikipedia or other suitable websites, and print them out.

## 14.2 The countries of Europe

### Core vocabulary

| Scandinavia | Escandinavia |
|---|---|
| Denmark | Dinamarca |
| Finland | Finlandia |
| Norway | Noruega |
| Sweden | Suecia |
| Iceland | Islandia |

| The Low Countries | Los Países Bajos |
|---|---|
| Belgium | Bélgica |
| Holland | Holanda |
| Luxembourg | Luxemburgo |

| The Iberian Peninsula | La Península Ibérica |
|---|---|
| Spain | España |

| | |
|---|---|
| *Portugal* | **Portugal** |
| **The United Kingdom** | ***El Reino Unido*** |
| *England* | **Inglaterra** |
| *Scotland* | **Escocia** |
| *Northern Ireland* | **Irlanda del Norte** |
| *Wales* | **el País de Gales** |
| **Europe** | ***Europa*** |
| *Greece* | **Grecia** |
| *Turkey* | **Turquía** |
| *Germany* | **Alemania** |
| *Poland* | **Polonia** |
| *France* | **Francia** |
| *Ireland* | **Irlanda** |
| *Austria* | **Austria** |
| *Italy* | **Italia** |
| *the Czech Republic* | **la República Checa** |
| *Hungary* | **Hungría** |
| *Slovakia* | **Eslovaquia** |
| *Switzerland* | **Suiza** |

## Insight

Once again, you might be able to learn these with a map to illustrate them. Note also that in most cases the names are recognizably close to the English version, simply needing appropriate adjustments to their spelling.

| | |
|---|---|
| **The European Union** | ***La Unión Europea*** |
| *the European Parliament* | **el Parlamento Europeo** |
| *the Common Market* | **el Mercado Común** |
| *Member of the European Parliament* | **Diputado del Parlamento Europeo / eurodiputado** |
| *the Common Agricultural Policy* | **la Política Agrícola Común** |
| *the euro* | **el euro** |
| *the European institutions* | **las instituciones europeas** |
| *the European bank* | **el Banco Europeo** |

## 14.3 The high seas

### Core vocabulary

| The points of the compass | *Las cuartas de la brújula* |
|---|---|
| north | **norte (+ noreste, noroeste)** |
| south | **sur (+ sureste, suroeste)** |
| east | **este** |
| west | **oeste** |

| The oceans and seas | *Los océanos y los mares* |
|---|---|
| Atlantic | **el Atlántico** |
| Indian | **el Océano Índico** |
| Pacific | **el Pacífico** |
| Mediterranean | **el Mediterráneo** |
| North Sea | **el Mar del Norte** |
| Baltic | **el Mar Báltico** |
| Red Sea | **el Mar Rojo** |
| English Channel | **el Canal de la Mancha** |

| | |
|---|---|
| navigation | la navegación |
| longitude | la longitud |
| latitude | la latitud |
| equator | el ecuador |
| northern hemisphere | el hemisferio norte |
| southern hemisphere | el hemisferio sur |
| tropics | el trópico |
| bay | la bahía |
| island | la isla |
| peninsula | la península |
| canal | el canal |
| the Suez canal | el Canal de Suez |
| the Panama canal | el Canal de Panamá |
| straits | el estrecho |
| currents | las corrientes |
| tides | las mareas |
| | |
| ferry | el ferry / el transbordador |
| liner | el transatlántico |
| cruise ship | el crucero |
| tanker | el petrolero |
| container ship | el portacontenedores |
| hazard | el peligro |
| iceberg | el iceberg |
| shipping | los barcos / la navegación |
| shipping forecast | el pronóstico marítimo |
| storm | la tormenta / la tempestad |
| gale | el vendaval |
| gale force (ten) | los vientos huracanados (de fuerza diez) |
| rough sea | el mar agitado / la fuerte marejada |
| calm sea | el mar tranquilo |

## Insight

In addition to **estrecho**, a typical example of a Spanish word needing **e-** before **-str-**, which is obviously a cognate of strait(s), there are many other cognates. However, there are a few words which need some explanation: the names of ships. Apart from **ferry**, a borrowing from English which is related to the Latin word *ferre* (to carry) they are peculiarly Spanish – but all are very logical.

- **transbordador** derives from **transbordar**, which means to change vehicles
- **transatlántico** harks back to the old days when many liners crossed the Atlantic
- **crucero** is logical for a cruise ship, but also means *cruiser* in the naval sense
- **petrolero** relates to the word **petróleo** = *crude-oil*, because that's what they carry
- **portacontenedores** does what it says – carries containers

### Useful verbs

| | |
|---|---|
| *to board* | **ir a bordo** |
| *to embark* | **embarcar** |
| *to disembark* | **desembarcar** |

## 14.4 The weather forecast

### Core vocabulary

| | |
|---|---|
| *weather forecast* | **el pronóstico del tiempo** |
| *rain* | **la lluvia** |
| *snow* | **la nieve** |
| *wind* | **el viento** |
| *fog* | **la niebla** |
| *sun* | **el sol** |
| *hail* | **la llovizna** |

| | |
|---|---|
| sleet | **la aguanieve** |
| thunder | **el trueno** |
| lightning | **el relámpago** |
| It is ... raining | **llueve / está lloviendo** |
| snowing | **nieva / está nevando** |
| sunny | **(está) soleado / (hace sol)** |
| warm | **caliente / caluroso** |
| cold | **frío** |
| cloudy | **nuboso** |
| overcast | **cubierto** |
| rainy | **lluvioso** |
| wet / damp / humid | **húmedo** |
| mild | **templado** |
| dry | **seco** |
| It is cold | **hace frío** |
| hot | **calor** |
| good weather | **buen tiempo** |
| bad weather | **mal tiempo** |

### Insight

Several of these need a bit of explanation to help you understand them.

• **llovizna** is derived from **llover** – *to rain*; **aguanieve** is half-way between water and snow – *sleet*

• **relámpago** is onomatopaeic – try saying it aloud with spirit!

You can practise and learn them all by looking at Spanish weather forecasts on the Internet.

| | |
|---|---|
| yesterday | **ayer** |
| today | **hoy** |
| tomorrow | **mañana** |

| | |
|---|---|
| over the next few days | **en los próximos días** |
| the weather is getting worse | **el tiempo está empeorando** |
|   improving |   **mejorando** |
| you can expect | **se puede anticipar** |
|   light / strong winds |   **vientos débiles / flojos / fuertes** |
|   rain / snow |   **lluvia / nieve** |
|   clouds |   **nubes** |
|   gusts of wind |   **rachas de viento** |
|   gales |   **vendavales** |
|   storms |   **tormentas / tempestades** |
|   heavy showers |   **los chubascos** |
|   floods |   **inundaciones** |
|   sunny intervals |   **intervalos soleados** |
|   bright periods |   **intervalos claros** |
|   prolonged spells of rain |   **períodos prolongados de lluvia** |
|   morning mist |   **bruma matinal** |
|   fog patches |   **bancos de niebla** |
|   frost |   **escarcha / helada** |
| dangerous driving conditions | **condiciones peligrosas para conducir** |
| | |
| risk of flooding | **el riesgo de inundaciones** |
| the temperature will be ... | **la temperatura será ...** |
| degrees | **grados** |
| Celsius / centigrade | **Celsius / centígrado** |
| Fahrenheit | **Fahrenheit** |
| the temperature is rising / falling | **la temperatura sube / baja** |
| maximum | **máximo** |
| minimum | **mínimo** |

## Insight

Most weather words and expressions are quite logical, being either cognates or derivatives, direct or indirect. So, how might you learn these? Given our obsession with the weather, it should be obvious: learn them by researching Spanish weather forecasts or inventing them, perhaps in conjunction with an event or situation. For example, as seems inevitable: **barbacoa – ¡lluvia y frío!**

# Test yourself

Match the countries with the seas / oceans or continents that they are associated with.

| | | | |
|---|---|---|---|
| 1 | Grecia | a | el Mar del Norte |
| 2 | Suecia | b | el Océano Índico |
| 3 | Inglaterra | c | el Pacífico |
| 4 | Italia | d | el Atlántico |
| 5 | China | e | el Mediterráneo |
| 6 | el Japón | f | el Mar Báltico |
| 7 | Islandia | g | Europa |
| 8 | Irlanda | h | el Ártico |
| 9 | Holanda | i | Asia |
| 10 | India | j | el Canal de la Mancha |

# 15

# Government and society

## 15.1 Politics and government

### Core vocabulary

| | |
|---|---|
| government | **el gobierno** |
| democracy | **la democracia** |
| state of law | **el estado de derechos** |
| dictatorship | **la dictadura** |
| monarchy | **la monarquía** |
| UK's parliamentary monarchy | **la monarquía parlamentaria del Reino Unido** |
| Spain's parliamentary democracy | **la democracia parlamentaria de España** |

## Insight

Spain's democratic state is modelled on the UK system in being a constitutional parliamentary monarchy. King Juan Carlos is well-loved, having successfully smoothed the path of Spain's return to democracy in the last quarter of the twentieth century.

Spain has two main political parties:

• **Partido Popular** – it stands for conservative values, a strong state, security and European commitment;

• **Partido Socialista Obrero Español** – this is the Socialist party, which is currently in government. It stands for social justice and equality, and is very committed to Europe. During its first period in power (1982–1996), this party introduced many social reforms.

| | |
|---|---|
| King | **(su majestad) el Rey** |
| Queen | **(su majestad) la Reina** |
| King and Queen | **los Reyes** |
| Prince | **el Príncipe** |
| Princess | **la Princesa** |
| Head of State | **el Jefe de Estado** |
| President | **el presidente (del Gobierno)** |
| Prime Minister | **el Primer Ministro** |
| Head of Government | **el Jefe del Gobierno** |

## Insight

• The Spanish Prime Minister is also known as **el presidente**, being president of the government.

• The King, of course, is the **Jefe de Estado**, aided in official functions by the Queen and their family. Try looking up the Royal Family on www.casareal.es to find out about the King, the Royal Family and their latest news.

• The Spanish parliament – **las Cortes** – has two chambers: the **Congreso de los Diputados** is the lower house, members of which (**diputados**) are elected by proportional representation for a four year term. The house elects its **presidente**, who is then invited by the King to form the government. The upper house is the **Senado**, whose members are called **senadores**.

Note that the current Consejo de Ministros consists of 50% women, so Spain has lots of **ministras**!

| | |
|---|---|
| Cabinet | **el Consejo de Ministros / el gabinete** |
| Minister of the Interior | **el Ministro del Interior** |
| Defence Minister | **el Ministro de Defensa** |
| Chancellor of the Exchequer | **el Ministro de Economía y Hacienda** |
| Justice Minister | **el Ministro de Justicia** |
| parliament | **el parlamento, las Cortes** |
| chamber | **la cámara** |
| Lower House (Spanish Parliament) | **el Congreso de los Diputados** |
| Upper House (Spanish Parliament) | **el Senado** |
| member of elected parliament | **el diputado** |
| member of the higher chamber | **el senador / miembro de la Cámara Alta** |
| ministry | **el ministerio** |
| Foreign Office | **el Ministerio de Asuntos Exteriores** |
| Home Office | **el Ministerio del Interior** |
| Ministry of Education | **el Ministerio de Educación** |
| Ministry of Defence | **el Ministerio de Defensa** |
| constituency (area) | **la circunscripción electoral / el distrito electoral** |
| election | **las elecciones (generales)** |
| vote | **el voto / la votación** |
| the armed forces | **las Fuerzas Armadas** |
| the army | **el Ejército** |
| soldier / tank / to march | **el soldado / un carro de combate / marchar** |
| the navy | **la Marina / Armada** |
| sailor / warship / to sail | **el marinero / el buque de guerra / navegar** |
| the airforce | **el Ejército del Aire** |
| airman / pilot / jet fighter / to fly | **el aviador / el piloto / el reactor / volar** |

**Useful verbs**

| | |
|---|---|
| to appoint one's government | **nombrar su gobierno** |
| to appoint one's cabinet | **nombrar su gabinete** |
| to defend | **defender** |
| to fight | **luchar (contra)** |
| to guard | **guardar** |
| to protect | **proteger** |
| to spy | **espiar** |
| to speak | **hablar** |
| to make a speech | **pronunciar un discurso** |
| to canvass | **solicitar el voto de ...** |
| to debate | **debatir / discutir** |
| to vote | **votar** |
| to pay taxes | **pagar impuestos** |

## 15.2 Local government and services

## Core vocabulary

| | |
|---|---|
| mayor | **el alcalde** |
| town / city councillor | **el concejal** |
| town hall | **el ayuntamiento** |
| local council | **el concejo municipal** |
| roads | **las carreteras** |
| transport | **el transporte** |
| tourist office | **la oficina de turismo** |
| council offices | **las oficinas municipales** |

## Insight

You could try googling some of these on www.google.es, or use www.elmundo.es or www.elpais.es to see them in context; http://es.wikipedia.org/wiki/Wikipedia:Portada might also be useful.

| | |
|---|---|
| telephone | **el teléfono** |
| taxes | **los impuestos** |
| council tax | **el impuesto municipal** |
| rates | **la contribución municipal** |
| bureaucracy | **la burocracia** |
| the small print | **la letra pequeña** |
| red tape, bureaucracy | **el papeleo** |
| civil servant | **el funcionario** |
| paperwork | **el papeleo** |
| permit | **un permiso** |
| certificate of residence | **un permiso de residencia** |
| receipt | **un recibo** |
| driving licence | **un permiso de conducir** |
| insurance | **el seguro** |
| medical insurance | **el seguro médico** |
| medical check | **la revisión médica** |
| solicitor | **el procurador** |
| lawyer | **el abogado** |
| criminal offence | **el delito criminal** |

| court | el tribunal / juzgado |
| sentence | la sentencia / condena |
| fine | la multa |
| imprisonment | el encarcelamiento |
| police | la policía |
| emergency services | los servicios de emergencia / urgencia |
| ambulance | la ambulancia |
| fire brigade | el Cuerpo de Bomberos |
| telephone | el teléfono |
| electricity | la electricidad / la luz (common usage) |
| gas | el gas |
| water | el agua |
| sewage | (el sistema de depuración de) aguas residuales |

## Insight

Many of these are cognates, of course: when you learn them make sure you take account of the spelling changes.

### Useful phrases

| I don't understand. | No entiendo. |
| I didn't know | No lo sabía. |
| I have already supplied you with this document. | Ya le he proporcionado ese documento. |
| I need help ... | Necesito ayuda / que me ayuden ... |
| Is there anyone who can help me? | ¿Hay alguien que pueda ayudarme? |
| When are the offices open? | ¿A qué hora se abren las oficinas? |
| Where do I need to go to get ...? | ¿Adónde tengo que ir para obtener ...? |
| What do I need? | ¿Qué necesito? |

| | |
|---|---|
| Where can I get it? | **¿Dónde puedo obtenerlo/la?** |
| a (rubber) stamp | **la estampilla de goma** |
| It has / hasn't been stamped. | **No ha sido aprobado (oficialmente).** |

**Insight**

Try practising these by using them to make up two-line dialogues.

## 15.3 Money

### Core vocabulary

| | |
|---|---|
| currency | **la moneda** |
| dollars | **los dólares** |
| sterling | **la libra esterlina** |
| euros | **los euros** |
| cash | **el (dinero) efectivo** |
| bank | **el banco** |
| bank account | **la cuenta bancaria** |
| current account | **la cuenta corriente** |
| deposit | **el depósito** |
| account | **la cuenta** |
| account number | **el número de la cuenta** |
| bank sort code | **el número de agencia** |
| cheque book | **el talonario** |
| credit card | **la tarjeta de crédito** |
| cheque card | **la tarjeta de identificación bancaria** |
| signature | **la firma** |
| number / code | **el número / código** |
| loan | **el préstamo / crédito** |
| overdraft | **el saldo deudor** |
| bank transfer | **la transferencia bancaria** |
| in credit | **con un saldo positivo** |

| in the red | con un saldo negativo / en números rojos |
| bankruptcy | la quiebra |
| mortgage | la hipoteca |
| household insurance | el seguro doméstico |
| stocks and shares | las acciones |
| stock market | la bolsa |
| prices | los precios |
| dividend | el dividendo, los beneficios |
| profits | las ganancias |
| loss | la pérdida |
| inflation | la inflación |
| accounts | las cuentas |
| accountant | el contable |
| annual accounts | las cuentas anuales |
| income tax | el impuesto |

## Insight

Notice **quiebra** from **quebrar** – *to break*, and also **cuenta** and **contable**, from **contar** – *to count*; in both cases the spelling changes are typical of root-changing verbs, and occur when the stress is on the 'stretchy' **e** ( → **ie**) or **o** ( → **ue**).

### Useful verbs

| to apply | solicitar *(ask for)*, **presentarse** |
| to be accepted | ser aceptado |
| to be refused | ser negado / rechazado |
| to win | ganar |
| to lose | perder |
| to make a gain | hacer ganancias / beneficios |
| to make a loss | hacer pérdidas |
| to buy / sell shares | comprar / vender ganancias |
| to save | ahorrar |

The Spanish are great gamblers – they invest a considerable amount of money in their **Lotería Nacional**. Tickets – or rather tenths of tickets (**décimos**) are sold in special shops and kiosks. The jackpot prize **el Gordo** is one of the biggest prizes in the world. Winning numbers for the Christmas lottery are sung out by choirboys or choirgirls and the ceremony is broadcast on television.

## 15.4 National holidays

### Core vocabulary

| | |
|---|---|
| saint's day | **el Santo** |
| bank holidays | **las fiestas nacionales** |
| national holidays | **las fiestas nacionales** |
| local holidays | **las fiestas locales** |
| holidays | **las fiestas nacionales** |
| Christmas | **(la) Navidad** |
| New Year | **el Año Nuevo** |
| Easter | **la Pascua (de Resureción)** |
| Easter Week / Holy Week | **Semana Santa** |
| Halloween | **la víspera de Todos los Santos** |
| January 6 - the Epiphany | **el día de Reyes** |
| Shrove Tuesday | **Carnaval** |
| Ash Wednesday | **Miércoles de Ceniza** |
| Good Friday | **Viernes Santo** |
| Easter Sunday | **el Domingo de Resurrección** |
| the April Fair in Sevilla | **la Feria de Abril** |
| the Crosses of May – celebrated in Andalucía | **las Cruces de Mayo** |
| St Fermín's day – July 7, in Pamplona | **San Fermín** |
| October 12, Our Lady of el Pilar, national day | **El Pilar / Día de la Hispanidad** |
| All Saints' Day | **el día de Todos los Santos** |

| | |
|---|---|
| Christmas Eve | **la Nochebuena** |
| Christmas Day | **el Día de Navidad** |
| New Year's Eve | **la Nochevieja** |
| village fête | **la fiesta del pueblo / la fiesta rural** |
| circus | **el circo** |
| concert | **el concierto** |
| band | **la banda** |
| gig | **el concierto** |
| festival of (music) | **el festival (de música)** |
| competition | **la competición** |
| championship | **el campeonato** |
| match | **el partido** |
| wine festivals... | **los festivales de vino / la vendimia** |
| national dress | **el traje nacional** |
| procession | **la procesión** |
| bullfight | **la corrida de toros** |
| bullfighter (3 roles) | **el matador / el picador / el banderillero** |

## Insight

Many of these are cognates, so should be easy to learn and remember. As for the various Spanish festivals, you will find most in http://es.wikipedia.org/wiki/Wikipedia:Portada

## 15.5 Environmental issues

### Core vocabulary

| | |
|---|---|
| the environment | **el medio ambiente** |
| environmentalist | **el ecologista** |
| environmental issues | **los asuntos medioambientales** |
| ecology | **la ecología** |
| ecosystem | **el ecosistema** |

| | |
|---|---|
| erosion | **la erosión** |
| foodstuffs | **los comestibles /** |
| | **productos alimenticios** |
| GM (genetically modified) | **alimentos transgénicos** |
| organic | **orgánico/a** |
| artificial fertilizer | **el abono / fertilizante artificial** |
| nitrate | **el nitrato** |
| pesticide | **el pesticida** |
| poison | **el veneno** |
| weedkiller | **la herbicida** |
| pollution | **la polución / contaminación** |
| environmental pollution | **la polución medioambiental** |
| acid rain | **la lluvia ácida** |
| air pollution | **la contaminación del aire /** |
| | **atmosférica** |
| car exhaust | **el escape del coche** |
| detergent | **el detergente** |
| global warming | **el calentamiento global** |
| greenhouse gas | **el gas invernadero** |
| nuclear testing | **las pruebas nucleares** |
| ozone layer | **la capa de ozono** |
| radiation | **la radiación** |
| radioactive waste | **los residuos radiactivos** |
| water pollution | **la polución de agua** |
| power | **la electricidad** |
| energy | **la energía** |
| nuclear power | **la energía nuclear** |
| hydro-electric power | **la energía hidroeléctrica** |
| solar power | **la energía solar** |
| wind power | **la energía del viento / eólica** |
| power station | **la central eléctrica** |
| recycling | **el reciclaje** |
| glass, cans, paper, plastic | **el vidrio, las latas, el papel, el** |
| | **plástico** |
| compost | **el compost, el abono orgánico** |
| resources | **los recursos** |
| sustainable | **sostenibles** |
| renewable | **renovables** |

| | |
|---|---|
| *the protection of the environment* | **la protección del medio ambiente** |
| *of animals* | **de los animales** |
| *of plants* | **de las plantas** |

---

### Insight

Not only are many of these cognates, but also this section includes just about every common noun ending in Spanish! Note the genders, as they are all quite reliable. Here are some examples:

- **la polución: -ión** words are always feminine
- **la electricidad: -dad** words are always feminine
- **la energía: -ía** words are always feminine
- **el reciclaje: -aje** words are always masculine
- **el calentamiento: -miento** words are always masculine

Note also the endings of the adjectives **sostenible** and **renovable:** one is the same suffix as in the English word, the other is different. Either way, they are just as easy to understand.

---

#### Useful verbs

| | |
|---|---|
| *to protect* | *proteger* |
| *to conserve* | *conservar* |
| *to destroy* | *destruir* |
| *to dispose of* | *deshacerse de* |
| *to throw away* | *tirar* |

---

## 15.6 Religion

#### Core vocabulary

| | |
|---|---|
| *religion* | **la religión** |

| | |
|---|---|
| beliefs | **las creencias** |
| faith | **la fe** |
| Buddhism | **el budismo** |
| Christianity | **el cristianismo** |
| Hinduism | **el hinduismo** |
| Islam | **el islam** |
| Judaism | **el judaísmo** |
| I am a / an | **soy ...** |
| agnostic | **agnóstico** |
| atheist | **ateo** |
| Buddhist | **budista** |
| Catholic | **católico** |
| Christian | **cristiano** |
| Hindu | **hindú** |
| Jew | **judío** |
| Moslem | **musulmán** |
| Quaker | **cuáquero** |
| Jehovah's witness | **testigo de Jehová** |
| God | **Dios** |
| Buddha | **Buda** |
| Christ | **Cristo** |
| Mohammed | **Mohama** |
| the prophet | **el profeta** |
| cathedral | **la catedral** |
| chapel | **la capilla** |
| church | **la iglesia** |
| mosque | **la mezquita** |
| synagogue | **la sinagoga** |
| temple | **el templo** |

## Insight

These names of places of worship could be learnt with the help of appropriate pictures.

| | |
|---|---|
| religious leader | **el líder religioso** |
| bishop | **el obispo** |

| | |
|---|---|
| *imam* | **el imán** |
| *monk* | **el monje** |
| *nun* | **la religiosa / la monja** |
| *priest* | **el sacerdote / el cura** |
| *rabbi* | **el rabino** |
| *prayer* | **la oración / el rezo** |
| *hymn* | **el himno** |
| *religious service* | **el oficio religioso** |
| *mass* | **la misa** |
| *baptism* | **el bautismo** |
| *christening* | **el bautizo** |
| *(first) communion* | **la (primera) comunión** |
| *wedding* | **la boda** |
| *funeral* | **el funeral / entierro** |

## Insight

As ever, many of these are cognates with spelling changes; try copying them but with the spelling differences highlighted in a different colour.

### Useful verbs

| | |
|---|---|
| *to attend church* | **ir a la iglesia** |
| *to believe* | **creer** |
| *to pray* | **rezar** |
| *to preach* | **predicar** |
| *to kneel* | **arrodillarse** (reflexive) |
| *to sing* | **cantar** |
| *to chant* | **cantar** |
| *to worship* | **adorar** |

# Test yourself

In Unit 15 find 10 words across and 10 down in this wordsearch, then translate them into English

```
J   E   F   E   B   O   L   S   A   C
I   X   E   F   A   N   S   O   K   I
M   P   R   I   N   C   E   S   A   R
M   A   I   D   C   A   N   F   Ñ   C
U   P   A   B   O   G   A   D   O   O
L   E   G   O   W   X   D   E   B   R
T   L   E   D   U   M   O   N   J   E
A   G   U   A   F   I   R   M   A   Y
J   E   U   R   O   S   U   L   F   E
F   I   E   S   T   A   P   F   D   S
```

# The media

## 16.1 The press

### Core vocabulary

| | |
|---|---|
| newspaper | **el periódico / diario** |
| magazine, review | **la revista** |
| comic | **el cómic / tebeo / la revista de historietas** |
| daily | **diario** |
| weekly | **semanal** |
| monthly | **mensual** |
| bi-monthly | **bimensual** |
| quarterly | **trimestral** |
| yearly | **anual** |
| publisher | **la editorial** |
| editor | **el editor** |
| journalist | **el periodista** |
| journalism | **el periodismo** |
| reporter (press) | **el reportero** |
| reporter (TV, radio) | **el locutor** |
| correspondent | **el corresponsal** |
| special correspondent | **el correponsal especial** |
| war correspondent | **el corresponsal de guerra** |
| critic | **el crítico** |
| press agency | **la agencia de prensa** |

| | |
|---|---|
| *front page* | **la portada** |
| *back page* | **la contraportada** |
| *headline* | **el titular** |
| *column* | **la columna / sección** |
| *article* | **el artículo** |
| *brief report* | **el reportaje en breve** |
| *advertisement* | **el anuncio** |
| *notices* | **los anuncios / avisos (clasificados)** |
| *obituaries* | **los obituarios / las necrológicas** |
| *small ads* | **los anuncios por palabras** |

## Insight

Notice the logic of **diario** and **periódico**. Note also the very logical derivatives based on expressions of time, and the many other derivatives and cognates; try listing them in groups of words which are cognates, words which are derivatives, and words which are both.

| **News items** | *Las noticias* |
|---|---|
| *natural disaster* | **el desastre natural** |
| *flood* | **la inundación** |
| *earthquake* | **el terremoto** |
| *eruption of a volcano* | **la erupción de un volcán** |
| *storm* | **la tormenta / tempestad** |
| *hurricane* | **el huracán** |
| *tornado* | **el tornado** |
| *torrential rain* | **las lluvias torrenciales** |
| *road accident* | **el accidente de carretera / tráfico** |
| *car crash* | **el accidente de coche** |
| *collision* | **la colisión / choque** |
| *plane crash* | **el accidente de avión** |
| *terrorist attack* | **el ataque / atentado terrorista** |
| *demonstration* | **la manifestación** |
| *strike* | **la huelga** |
| *a call to go on strike* | **la convocatoria de huelga** |
| *fire* | **el incendio** |

Visual images will help you to learn and recall many of these.

• Spanish newspaper reports often use unexpected tenses; the present tense gives vividness to narration of incidents, and the imperfect is sometimes used with similar effect.

• The distinction in the British press between tabloid and broad-sheet newspapers does not exist in Spain, where most papers are the same size – smaller than a broad-sheet, but larger than a tabloid paper. There is no division of style and tone as in the UK press.

• Spanish newspapers tend to focus on news rather than on celebrity gossip, which is left to magazines like ¡Hola!. Even regional papers contain lots of national and international news, as well as local news and information; as a result, many Spanish people buy local rather than national papers.

• Many national and local newspapers have websites; as well as www.elmundo.es and www.elpais.es , try http://www.heraldo.es/ , http://www.diariodesevilla.es/ or http://www.diariodenavarra.es/ Then again, there are digital papers such as: http://www.estrelladigital.es/ED/diario/portada.asp

## 16.2 Books

### Core vocabulary

| | |
|---|---|
| book | **el libro** |
| title | **el título** |
| author | **el autor** |
| writer | **el escritor** |
| illustrator | **el ilustrador** |

| | |
|---|---|
| cartoonist | **el dibujante (de dibujos animados)** |
| paperback | **el libro en rústica** |
| biography | **la biografía** |
| autobiography | **la autobiografía** |
| novel | **la novela** |
| short story | **el cuento** |
| dictionary | **el diccionario** |
| encyclopaedia | **la enciclopedia** |
| atlas | **el atlas** |
| guide book | **la guía turística** |
| (road) map book | **la guía de carreteras** |
| fiction | **la ficción** |
| non-fiction | **la literatura no novelesca** |
| | |
| **Literary genres** | *Los géneros literarios* |
| novels | **las novelas** |
| mystery novels | **las novelas de misterio** |
| detective novels | **las novelas policíacas** |
| short stories | **los cuentos** |
| foreign literature | **la literatura extranjera** |
| literary review | **la crítica literaria** |
| poetry | **la poesía** |
| epics | **las epopeyas / novelas épicas** |
| essays | **los ensayos** |

## Insight

Lots of logical cognates and derivatives here, and even those which are less obvious are guessable!

### Useful verbs

| | |
|---|---|
| to write | **escribir** |
| to edit | **editar** |
| to print | **imprimir** |
| to publish | **publicar** |
| to sign | **firmar** |

### Useful phrases

| | |
|---|---|
| What sort of books do you like to read? | ¿Qué tipo de libros te gusta leer? |
| Who is your favourite author? | ¿Quién es tu / su autor preferido? |
| I like reading books about ... | Me gusta leer libros sobre ... |
| I like reading books where ... | Me gusta leer libros en los que ... |
| I like reading books that ... | Me gusta leer libros que ... |

## Insight

Notice the patterns here: sometimes the words are more or less in the same order as in English, whilst the structure of **gustar** expressions reflects the 'back to front' nature of this verb and others like it. They need a special effort to learn them.

## 16.3 Cinema and television

### Core vocabulary

| | |
|---|---|
| the cinema | **el cine** |
| auditorium | **el auditorio** |
| (big) screen | **la pantalla (grande)** |
| seat | **la silla / el asiento** |
| foyer | **el vestíbulo** |
| ticket | **la entrada** |
| booking office | **la taquilla** |

| **Films** | *Las películas* |
|---|---|
| thriller | **la película de suspense** |
| romance | **la película sentimental** |
| love story | **la historia de amor** |
| historical film | **la película de historia** |
| science fiction | **la película de ciencia ficción** |
| horror film | **la película de horror** |

| | |
|---|---|
| *war film* | **la película de guerra** |
| *comedy* | **la película de humor** |
| *detective film* | **la película policíaca** |
| *drama* | **la película dramática** |

## Insight

These names of film types are all logical, even when different from English, so should be easy to learn and remember.

| | |
|---|---|
| *adverts* | **la publicidad** |
| *the cast* | **el reparto / los actores** |
| *film star* | **una estrella de cine** |
| *actor / actress* | **un actor / una actriz** |
| *leading role* | **un papel principal, protagonista** |
| *supporting role* | **un papel secundario** |
| *singer* | **un(a) cantante** |
| *dancer* | **un bailarín / una bailarina** |
| *director* | **el director** |
| *producer* | **el productor** |
| *cameraman* | **el cámera** |
| *sound recordist* | **el registrador de sonido** |
| *the crew* | **el equipo (de cámera)** |
| *video rental / shop* | **el videoclub** |
| *video* | **el vídeo** |
| *dvd* | **el DVD / disco de vídeo digital** |
| *dubbed / subtitled* | **doblado / subtitulado** |

| **Television** | *La televisión* |
|---|---|
| *television set* | **el televisor** |
| *small screen* | **la pantalla pequeña** |
| *cable* | **el cable** |
| *satellite* | **el satélite** |
| *dish* | **la antena parabólica** |
| *video recorder* | **el aparato de vídeo** |
| *dvd player* | **el lector (de) DVD** |
| *remote control* | **el mando a distancia** |
| *channel* | **el canal** |
| *credits* | **los créditos / titulares de crédito** |

| | |
|---|---|
| *commercials* | **los anuncios / spots publicitarios** |
| *cartoons* | **los dibujos animados** |
| *children's programmes* | **los programas infantiles** |
| *chat show* | **el programa de entrevistas** |
| *documentary* | **el documental** |
| *feature film* | **el largometraje** |
| *short film* | **el cortometraje** |
| *game show, quiz programme* | **el programa de concurso** |
| *news programme* | **el programa de actualidad** |
| *soap* | **la telenovela** |
| *weather forecast* | **el pronóstico / la previsión del tiempo / el boletín meteorológico** |
| *news reporter* | **el locutor** |
| *newsreader* | **el locutor** |
| *presenter* | **el presentador** |
| *interviewer* | **el entrevistador** |
| *commentator* | **el comentarista** |
| *disc jockey* | **el DJ / discjockey / pinchadiscos** |
| *game show host* | **el presentador de un programa de concurso** |
| *the viewer* | **el telespectador / televidente** |
| *radio* | **la radio** |
| *station* | **la emisora** |
| *programme* | **el programa** |
| *frequency* | **la frecuencia** |
| *on FM* | **en FM** |
| *on LW* | **en onda larga** |
| *on MW* | **en onda media** |

## Insight

Most of these are quite logical, but notice **largometraje** and **cortometraje**. Also think about **pinchadiscos**, probably coming from the idea of sticking a needle onto a vinyl record in the same way as a cocktail stick is stuck into a snack! (**pincho** = a snack on a stick). Try looking for explanations of other 'complex' words; the trick is always to start by breaking them up into their component parts.

### Useful verbs

| | |
|---|---|
| to change channels | **cambiar de canales** |
| to graze / channel hop | **hacer zapping** |
| to turn on / off the telly | **encender / apagar la tele** |
| to turn the sound up | **subir el volumen / poner más fuerte** |
| to turn the sound down | **reducir / bajar el volumen** |
| to broadcast | **transmitir / emitir** |
| to record | **registrar** |

### Useful phrases

| | |
|---|---|
| What is your favourite programme? | **¿Cuál es tu programa favorito / preferido?** |
| Do you like documentaries? | **¿Te gustan los documentales?** |
| Who is your favourite presenter? | **¿Quién es tu / su presentador(a) preferido/a?** |
| He / she is partial / impartial. | **(El / ella) es parcial / imparcial.** |

## Insight

Just a couple of items to comment on: first, notice how **emitir** is a logical expression for transmit or broadcast. Then, how about the typical 'pseudo-borrowing' from English: **hacer zapping**? Perhaps the TV remote control is being likened to an electronic gun! Weird, but logical in a way.

# Test yourself

Work out which Spanish word goes with which; they are all logical pairs! Then translate them into English.

1 la novela
2 el locutor
3 el auditorio
4 la estrella de cine
5 escribir
6 la entrada
7 el lector de DVD
8 el periodista
9 el programa de concurso
10 editar

a el presentador
b el cine
c el escritor
d el diario
e el televisor
f el autor
g el asiento
h el editor
i la película de ciencia ficción
j las noticias

# Test yourself

## Answer key

### Unit 1

**a** Te presento a mi mujer; **b** ¿Qué vamos a hacer esta tarde?; **c** ¿Adónde te gustaría ir?; **d** Por favor, hable más despacio.; **e** ¿De qué nacionalidad eres?; **f** No encuentro mi bolsa.; **g** Nos gustan mucho las vacaciones.; **h** No pienso que tengan miedo.; **i** Ojalá que pudiera estar de acuerdo.; **j** Es peligroso bañarse aquí.

### Unit 2

**1 c** mi anillo; **2 b** mi hijo; **3 c** mi pareja; **4 a** el viudo; **5 d** querido; **6 d** eructar; **7 a** divertirse; **8 d** el biberón; **9 e** Madrid; **10 b** el ayuntamiento.

### Unit 3

**1** g; **2** i; **3** f; **4** j; **5** h; **6** c; **7** e; **8** b; **9** a; **10** d.

### Unit 4

**a** el maestro **b** el trimestre **c** la Ciencia **d** el ordenador **e** copiar **f** el licenciado **g** explicar **h** una carrera **i** traducir **j** la facultad

### Unit 5

Group 1: la escalera, el balcón, el hogar, la ventana, la calefacción
Group 2: el sótano, el dormitorio, el despacho, el vestíbulo, el comedor
Group 3: la butaca, la lámpara, la cama, el armario, el espejo
Group 4: la nevera, la secadora, la pila, la lavadora, el tazón
Group 5: la flor, el césped, las malas hierbas, el bulbo, el roble

### Unit 6

**1** a, c, d **2** b, c, e **3** a, b, c **4** b, d, e **5** a, b, d **6** a, c, e **7** c, d, e **8** b, c, d **9** a, b, e **10** b, c, e

**Unit 7**
**1** j, **2** i, **3** f, **4** h, **5** g, **6** d, **7** a, **8** b, **9** c, **10** e.

**Unit 8**
**1** h, **2** d, **3** f, **4** i, **5** b, **6** c, **7** j, **8** a, **9** g, **10** e

**Unit 9**
**1** hacer baile moderno – to do modern dancing **2** dibujar – to draw
**3** ver la tele – to watch the TV **4** el crucigrama – crossword puzzle
**5** ser aficionado a – to be keen on **6** es fantástico – it's fantastic
**7** marcar un ensayo – to score a try **8** el levantamiento de pesas
– weight lifting **9** la plancha de surf – surf board **10** el tobogán –
toboggan

**Unit 10**
**1** vestido **2** sostén **3** vaqueros **4** impermeable **5** guantes **6** sudadera
**7** zapatillas **8** ancho **9** cremallera **10** descalzo

**Unit 11**
**1** el andén, la estación, el horario, el rápido, el vagón TRAINS
*platform, station, timetable, express, waggon/carriage* **2** el
registro de equipaje, la sala de embarque, el avión, el vuelo,
el asiento PLANES *baggage check, departures lounge, plane,
flight, seat* **3** el coche, el todoterreno, las luces, el parabrisas,
el cuentakilómetros AUTOMOBILES *car, off-road vehicle,
lights, windscreen, speedometer* **4** el acelerador, el volante, los
faros, los neumáticos, la gasolina AUTOMOBILES *accelerator,
steering-wheel, headlamps, tyres, petrol* **5** el chaleco salvavidas,
los auriculares, despegar, la azafata, la turbulencia PLANES
*lifejacket, earphones, to take off, air-hostess, turbulence* **6** el
maquinista, la vía, el revisor, la consigna, el paso a nivel TRAINS
*engine-driver, track, ticket inspector, left-luggage, level crossing*
**7** el ferrocarril, el jefe de tren, el vagón restaurante, el pasajero,
el intercity TRAINS *railway, guard, restaurant car, passenger,
Intercity train* **8** navegar, el ferry, el barco, el pasajero, el chaleco
salvavidas BOATS *to navigate, ferry, boat, passenger, life-jacket*
**9** la fila, la salida de emergencia, el piloto, el aeropuerto, la
puerta PLANES *row, emergency exit, pilot, airport, door* **10** el

espejo retrovisor, el maletero, la matrícula, la batería, el encendido
AUTOMOBILES *rearview mirror, boot/trunk, number plate, battery, ignition*

## Unit 12
**1** a, **2** c, **3** c, **4** b, **5** b, **6** a, **7** c, **8** b, **9** a, **10** b

## Unit 13
Ailments: 3 Flu, 4 mumps, 6 stomach ache, 7 cold, 9 measles.
Body Parts: 1 eyelids, 2 knees, 5 lungs, 8 thighs, 10 cheeks.

## Unit 14
(alternative answers are given where appropriate) **1** g, e **2** f, g **3** j, a, g **4** e, g **5** i, c **6** c, i **7** h, d **8** d, g **9** a, g **10** b, i

## Unit 15

```
J E F E B O L S A C
  E   A   S     I
  P R I N C E S A R
M A I   C   N Ñ C
U P A B O G A D O O
L E   O   D     R
T L   D   M O N J E
A G U A F I R M A Y
  E U R O S     F E
F I E S T A     S
```

<u>across</u>: chief; stock market; princess; lawyer; monk, water; signature; euros; faith; fiesta
<u>down</u>: festival; bank; circus; senate; paper; year; fine; wedding; king and queen; mass

## Unit 16
**1** novel **f** author  **2** newsreader **j** news  **3** auditorium **b** cinema
**4** film star **i** science fiction film  **5** to write **c** writer
**6** (entry) ticket **g** seat  **7** DVD player **e** television set
**8** newspaper reporter **d** daily newspaper  **9** TV games show
**a** presenter  **10** to edit **h** editor

# Taking it further

## Books

For an introduction to Spanish history, geography, language and culture, and modern-day society, try:

*World Cultures: Spain*, Mike Zollo and Phil Turk (Hodder & Stoughton Ltd, London, 2000).

*The New Spaniards*, John Hooper (Penguin, London, 1995).

Those wanting more in-depth knowledge of the language might enjoy:

*How Spanish Grew*, Robert K. Spaulding (University of California Press, 1967). An old but thorough text.

*The History of the Spanish Language*, Ralph Perry (Cambridge University Press, 1991).

The *Teach Yourself* series covers many aspects of learning Spanish, including the comprehensive *Complete Spanish*, *Complete Latin American Spanish* and *Essential Spanish Grammar* – the natural partner title to this book (all titles by Juan Kattán-Ibarra, Hodder & Stoughton, London, 2010).

## Watching and listening

In the UK, Televisión Española 2 and several others are available on Eutelsat FII / Hotbird on satellite television channels. Some systems can also access Hispasat, which broadcasts Spanish and Hispano–American channels. In some areas of the UK, Spanish channels are available on cable television. In the US, Spanish language TV is available in most areas.

Radio reception on a normal set in the UK is variable, though in some areas Spanish national stations can be received quite clearly, depending on atmospheric conditions. Spanish radio and TV are available on Satellite TV, and both radio and TV can be accessed via the Internet. Just try starting with http://www.rtve.es/ Listen to a variety of material or programmes. Try watching or listening to the news, having already seen or heard it in the English-speaking media, as many international news items will be shown on both. This will help your understanding and give you confidence.

If you are interested in literature, particularly poetry, the work of many Spanish poets has been recorded in the form of song; CDs will be easily available in Spain, but a specialist music shop may be also able to help. Here are some suggestions:

**Antonio Machado:** Joan Manuel Serrat – *Dedicado a Antonio Machado* on LP or CD, comprising eleven of Machado's poems set to music, or try *Campos de Castilla*, or any anthology of Machado's poems.

**Federico García Lorca:** one of his poems, *Chove en Santiago*, is featured on the CD *Cabo do Mondo* by Luar na Lubre, published in 1999; or try any anthology of Lorca's poems (look for one including this poem).

**Rafael Alberti:** Joan Manuel Serrat – 'La Paloma' on the LP *Joan Manuel Serrat* (1969), or any anthology of Alberti's poetry.

Many Spanish and Latin American films are available on video and DVD, most with English sub-titles if you really need them!

## Places to go

Look out for performances of Spanish culture in local venues, e.g. Flamenco dancing, films, South American films and music and so on. Also watch out for Spanish (speaking) films at local film clubs and on television.

Spanish paintings are sometimes displayed in galleries outside Spain, including the USA and UK; there are paintings by Velázquez in the National Gallery, London, and the National Gallery in Edinburgh, others are in Glasgow.

## Reading

Obviously, this will depend on whether or not you can read Spanish well enough to keep your interest going! Try short, simple items in the press, such as advertisements, small ads and short articles on well-known subjects. Another very useful source of reading material is the Internet, where there is plenty of visual material to support your understanding. Try tourist and hotel websites, or go to a site which deals with your hobby or your work specialization: you will already know a lot about the topic, so even understanding new words will be easier as you are familiar with the context. You could also try catching up with the gossip on celebrities on www.elmundo.es : go to *fotos del día*.

If you wish to read literature in Spanish, the best approach is to go for a 'school text' if one is available, that is one which has been set for Spanish literature examinations: such editions have a useful introduction, explanatory notes and glossaries.

# Websites

The web is very popular in Spain, so there is plenty of good material in Spanish available, and much also from Latin America – all good practice. Choose your subject and do the necessary search, but be prepared to be bombarded with Spanish. There are Spanish websites relating to many of the subjects covered in this book. You can either do a search using your favourite search engine, preferably one with Spanish links, or if you can cope with the language well enough to use a Spanish search engine, go direct to one of those listed below.

Be warned, that websites come and go, and their addresses often change. These were all fine at the time of going to press!

The website address of the Spanish Embassy Education Office, the *Consejería de Educación*, is:
http://www.educacion.es/exterior/uk/en/home/index.shtml

On certain specific topics the *Consejería de Educación* (Education Advisory Service) publishes booklets and work-packs in Spanish on certain subjects such as: *Las mujeres* (Women); *La juventud* (Youth); *El medio ambiente* (The environment); *La familia y las relaciones personales* (The family and personal relationships).

### Spanish Press

| | |
|---|---|
| El País | http://www.elpais.es |
| El Mundo | http://www.elmundo.es/ |
| ABC | http://www.abc.es/ |
| La Vanguardia | http://www.vanguardia.es/ |

### Spanish search engines

Using a Spanish search engine may speed up your search for a specific Spanish site.

http://www.google.es/

http://es.yahoo.com/
**Red iris** http://www.rediris.es/

## Language learning on the web

For basic language practice, try:

http://www.languagesonline.org.uk
http://www.bbc.co.uk/education/languages/
http://www.studyspanish.com/index.htm
http://www.spanishlanguage.co.uk
http://www.wordreference.com

Try making your own word-search games to practise vocabulary, on: http://www.makeyourownwordsearch.com

A useful UK site for more advanced Spanish is:
http://www.mepsyd.es/exterior/uk/es/tecla/tecla.shtml. This site offers dozens of short articles on various topics, followed by vocabulary lists and exercises in Spanish.

Among other sites offering more advanced information and practice is:

http://www.well.ac.uk/

For information on the state of Spanish and links to literature, try:

http://www.el-castellano.com/